READY, FIRE, AIM

OTHER BOOKS BY HARRY LEVINSON

Executive
Executive Stress
Organizational Diagnosis
The Great Jackass Fallacy
Emotional Health in the World of Work
Psychological Man
Casebook for Psychological Man
Casebook for Psychological Man: Instructor's Guide
CEO: Corporate Leadership in Action (with Stuart Rosenthal)

These books may be ordered directly from:

The Levinson Institute, Inc.
Box 95
Cambridge, MA 02138

Harry Levinson

READY, FIRE, AIM

Avoiding Management by Impulse

From The Levinson Letter
Compiled and Edited by Janet E. Robinson

The Levinson Institute, Incorporated
Cambridge, Massachusetts

Library of Congress Cataloging in Publication Data

Levinson, Harry.
  Ready, fire, aim.

  Bibliography: p.
  Includes index.
  1. Psychology, Industrial—Collected works.
  2. Management—Collected works. I. Robinson, Janet E. II. Title.
  HF5548.8.L386   1986   658   86-10593
  ISBN 0-916516-06-7
  ISBN 0-916516-07-5 (pbk.)

To the staff of The Levinson Institute
whose commitment reflects their dedication
to the standards we share.

Contents

Preface

Most managers say they like people. They feel that they understand people and are good at managing them. At the same time, every manager sometimes finds people's behavior perplexing. Usually this is because the behavior is a product of *unconscious* feelings—feelings that are just as real and powerful as the ones we are conscious of feeling, but that go on outside our awareness.

A major shortcoming of much contemporary psychological thinking is that it has no way to explain unconscious processes. It assumes that behavior is simply a product of the external environment. And unfortunately, it leads to managerial decisions and practices that are erroneous at best, but at times terribly destructive. By focusing on the outside, it supports the tendency toward management by impulse: ready, fire!...aim. It allows people to come up with quick answers which all too often are wrong answers. And that's because they have answers before they really know what the questions are.

What managers need instead is a comprehensive theory of personality that takes into account what goes on *inside* people as well as outside. The purpose of this book is to give you some simple tools to help you think about some of the most complex and refractory problems you have to handle. Our goal is to give you enough theory of personality to enable you to apply it thoughtfully to everyday problems. Many managers think quick decision making is the mark of a good manager. It isn't. The mark of a good manager is thoughtful, reasoned decision making.

This book is made up of items originally published in *The Levinson Letter*, a twice-monthly publication devoted to exploring psychological aspects of leadership and management. It includes some theoretical explanations and many, many practical applications of theory to actual managerial situations. Many of the situations described come from my direct experience consulting to organizations and teaching managers for more than thirty years. In addition, my editorial colleagues and I read widely. We cover a variety of publications—books, technical papers, business and clinical periodicals, and daily newspapers—perhaps 75 in all each month. The topics range from reviews of obscure literary tomes to sports columns. Ideas from clinical journals and ancient history are as important for the lessons they teach as interviews revealing the feelings of inadequacy suffered by artists or corporate chief executives. In *The Letter* we use what we read and experience to illuminate common managerial problems and puzzles, with the emphasis always on the practical: what can you as a manager *do* in such a situation?

The Levinson Letter is written for busy people—items are brief and concise, like snapshots of managerial experience. In addition, a monthly feature called "Focus On . . ." devotes two pages to the discussion of a particular topic, and alternate issues of *The Letter* include a two-page Case Study. A quarterly *Addendum* to *The Letter* presents a four- to eight-page treatment of a special topic. For space reasons we could include only a few of these longer pieces in this volume. For those who are interested in exploring in greater depth some of the issues raised here, "Focus On . . ." and *Addendum* articles are available from The Levinson Institute. A list of titles can be found at the back of this book.

Each issue of *The Levinson Letter* seeks to provide timely information on an interesting variety of topics. This book organizes the best of that material according to the enduring themes of *The Letter*. By pulling together everything I've said on a given topic and bringing it up to date, I hope to provide an important reference source for longtime subscribers to *The Levinson Letter*, as well as a fairly complete introduction to the subject for new subscribers and nonsubscribers. Naturally, I hope you will read from cover to cover. In addition, it will be useful to review specific topics when you come up against those particular problems.

This book is an important part of my self-imposed professional task: to translate what my colleagues and I know clinically into principles and practices that managers can understand and apply. *The Levinson Letter* grew out of a quarterly *Follow-up* publication for managers who had attended The Levinson Institute's executive seminars. After numerous requests to publish *Follow-up* more frequently and to make it available to people who had not attended seminars, I decided to publish *The Levinson Letter*.

Over the years I've had the advantage of collaborating with five associate editors. Carole Garlington had the strenuous task of helping to start *The Letter*, handling the many unforeseen problems and setting the precedents for later editors. Joan Lautman started the move toward a more informal style, while adding a scholarly touch. Katherine Kush refined the writing style and evolved a more collaborative relationship that resulted in shared contributions thereafter. Janet Robinson brought both greater psychological knowledge and a more immediate conversational quality. John Elder added both breadth of classical knowledge and a tongue-in-cheek sense of humor. Each built well.

Janet Robinson sifted through the massive amount of material that made up ten years of *The Levinson Letter* in order to conceptualize this book, then selected the best material and organized it as it appears here. She wrote the chapter and section introductions and conclusions, compiled the footnotes, and made the style consistent throughout.

Barbara Taylor and Kristen Walter clipped the many articles from *The Letter*. Parts of the manuscript were typed by Betsy Black and the whole by Vinnette Gordon. They were checked with painstaking care by Marilyn Farinato, Marie-Claire Ording, Linda Kay McCormick, Donna Teague, Marcia Atwood, Jody Liu, and Betsy Black, a task coordinated by Marilyn Farinato. Linda Kay McCormick copyread the whole. John Elder and Anne Friedman reviewed it for organization and content. Bill Rutherford, senior vice president of human resources of Sun Co., took a critical look at the draft manuscript. Ann Walter coordinated the whole with her usual careful attention to quality and detail. I am indebted to all of them.

Harry Levinson
Cambridge, Massachusetts
May 1, 1986

READY, FIRE, AIM

More Than Meets The Eye

Why do your subordinates do the things they do? Or your manager, for that matter! Do you ever wish you could look inside their heads to see what makes them tick? I can't offer you that, but I can show you a practical way to think about what motivates some of the apparently nonsensical things people do. Even your own behavior doesn't always seem entirely under your control, and sometimes your feelings don't make sense even to you. Whether it's yourself, your peers, your subordinates, or your manager who's driving you a little bit crazy, chances are there are some unconscious feelings at work.

Many people find the idea of unconscious feelings both difficult to believe and difficult to understand at first. After all, you can't see or feel them in yourself. Yet great literature through the ages has shown us, and you know from your own experience, that people are powerfully motivated to do things that make no rational sense, and which they themselves cannot explain. You can learn enough about unconscious feelings and how they show up in action to shed some light on your most perplexing managerial problems, and to come up with some new solutions—or at least some ways to live with the things that aren't likely to change.

This introductory chapter presents a sampling of the dilemmas and puzzlements of management that are explored more fully in the following chapters. It presents the rationale for my approach to managerial problems, and ways to check my approach against your own experience.

The Operation Was A Success, But The Patient Died

To combat drug abuse and racial unrest, one U.S. Army commander spontaneously ordered his subordinate commanders to move into the barracks with their men. Officer morale plummeted, while drug use and racial hostilities remained unchanged, according to an Army psychiatric consultant. The program quickly died.[1]

Too many managers, like this commander, are quick to prescribe a solution before they've diagnosed the problem. Then they're surprised by the unwanted side effects. This commander assumed that increased discipline would rectify the situation. He didn't look at the motivations behind the drug abuse and racial hostility, and he didn't see that the subordinate commanders would feel stripped of prerogatives and power.

Most problems involving people are complex, and simple solutions rarely work. You can't influence behavior in appropriate directions if you don't understand how people must feel in order to act as they do. Those feelings are usually complex and ingrained; they are often impervious to rational thought processes. That's why managers can change the rules, only to find the new rules haven't affected behavior at all. And their efforts often boomerang, because when managers create pain, their subordinates make sure the pain returns to the managers' shoulders.

Piece Of A Puzzle

When a subordinate exhibits a piece of puzzling behavior, your first thought might be, "Why the heck would he do that?" My colleague Dr. Arthur Kovacs suggests asking the following more specific questions: "What is he or she trying to do for me and others (or tell me and others) with this? What is this going to get him or her? What are its consequences? What kind of response is he or she looking for?"

All behavior is adaptive—that is, an attempt to master oneself or the environment. These questions help you see how individual acts are part of that overall mastery effort. You may not come up with good answers every time, but if you keep asking the questions, you gradually will come to a better understanding of motivation.

"Don't Shoot Me, I'm Only The Boss"

Many newly promoted managers ask, "Why do my subordinates resent my position? I haven't changed anything, but they've acted suspicious ever since I joined the unit." People are always ambivalent about those who have power over them. They worry about how that power will be used. These feelings are beautifully dramatized in Morris L. West's novel about the first Russian Pope, *The Shoes of the Fisherman.* A fictional cardinal expresses sentiments that many subordinates feel: "We elected him in the name of God, and now suddenly we're afraid of him. He has made no threat, he has changed no appointment, he has asked nothing but what we profess to offer. Yet here we sit, weighing him like conspirators and making ready to fight him. What has he done to us?"[2]

The manager who guides careers, sets salaries, and makes assignments exerts considerable power over people. Subordinates are in the psychological position of children, dependent on the parental manager to take care of them and watch out for their interests. We all start out in life totally helpless and therefore afraid. A playful adult might unintentionally hurt us, our parents could suddenly reject "babyish" behavior, a teacher could give us a bad grade. Even when adults were trustworthy, they controlled situations and we did not. Unconsciously we remember being small and helpless, and we don't like being reminded of it. Wise managers know it's natural for subordinates to fear and resent them. They don't become angry or defensive in response, but communicate with their people to quiet those fears. When people trust their managers, it's easier for them to accept the power differences between them.

Look To Your Own Conflicts First

When there is conflict between parents, the effects often are felt downward—that is, their child develops a problem. So one of the principles of family therapy is to deal with the conflict between the parents as a way of helping the child. With an organizational problem, it's important to examine what is going on among authority figures that makes it impossible for subordinates to act in ways that they might otherwise act. Subordinates may be caught in the middle of a struggle that has nothing to do with them, or they may be drawing fire for their manager, or their needs for direction and support may be neglected while their superiors are embroiled in other matters. An outside consultant is usually helpful, because he or she has both the perspective and the power needed to point out a conflict at high levels. Subordinates will show symptoms of an organizational problem first because they are vulnerable, but they are not always the cause.

When The Best Rx Can't Help

An attitude survey reaffirmed for one company's management that their quality of work life improvement effort was indeed successful. Morale was high; attitudes were positive. But a few months later it was publicly reported that the effort had failed.

How could the effort fail despite such high morale? You can always have high morale when people are engaged together against a common enemy. In this instance, the common enemy was higher management.

Whatever information you have, it must be interpreted in the context of the entire system. And you must think about the system in psychological terms.

The Whole Person

Managers are often tempted to put aside the messy human angle of problems they are trying to solve. A straightforward, logical approach is so much easier; there is a clear-cut answer. After all, you can't argue with facts!

But the fact is, leaving out the human factor spoils the solution as much as leaving it in spoils the equation. The clear-cut answer is an illusion—a solution to a different problem than the one that exists. The Rev. Gerald Molgren, Illinois Synod, Lutheran Church of America, speaking to the Institute of Medicine of Chicago, noted that physicians "are treating the whole person—either doing it well or badly. There isn't an option."[3] The same is true in every human situation, including management. Much as you might like to leave people's feelings, especially those elusive unconscious ones, out of the picture, that's not an option. You are managing "the whole person—either doing it well or badly."

Understanding Is No Luxury!

When psychologists talk about understanding people, many managers get the impression that we're advocating an impractical idealism. This common misconception is reflected in a letter I received which quotes a corporate human resources director as saying, "Yes, motivation is great, but our managers have to work under heavy pressure to get production results. . . . Maybe someday we can move toward an ideal environment where jobs can be structured and assignments made on the basis of employee motivation factors, but today we can't afford the luxury of such idealism!"

I am not saying every problem would be solved if managers could only be nice to their people. I am saying: if you understand the psychological realities of a situation, you'll have a better idea how to handle it. Circumstances can and do require managers to be firm and consistent, sometimes to the point of being hard or even firing people. But finding the most effective solution to a problem depends on understanding the people involved.

Who, Me?

From time to time people ask me whether managers should be expected to learn psychoanalytic theory. They're astonished when I say, "Yes."

I don't know why managers and executives who don't think twice about the need to understand complex marketing models, econometric models, and so on, think that understanding people is just too complex a task. Certainly it's complex, but not above being learned. Those kinds of questions reflect a reluctance to learn—perhaps motivated by a reluctance to look at oneself.

Mixed Feelings

If there's one common denominator to everything I say, it's that psychological phenomena are real, and will no more go away if you ignore or deny them than will a bad heart or a barrel of toxic waste. The first step is always recognizing and admitting your own feelings. Drs. Ellen Bassuk and Samuel Gerson studied chronic patients in a psychiatric emergency ward of Beth Israel Hospital, Boston, and commented on the difficulties faced by the therapists who deal with them. "Because these patients are often intensively hostile, manipulative, uncooperative, and devaluing, the therapist experiences anxiety, helplessness, and even hate. . . . The therapist should make every attempt to bypass the struggle while acknowledging to himself or herself the intensity and discomfort of these feelings."[4]

While few offices and organizations resemble psychiatric emergency wards (despite the jokes many employees make), the point remains valid. It may or may not be advisable or even useful to confront a person who makes you feel anxious, helpless, or full of hate; but it is definitely necessary to confront yourself with these feelings. There's a venerable tradition of dormitory bull sessions in which each person says what he or she dislikes about the others. Try carrying on such a session by yourself. By putting your feelings into words, even silently, you can force yourself to make them specific, to give reasons. Possibly you may see the other person's side for the first time. You might even try defending him or her against your own attack.

It's especially hard to admit feelings of dislike, dissatisfaction, or distrust about a person we like and respect—a spouse, a child, a friend, a buddy at work, the boss who gave us our start. It seems wrong to have such feelings. But that won't make them go away, nor should it. The feelings are frequently justified. The trick is to work them out and be done with them. (See "Troubled Waters," beginning on p. 153, for more about how to do this.) Healthy relationships, professional and personal, can survive all sorts of lapses and hurt feelings, but are often destroyed by unspoken grievances.

The Therapeutic Commander

With all my emphasis on understanding what motivates people's behavior, some managers get the impression that I want them to be therapists to their coworkers. That's not the case. I'm suggesting that managers use their understanding of human behavior to help them manage better—not that they try to change their coworkers' basic style of behavior. That requires professional psychological help, and even then it's not always possible.

Too often, managers try to *be* understanding (which may amount to excusing unacceptable behavior), rather than *use* their understanding. The difference is well stated in this comment by a longtime Army psychiatrist, Col. Kohler, which a reader shared with us: "A commander of troops must, by the very nature of his job, be 'anti-therapeutic,' for if he becomes a 'therapeutic commander' he may or may not help the person upon whom his energies are directed, But! This commander isn't commanding anything."

Managers don't have to go so far as to be "anti-therapeutic"—you can foster mental health without giving up authority. But I am not trying to teach you to be nice. As a manager, you do have to take charge, whether people like it or not. And if they don't like it, you don't have to accept hostile gestures from them. It's not up to you to teach them how to act, only to tell them what behavior is acceptable and what is not.

Friendly Atmospheres Aren't Built Of Niceness Alone

It's a rare treat to walk into a company and find a whole group of people who obviously enjoy working together day after day. What's so special about the place? Is it luck? A big part of it is almost always the manager. She likes all her people, and they like her. But that's not enough. That manager will also be open with her people. While she tries to help them with plans and choices, she does not ask them to become completely dependent on her or her organization and thereby increase their vulnerability. They run their own lives. As a result, people are apt to come to work early and stay late. They have a spontaneous interest in work. It's a place where they get a sense of continuous growth and increasing competence as well as group solidarity. This kind of company makes money, too!

Profitability Will Take Care Of Itself

"Take care of the sense and the sounds will take care of themselves," advises Lewis Carroll in *Alice's Adventures in Wonderland*. That's an example of an epiphenomenon: sounds are the secondary result of the primary concern with sense. Profitability is also an epiphenomenon. The primary consideration for any business—and any manager—is perpetuation of the organization. Take care of that, and profitability will take care of itself.

This contradicts the short-term focus of most American businesses. But a general rethinking of that focus was stimulated by Profs. Robert Hayes and William Abernathy of Harvard Business School in 1980 with "Managing Our Way to Economic Decline."[5] All the fuss about quality circles and similar competitive issues, they pointed out, is irrelevant. The basic issue is managing the business. The Japanese pay attention to the management process, while we emphasize short-term financial ends. The result, Hayes and Abernathy argued, is that we have not been replacing our adaptive and productive capacity.

We are going to have to relearn the primacy of managing, as opposed to controlling costs. Managers will have to interact more effectively with their people. Those who have a greater capacity for human interaction and a greater understanding of human behavior are more likely to succeed in the future. We have reached the limits of the heavy emphasis on financial efficiency. That orientation becomes ineffective as work becomes more fractionated, more boring, and more controlled. Isolation, boredom, and frustration—and the anger they induce—push people to demand higher pay. That in turn makes companies noncompetitive, without doing much for the anger, isolation, and boredom. Advances with robots don't change the fact that we will still depend on people to manage and to operate our organizations. There's no substitute for understanding people, and for working with them rather than pressuring them.

Tools For Your Trade

Managerial problems are often complex; human beings always are. One way to begin to understand this complexity is to focus on the actual behavior of the people involved. From a pattern of specific actions we can infer the meaning of the situation to the people involved, and their motivations for action—or inaction! Once we understand why people will not or can not follow a logical and apparently reasonable course of action, we can look for a psychologically reasonable course of action that they may be able to follow.

I have found it useful to categorize behavior in four dimensions: the ways people handle their basic feelings of affection, aggression, and dependency, and the ways they strive (or give up striving) toward their ego ideals (their ideal selves). The terms affection, aggression, and dependency are used here with specialized meanings, which are actually broader than their meanings in general usage. Although I avoid the use of jargon as much as possible, these terms and a few others are central enough to be worth defining and using. This chapter is devoted to clarifying these key concepts.

Of course, behavior doesn't divide neatly into categories. A single event can give us information in several dimensions. The way the person handles affection may require him or her to handle aggression in a particular way. Handling aggression that way may have implications for the handling of dependency and consequences for the person's ability to approach his or her ego ideal. As we begin to see how interconnected the various behaviors are, we realize what an enormous thing we are asking if we ask the person to change a particular behavior. That behavior results from a particular balance of forces, and this particular balance gives us what is commonly called the person's personality (a generalization based on what I would call his or her characteristic way of behaving). If one part changes, there may be repercussions throughout. Or the whole structure may come crashing down. People know this, whether or not they are conscious of it, and they will defend their particular balance of psychological forces as they would defend their lives.

Affection: The Need For Human Contact

All people must manage their relationships with other people. A major aspect of relationships is how people give and receive affection. They do this through physical contact, gestures, and words. Actions can also convey affection, when it is clear that they are undertaken with other people in mind. And it is possible to put forth the appearance of being in contact without being in contact at all—when one party manages not to pay attention to or recognize the other.

People vary considerably in the amount of contact they need and in their style of obtaining (or limiting) contact. There are people who have such a great need for contact with others that they can hardly sit down by themselves and work. Some people need to be liked to such a degree that they can't say anything the listener might not want to hear, be it criticism or simply a different opinion. For these people, taking charge is nearly impossible. Other people need to be liked, but are so afraid they won't be liked that they find ways to keep themselves at a considerable distance from others. And then there are people who completely deny their need for affection; at best they are isolated, and at worst they have no reason to keep a rein on their aggression.

Take notice when descriptions of behavior contain words that convey closeness or distance, warmth or coolness, being in touch, isolation, barriers, or gregariousness. The issue is affection.

Golden Thread

A spider sits at the center of its web, "listening" for vibrations that indicate the presence of prey, or its mate, or an enemy. Scientists study how this information transmitter, the web, works: what type of vibration travels best along the radii of the web, and is therefore most important to the spider?[1]

Every person sits, like the spider, at the center of a web of connections with other people. Some of the people are nearby, some are far away; some are close emotionally and send clear signals from any distance, while others are emotionally distant, so their signals are not very strong or clear no matter how close they are physically. Some of us pay more attention to the vibrations that travel through this web of connections than others, and some are more sensitive to the meanings of the vibrations that come through. But these connections are important to everyone. They are the source of affection and support, as well as information on various topics. These vibrations keep us from being isolated, left alone with what goes on in our own heads. Without interchange with the external world, our own thoughts and fantasies become too difficult to manage. Sometimes the results of isolation are creative, but more often people simply become distressed if they can't act on those fantasies and interact with other people.

It would be interesting to study the important vibrations of your own web—to map out your social network. Who are you in touch with, both closely and more distantly? How clearly are the vibrations transmitted? Who sends what kind of information, what kind of support? If a connection is lost, through death or changing circumstances, what kind of support will you lose and who could replace it? From some people we need intimacy, from others approval, and from still others we need job interaction. From some people we need specific information, while from others we need the assurance that they are keeping an eye out for the information we need. But perhaps the most important thing is the knowledge that the web exists—that we will pick up whatever vibrations are sent out, because we are connected.

Touching

People find it hard to express affection except in conventional ways. There are definite social rules about how one may do so, and to whom. Men are especially constricted in the ways they can show affection to other men. But the affections themselves are not so limited, and it seems a shame that a man can hug a woman he is fond of at the stroke of the New Year, but would be looked on askance for hugging a man he likes equally well.

Touching is the fundamental expression of affection. Not only is it pleasant and gratifying, but in some ways it is necessary, or at least beneficial. Scientists have demonstrated the ill effects suffered by infants deprived of being touched. Other research, on adults, indicates that being touched slows the heart rate. And this effect was independent of the gender of the people involved.[2]

There are many situations at work where you might wish to show your affection for someone: for a manager who has really helped you out or shown confidence in you, for a subordinate who has done a great job or is doing battle with some problem (or machine), for a peer with whom you've shared an experience that binds you. If the affection is truly felt, a hand on the shoulder, a touch on the arm, a warm handshake are among the best ways to convey it.

The social rules about touching do mean you have to be careful though, especially if you're a man touching a woman. A sexual harassment suit can result from a touch that is self-indulgent or condescending. People must feel that you like and respect them and are pleased with what they've done, not that you're just looking for an excuse to touch a body. And there are some people who just do not like to be touched. So even with the purest of intentions, one must be careful to read the response.

When Does The Men's Movement Start?

Men rarely share the same poignant relationships as women because, for men, our culture sanctions either standing alone or standing together as a team, comments Elliot Engel, N. Carolina State U. "The male two-some is rare and seems designed more for combat than for comfort," he says; and for that reason male relationships almost never deepen into intimacy, but rather stay at the superficial and guarded level. He argues that "men nurture their feelings only inwardly and later harvest ulcers or heart attacks." They cannot express their needs for warmth, security, and other deep emotions. He argues further that "there is a little boy within all men" (and certainly we know that), who "never completely stops looking for a pal." He urges that men "personalize the concept of brotherhood by seeking more fraternal bonds with other men."[3]

Engel's thoughts and ideas are fine. The problem is that in all species (except the lobster) males are competitive. They compete with each other for food, turf, and mates. Men have to work hard to temper their competitive feelings—but they can and do, in our civilized world. The question is, how much can feelings be tempered? Certainly men can be close friends, but they do better in circumstances where their competitiveness can be directed against a common enemy, which they can support each other in opposing. In order for men to share the level of intimacy women more commonly share, they must learn to trust each other enough to expose the fears and hurts that make one vulnerable and open the way for intimacy and support. This isn't going to happen en masse, through advocation and public education. This kind of change happens on a more individual basis. One man might learn from a woman that it can be comforting and strengthening to admit "weaknesses" rather than hide them, and try it with men. Another might learn the same thing in psychotherapy. A third might suffer enough pain from divorce to be forced to seek support from male friends. Others might have some personal experience which legitimizes the expression of feelings, making it "all right" and worth trying.

People benefit from sharing their pain: they find strength in the ability to ask for help, not because they can't do without it, but because mutual support makes both parties stronger, both lives easier, and both lives richer. I'm not saying it's easy. Taking risks never is. But you have to start somewhere.

Rerouting Means Rerooting

Coping with detachment is one of the hardest problems we face. We feel detached, alone, and floating when we leave one job for another, one home for another. People who break off long-term relationships with organizations can feel that they are no longer attached to anything. They often feel that they have no hold on life because they don't know where they belong. And they feel empty inside to boot.

Detachment is an occupational hazard for many managers and their families. When managers relocate, the spouse who lacks the continuity of work and the organization feels detached. And when managers relocate without their families in order to let their kids finish out the school year, they feel detached. Alone for months, they're not rooted to their families and not rooted to their new homes. They feel empty and inadequate—but their companies rarely recognize this problem. It's important for people in organizations to make contact with these newcomers, invite them to their homes, and help them get anchored and established in their new communities.

Because detachment often leads to anxiety and depression, it's important for people who feel detached, lost, and alone to reattach themselves as quickly as possible. Short-term therapy often helps transplanted people reroot themselves. When detached people allow the depression to continue, it can last for years. But when they take these feelings seriously and respond to them therapeutically, people can master them, and soon learn to flourish in new soil.

Aggression: The Need For Mastery

Aggression refers to the attacking aspect of the personality. As with affection, it must be carefully managed. Managers get into difficulty mismanaging their aggression more than other aspects of their personalities. Aggression is best known as the "fight or flight" impulse, which probably accounts for the negative connotations of the word. But aggression makes life possible, when we channel the "fight" impulse into mastering our environment. It enables us to feed and clothe ourselves and make ourselves more comfortable, as well as defend ourselves against threats of harm. Aggression can be used to master oneself: to behave as one intends to behave. It can be used to master others: to give adequate guidance, direction, and leadership. And it can be used to master aspects of the environment: to make the world the kind of place one wants it to be. Aggression itself is neither bad nor good; it's a force that must be directed, and can be used constructively or destructively. But actions that are constructive for one are often destructive to another. And when action is thwarted either internally or externally, it is likely to appear as anger.

Work is aggressive behavior. It is a matter of making things happen. So understanding how a person handles aggression is an important key to the person's behavior at work and his or her motivation to act or avoid action. Take notice when descriptions of behavior include action words or inaction, anger or emotional unavailability, people getting hurt (even

*by apparently unintentional means), competition or comparison, power-
or control-seeking, or an emphasis on success or failure. The issue is likely
to be aggression.*

American As Apple Pie

"Exactly what has always seemed most overwhelmingly American about
America—its devotion to the rough mythologies of winning and progress
through the medium of democratic capitalism—is what has always most
mystified visitors here."[4]

This capacity for continuing to advance through open competition
allows aggression to be directed into mastering the environment. The
alternative would be the overcontrol of aggression through political structure (as we see most vividly in Scandinavia and the Communist countries), which makes for great passivity. The capacity to direct aggression
into creative and constructive competition gives us our strength. There
is great need for this competitive energy in peacemaking and in resolving problems that confront us as a nation and as members of organizations. We get into difficulty when this energy is misdirected into areas
of conflict that don't resolve or master or innovate anything. And this
is the issue in the psychology of organizations—how to focus energy on
solving problems. The vitality of organizations can best be sustained by
recognizing that they are fundamentally fueled by underlying aggression. When that aggression is damped down, overcontrolled, or misdirected, then organizations, like people, get into great difficulty.

Madder Than A Hornet

Most people don't know how mad they are—and how often. But if we
look carefully at primitive organisms, we can see clearly the kinds of
responses we've learned to suppress. For instance, when male blackbirds
are spurred to attack, their hormone levels change considerably, research
zoologists say.[5]

We're taught to dampen aggression, to detoxify it; we learn to be nice,
to be reasonable. But we also feel primitive rage, and, like the blackbirds,
want to attack the offending object. And even when the cultural prohi-
bitions are so strong that we're not aware of the strength of our feelings,
our chemical balances shift and prepare our whole organism for defense
or attack.

Though we rarely see the strength of our anger, that powerful, primitive rage is nevertheless there, and the changes it creates cause considerable wear and tear on our systems. For that reason, we all need to be
alert to signs of suppressed, repressed, and detoxified anger. You can look
for common warnings: when you find yourself using words like "frustrated," "irritated," or "gets on my nerves," you can bet that you're

dealing with some mighty powerful feelings in a highly controlled, civilized way. When we see that and admit to it, we can find appropriate outlets for anger. But the cost of simply squelching those feelings is just too high.

Anger: It's Necessary

Anger is a fundamental and necessary emotion. It stems from the basic aggressive drive, which we need in order to master the environment and to defend ourselves against dangers. To be angry is not by definition to be bad. Many people believe they should be free of anger, but that's impossible. Here are some principles which may be helpful in understanding and accepting your own anger:

1. Anger is universal. Everybody gets angry, and does so frequently, with varying degrees of intensity. Some people have come to overcontrol their anger so tightly that they are not aware of being angry at all, let alone how intensely angry they are. Their anger may come out in the form of psychosomatic symptoms, or it may result in such overcontrol of behavior that they are very passive.
2. The problem, therefore, is not to avoid becoming angry or to try to get rid of anger by some magical device, but rather to learn to manage it.
3. An important way to manage anger is not to speak while you feel angry. To do so is often to speak impulsively and without good judgment. One of the best ideas I've heard is to dictate or write a letter, and then hold onto it. On cooler reflection you may think better of sending it. In the meantime, you had a safe place to express your feelings. Differences with others are better settled when you have cooled down somewhat.
4. You can check your angry feelings with somebody else, a friend or other neutral party, and try to assess with that person whether your anger is appropriate to the situation. Sometimes just talking about it that way eases the intensity. Then it becomes possible to deal with the problem in a more balanced way.

One important exception to all this is: people do have to stand up for themselves when they are being mistreated. When treated discourteously, unfairly, manipulatively, disrespectfully, or in any way other than as mature human beings, people should express clearly and directly the intensity of their feelings about the other person's behavior. When people express their feelings of anger about issues that really matter to them, they help the other person know where the boundaries are—what is acceptable behavior and what is not.

Fire Or Ice

"A man has trouble showing grief and loss, and a woman has trouble showing anger," says my former colleague Dr. Teresa Bernardez, Michigan State U. Bernardez sees men making more progress in this area than women. As men begin to see the importance of expressing feelings, "society isn't throwing up roadblocks," she notes. Yet society still sends women the message that it's not nice to express anger. That doesn't make the anger go away—and if a woman can't direct her anger at someone else, she has to hold on to it or direct it at herself. The result is depression, anxiety, headaches, and crying for no apparent reason. Bernardez, who is originally from Argentina, sees American cultural values from an outsider's perspective. She notes that Americans assume that the angry person tries to hurt the other; since women are taught to make others happy, they find it extremely difficult to allow themselves to do something that is assumed to be harmful to others. However, anger can be expressed in a constructive manner, by telling the other person how it feels to be unfairly treated.[6]

Another fear about expressing anger is that there will be no end to it—that if you begin to let the anger out, you will be a screaming virago forever. (*Virago* is a perfect example of our cultural prejudice against women expressing their aggression: it originally meant "a woman of great stature, strength, and courage," but has come to mean "a loud overbearing woman.") But the anger won't go on forever. Safe situations can be created with the help of a therapist, where expressing the anger can't hurt anyone. When the backlog of anger and hurt has been reduced and some practice has been obtained at expressing anger constructively, the likelihood of flying off the handle when things get to be too much will be greatly reduced. This leaves a woman devoting much less energy to controlling angry feelings, and consequently more energy is available for creative work.

Move Over, Baby!

Many people have assumed that overcrowding contributes to urban crime and other undesirable behaviors. A wealth of studies, from animal experiments to cross-cultural observations, has tried to establish this link. But the results of these studies aren't very compelling, says sociologist Avery Guest, U. Wash. Hard data about aggressive and aberrant behaviors of rats living in overcrowded cages don't necessarily apply to humans, says Guest. And field studies of overcrowding among humans, while often provocative, have actually generated only impressionistic results, he adds.[7]

Animal behavior can tell us about the primitive underpinnings of human behavior, but we must take care when making assumptions about human behavior on the basis of animal experiments. Humans living in crowded cities or working in close quarters do not suffer the same constraints as rats crowded into cages. People can move from one place to another; they can often vary their activities. And, significantly, they can think about their situations and seek out ways of coping. Because people can daydream and fantasize (unlike lower animals), overcrowding is bound to affect them differently.

Humans also have the capacity for symbolic communication. In the animal world, every act of aggression is a threat. But human beings invent special customs and practices that make it possible to be aggressive without others jumping to the conclusion that we are attacking them. Saying "Excuse me, may I get through here?" is far different from plowing through a crowd of people who haven't the remotest idea what you might intend. People's defenses aren't activated. The more crowded conditions become, the more rules we work out for stepping down the effects of our aggression.

Nip It In The Bud

"I hate to be rude, but," said a Soviet diplomat to Donald McHenry, when he was new as U.S. Ambassador to the U.N. McHenry quickly replied, "If you hate to be rude, don't."[8]

People often preface hostile comments by giving themselves permission to be rude, as if the warning softens the remarks. McHenry gave the wise response. He quietly made it clear that no one has permission to offend him. This is the best way to ward off hostile comments, which rarely profit anyone.

How A Good Idea Can Win In The End

Matthew Maury (1806-1873) was a troublemaker from the start. While still a midshipman, he contradicted what was then the Bible of navigation. Later he wrote a series of newspaper articles advocating Navy reform and criticizing graft. The Navy retaliated by assigning him to one of its most obscure backwaters, the Depot of Charts and Instruments. There he found thousands of captain's logbooks gathering dust. With the data from these, he wrote *Wind and Current Charts,* which soon revolutionized world shipping.[9]

Maury's career is instructive:
1. He attacked sacred cows, but he proposed improvements or replacements. After criticizing Bowditch's navigation textbook, he wrote a new one, which Bowditch himself recommended to the Navy.
2. He identified a real need. American naval charts and maps were inadequate.
3. He put in the hard work that guaranteed his suggestions would be workable. Captains using his *Charts* cut weeks and months off their voyages, savings thousands of dollars.

4. He involved beneficiaries of his innovations in his efforts. Many captains collected data for him (on charts he provided) in return for free copies of *Charts*.
5. He stuck with the organization where his work would be most significant, even while it was against him. Maury could have quit the Navy, but he probably would not have achieved elsewhere what he did in the Navy.

Maury's is a textbook case of aggression channeled into positive directions. He was driven to expose others' errors, but driven as well to create solutions. People like that make some enemies, many friends, and a big difference.

The Last Laugh

What do we mean when we say humor is tempered aggression? Sometimes it's a socially acceptable way of expressing otherwise unacceptable emotions—hostility, bitterness, anger, anxiety, envy, desire. (Sometimes the attempt to reach social acceptability is not entirely successful). But some humor expresses a sense of mastery, which is another aspect of aggression. As Freud pointed out in *Jokes and their Relation to the Unconscious* (1928): "Humor . . . has also something fine and elevating . . . the triumph of narcissism, the ego's victorious assertion of its own vulnerability. It refuses to be hurt by the arrows of reality or be compelled to suffer. It insists that it is impervious to wounds dealt by the outside world, in fact, that these are merely occasions for affording it pleasure."

License To Kill

Most people feel the urge to kill from time to time, but mentally healthy people use psychological defense mechanisms to keep from doing it, and even from thinking about it very much. If those defenses are broken down—in combat, for example—the person may have trouble restoring them. One Vietnam veteran, participating in a study at VA Medical Center, Montrose, N.Y., found himself so wary of unleashing his proven aggression that he had trouble at work just telling people what to do or correcting their mistakes. This man had feared his own violence even before going to Vietnam, and "combat had given him a license to be destructive." However, after the war he "did not become violent; rather he paid an internal price through . . . inhibition and constriction" of his aggression.[10]

People reach an internal balance of drives and controls which they can live with, resulting in what we call their characteristic behavior. It can range from uptight to laid back, from bully to pushover, from prude to flirt. If a person is unhappy with the style he or she has developed, change may be possible. But during the process, the old balance will be upset, leaving the person vulnerable until a new balance is achieved. Without one's usual set of controls, basic aggressive and sexual drives are very powerful and frightening. That is why change must be worked gradually and with a good deal of experienced support, most likely from a professional.

In organizations, a number of circumstances can serve to upset the balance:

1. Managers may be given a "license to kill" and pressured to be tougher than they feel is right.
2. Those who work for authoritarian managers may come to identify with the manager's successful use of verbal and psychological violence.
3. Overcontrolled coworkers may be pressured to compete with each other, in an effort to "bring out the best" in them.
4. Overcontrolled salespeople may be pressured to aggressively vanquish customers, in an effort to turn up the marketing heat.
5. Affection can be unleashed when a team works closely together on an intense effort, especially if there are both men and women members. Affection that exceeds one's control can be just as damaging to oneself and others as unleashed aggression.
6. T-groups, encounter sessions, retreats, and other semitherapeutic activities can unleash feelings that were being controlled for a reason. This can be quite damaging when the leader doesn't have the training necessary to help people regain control.[11]

When a person's defense mechanisms are overridden, one possibility is that he or she will lose control. Another is that the person will desperately clamp on tighter controls, and a manager held in these "mind-forged manacles" may well be less able to supervise, to cooperate, to listen, to accept change, or to think creatively.

FOCUS ON . . . . The Too-Tough Boss

" . . . a group of about 10-15 professional, managerial and technical people who left the company during 'Attila's reign' have all returned in the last few months. Most . . . are in the 35 to 45 age group and had between 10 to 15 years of service with the company when they departed. . . . The families of three men [who] died of heart attacks during this 'reign of terror' all attribute their breadwinner's deaths to this man's management style. Those of us who left suffered a lot of stress, but we did survive. . . . "

Tough vs. Bully
Top managements often prize tough-minded managers. Unfortunately, they don't always distinguish between being tough and being a bully—and there's a real and important difference. Being tough, managerially

speaking, means making up one's mind, taking a stand, having high standards and insisting that people meet them, and dealing with the organization's internal and external problems in a firm and consistent way. But some managers, in the name of high standards, berate people, humiliate them, and in various ways beat on them psychologically, sometimes to the point of destroying them. Some managers, in the name of taking a stand, refuse to listen to any advice, criticism, or divergent points of view, and attack those who dare to speak up. That's not being tough, that's just being a bully. *Fortune's* updated article on "The Toughest Bosses in America" acknowledges the difference between tough and too-tough, and points out that a too-tough boss doesn't necessarily get better financial results.[12] Yet that is almost invariably the justification for treating subordinates abusively. In fact, the cost to the organization can be very, very high. The cost to the people in the organization also can be very high, as the letter quoted above so vividly illustrates. Working for a too-tough boss can be particularly difficult for people who identify with the organization and who have some integrity. They can be torn apart by the conflict between staying and doing what they can for their organization, and leaving to protect their own values and self-respect.

Attila's Reign

In consultation, we hear about such managers quite regularly. What surprises me in the example above is not that such a manager existed, but how long he could go on wreaking financial and psychological havoc on his organization before his superiors decided to do anything about the situation. "Attila" had already led his organization into the first strike in 20 years at its largest plant, costing the company nearly $200 million, and was headed for the second strike in three years when the author of the letter left his organization. From his new position, he was still in touch with many former coworkers, and was able to watch the situation develop. He had predicted to his immediate boss that the second strike would occur—which it did, costing the organization $350 million this time. This was sufficiently painful to senior management that they removed Attila from that division, but installed him in another. That only postponed the inevitable. The move was encouraging to the author of the letter, who returned to his company on the faith that the abrasive manager would eventually quit or be fired. Difficult as it was—the company had never fired anyone at that level before—they did fire him.

Not Condemning Is Condoning

The firing of this executive did a great deal to restore people's faith in the company and to enhance the credibility of the man who had to fire him. When senior executives allow a manager in their purview to bully his or her subordinates, they condone those management practices. Furthermore, their passivity actually encourages the spread of this managerial style. It is a well-documented fact that abusive parents generally were abused as children; it's easy enough to see the same "generational" pattern between levels of organizations. *Fortune's* original "tough bosses" article quotes one subordinate manager as saying: "The boss will negotiate the standards with us for an outstanding performance. We'll buckle under them, then turn around and do the same to our people."[13] It happens with the standards, it happens with the response to a less-than-outstanding performance. Depending on the bully's place in the hierarchy, he or she can determine the managerial style of large parts, or even all, of the organization.

Organizations increasingly are being held responsible for the emotional stress they create for individual employees through management practices, as well as in other ways. I would not be surprised to see an increasing flow of lawsuits against corporations for psychologically destructive behavior on the part of their managers. Management makes itself vulnerable when it tolerates such behavior. The justification for tolerating the behavior is similar to the bully's justification for the behavior itself— the person is brilliant, rescued the operation from a disastrous downhill slide, has particular talents or skills the company can't do without or doesn't want to lose, and so on. The fact is, no one is indispensable or irreplaceable. And in tolerating a bully, the company always loses.

Learning The Lessons Of Experience
The managers who survived Attila are thinking of getting together periodically to talk over their experiences. I hope they do. Checking out your understanding of a difficult situation with others who shared it validates your feelings and perceptions. It also relieves your guilt and fears that somehow you were responsible for what happened, or responsible for those who did not survive as well. Whether a manager leaves or stays, for whatever reasons, there are difficult feelings to be faced. But facing them can salvage some benefits of personal growth from an otherwise destructive experience.

The moral of the story is that managers of such authoritarian bullies should recognize that behavior early (see my article, "The Abrasive Personality," *Harvard Business Review,* May-June 1978). Only very rarely can such people change and, even then, not without intensive psychotherapeutic help. Those who applaud such behavior are usually of the same stripe. An executive who praised one of the *Fortune* ten toughest had himself been fired from two high-level executive roles for his abrasiveness. Sometimes the person who hires an abrasive manager is hell-bent on having someone whip into shape those he couldn't whip himself—like parents hiring a tough babysitter to control the kids they can't handle. Henry Ford II tried that by hiring Bunky Knudson to control Lee Iaccoca. It doesn't work. There is no substitute for decent treatment.

Anything else exemplifies the Great Jackass Fallacy—the mistaken idea that you can rely on rewards and punishments to maximize performance. Carrots and sticks work fine with donkeys, but not with people who really have something to offer.

FOCUS ON . . . . The Manipulative Personality

You liked him the minute you set eyes on him. He was charming. You felt valued and interesting; working with him would be great. Then you began to see another side—when he altered your report slightly so it gave a very different impression. . . . To put it bluntly, he's a manipulator.

Now What Do You Do?
The next thing most people do is nothing. It's just too unpleasant to contemplate a grown person lying, sweet-talking, and conning people, just to look good or to get his or her own way. The words we use to describe such people—slimy, snake-in-the-grass, two-faced—indicate our disgust and sense of betrayal. A certain level of trust is necessary for people to live and work together. But manipulators betray that trust, actually using others' willingness to trust them to further their own ends.

Once you see a coworker manipulating others, you realize that you're probably a victim, too. You may be embarrassed that you didn't catch on sooner. But manipulators typically are charming and convincing. It's unreasonable to expect always to see through this facade. Or you might feel embarrassed by your associate's behavior. But you cannot be responsible for others' actions—even if you are responsible for their work.

Manipulators assume a right to use others. That implies a sense of superiority—but it is a false one, a defense against actual feelings of inferiority. They see themselves as unable to get their way by direct action, and resort to outsmarting others. They may take great pride in their ability to maneuver, but this never gives them a feeling of self-worth—only a sense that others are rather stupid. If the manipulator allows you to see his or her machinations, that assumes: 1) you don't object to the behavior; 2) you won't dare do anything about it, if you do object; or 3) no matter what you think or do, the manipulator will always come out on top. These assumptions arise from unconscious contempt. If this condescension embarrasses you, you are accepting the manipulator's low opinion of you. But ask yourself, have you given the person cause to disrespect you so? Probably not. At that point, your embarrassment or shame is likely to give way to anger.

You may also be angry because you realize that you have borne the blame for mistakes you didn't make, or missed recognition you deserved. You may even have felt obliged to work against your own interests. Manipulators often ingratiate themselves with compliments or favors, then ask for something. You'd rather not do it, but you feel guilty refusing—so you're angry at yourself either way, until you see through the con.

Your anger may be so great that you fear it could get out of hand, once you start talking about the situation. So you may still keep your mouth shut. But anger can also be the impetus to action.

When You Decide To Speak Up

Taking action against a manipulator can be extremely difficult. The behavior usually is not public, so it's difficult to document without revealing your sources and exposing those people to retribution. And deceit is often a matter of *how* things are said and done more than *what*. Manipulators are experts at inventing plausible explanations, even in the face of written evidence. Confrontations can easily degenerate into assertions and counterassertions ("You did"; "I didn't!") that can't be proven.

If you must report the situation to higher management, you cannot assume their unqualified support. They are likely to experience the same feelings you did, and be equally reluctant to get involved. They may feel added embarrassment or guilt at having hired and promoted the person. They may be aware of the manipulator's behavior but avoiding the hassle of taking action. Or they may be in the process of gathering evidence. They may react to your exposing the situation with anger, both at their own helplessness to act thus far and at having their hand forced. They may turn a deaf ear to your story, or even challenge it.

Whether presenting information to higher management or confronting a manipulator yourself, it's important to steer clear of labeling and name-calling ("You're always manipulating people"). Instead, stick to descriptions of behavior (on this occasion you said this or did that). Otherwise, you may find yourself debating the labels rather than the issues. It's better to talk in terms of the effects of the behavior on coworkers and the resulting costs to the organization.

Costs To The Organization

Because manipulators are so good at getting people to do what they want, they can do quite well in management. Higher management may approve of their successes, without recognizing the cost of substituting manipulation for leadership. The most important difference is that a leader has a long-term goal. He or she communicates that vision to subordinates and inspires them to join in pursuing it. Manipulators are interested only in short-term gains. Their subordinates have a sense of drifting. Without a common purpose, their efforts will never amount to anything. With little support from their manager (because manipulators see no reason to help others advance), they can't expect their own careers to progress, either. They feel victimized. This undermines their motivation and increases the need for the manager to manipulate.

The manipulator has a characterological problem; this is the only strategy the person has learned for coping with life. That doesn't excuse the behavior. It does mean manipulators are not in voluntary control of their behavior; and that means the behavior is very difficult to change. It requires considerable, usually painful, psychological work. And why should manipulators undertake this arduous process? The behavior isn't a problem for them; it gets them what they want. The only way to get any leverage on manipulators is to point out the negative consequences of their behavior for the organization, and to specify improvements as requirements for continued employment.

If you are not in a position to take action and if higher management doesn't respond, what can you do to make your situation bearable?

1. Avoid being pulled into the manipulator's schemes, if at all possible. At least you won't have to be angry at yourself.
2. Maintain your perspective about your own worth—don't fall for the manipulator's contemptuous view of you. Remember that the behavior is not voluntary, and therefore is not a response to you.
3. Avoid plots or conspiracies against the person. It's hard to beat manipulators at their own game; you're better off refusing to play.

In short, the best you can do is to keep your distance and mind your own business.

Dependency: The Need To Share And Cooperate

Another aspect of managing relationships is the degree of help we are willing to give or accept from others. Physical care, financial support, guidance and assistance at work, a friendly ear or a shoulder to cry on—all are ways of depending on each other. Letting someone else share our burden means that we become vulnerable—the other person can let us down. If we need help we may feel helpless, especially if we can't trust others to come through for us. To avoid feeling helpless, some people seek to control everything around them, from feelings to objects to tasks to people. In order to maintain control, they may seek various forms of power. Other people need so much support and guidance that they can't make a move without someone else's assistance—working with them is more like having another job to do than having a coworker. There are also people who are basically independent, who do well working on their own or as consultants, but have trouble working as a team—but these people are less likely to end up in organizations, simply because they do not have a strong need to belong or to share in a mutual project.

Take notice when descriptions of behavior include words that convey a sense of belonging, sharing, mutuality, or the lack of these, trust or mistrust, helpfulness or helplessness, feeling needed, not feeling needed or appreciated, support, control, power or powerlessness, independence, clinginess, or extreme avoidance. The issue is likely to be dependency.

A Need To Share

Many people still seem to think that workers' grievances result from jobs that are made unpleasant, repetitive, strenuous, dirty, or exacting by changes in technology. But as long ago as 1958, Leonard Sayles argued that it was the social structure derived from the technology, not the technology itself, that determined the level of grievance activity.[14] A more recent study by Nels E. Nelson, Cleveland State U., supports Sayles' findings. Groups of highly skilled employees working fairly independently had few grievances in comparison to semi-skilled workers in similarly scattered work situations, whereas semi-skilled workers who coordinated their tasks with coworkers had a level of grievances similar to that of the skilled workers.[15]

When a task itself is satisfying, that can be enough to keep people who don't like or want to work with others from complaining about things; but most people require supportive contact with others—the opportunity to share problems and develop ties. That's what we described in *Men, Management, and Mental Health* as legitimate dependency needs.[16] When employees have limited contact with each other, most need more contact with supervisors. They need to discuss their progress, not only for advice, but for reassurance that someone is concerned about them.

Matching Socks

There's a lot of talk about organizations suppressing individuality or over-controlling people. As Jane Bensahel points out, people generally need to feel individually different from others in their group, but not *too* different.[17] There's a reason for a certain amount of conformity in organizations. Anything done in an organization requires group effort, or there would be no need for an organization. Group effort requires trust, and that in turn means people need to feel that others are not hostile to them. Conformity in dress, manner, hours, and so on says, "I'm with you." But people don't need to be clones of each other in order to trust each other. Individual differences within an understood range of acceptability are part of the stimulating and enjoyable variety of life.

Bensahel believes that most organizations lean too much toward uniformity, and suggests that the company, or the manager, allow or encourage harmless individuality in dress, decor, work hours (when possible), and so on. I wouldn't go so far as to say *most* organizations, but some do go overboard on uniformity and control, at the cost of innovation. And it's probably not necessary to encourage individuality, because it occurs naturally—just avoid suppressing it as long as it isn't distracting. Often the people who need to present a conspicuous negative image are still unconsciously fighting the battles with their parents over dress, hours, and so on. Managers shouldn't allow themselves to be put in a win/lose situation, but should talk about the image and its cost. There is a significant difference between the freedom required for innovation and rationalized hostility.

A Boss And Blue Cross

Do you ever find yourself thinking you're not needed as a boss, not important to your subordinates? Think again. A freelance writer once told me that all she wanted was a boss and Blue Cross. What she missed, working on her own, was the direction and guidance she now had to supply for herself. She missed having someone else set the deadline and the dimensions of her assignment, require her to be at her desk at 9:00, show her she's in a rut, inspire her out of a slump, focus a directionless manuscript. Without a boss, she had to rely on her own conscience, her own inner drive to work—or the paychecks would stop coming in. She also missed the security of the health insurance most organizations provide. If she were injured or sick, the bills would pile up and her income would stop.

If people complain about the organization, if you feel they resent your enforcing the rules or defining their roles, take it with a grain of salt. Down deep, most of them want a boss and Blue Cross—or they wouldn't be in an organization in the first place.

Contradiction In Ideals

Type A behavior has been linked to heart disease in a variety of studies, but many Type A people never suffer coronaries. Researchers have identified one factor that seems to further distinguish Type As who will have coronaries from those who won't. They subdivided Type As into those who depend mostly on external frames of reference (field dependent) and those who depend mostly on internal ones (field independent). The field dependent group (which I see as leaning more heavily for approval on the outside world) had higher cholesterol levels, regardless of gender.

The researchers suggest that hard driving, competitive, aggressive behavior combined with a field dependent style of processing information "reflects a basic conflict in personality functioning"—in our terms, the simultaneous wish to be aggressive and to be loved. Such people "may be attempting to deny or repress underlying passive, dependent tendencies"[18]—that is, their unconscious wishes to be cared for.

The wish to be nurtured and cared for is a powerful one. But the cost is the possibility of control by those who nurture and care. The period of the "terrible twos" reflects the effort of the child to escape that control and to become autonomous. That effort is given further fuel by the value our culture places on independence. The more powerful the wish to be dependent, the more powerful the compensatory effort to deny it. Workaholic behavior, characteristic of Type As, is one consequence. Since the underlying conflict is unconscious, professional help is required to bring it to the surface so the person need not be so intensely driven and coronary-vulnerable.

Those who are more aware of their strong dependency needs have another option. With success being so clearly defined in our culture as a matter of independence and the money and power that come with positions of leadership in business, it can be difficult to accept the reality that you do *not* fit the "ideal." But the fact is, success can be measured in many ways, and it may be more worthwhile in the long run to recognize that, for example, you are a superior chemical engineer. You can be an expert in your own field, where you must lean on knowledge and organizational structure, rather than force yourself into a managerial role for which your personality is poorly suited. And higher management can support those kinds of wise choices by recognizing (with money, prestige, input into decisions) the expertise and contributions of those who do best in structured roles, rather than "rewarding" professional competence with ill-fitting managerial opportunities.

Faulty Towers

Some men who are towers of strength in their companies and communities are really psychological leaning towers of Pisa. H. Waldo Bird, Peter Martin, and Anthony Schuham call them "collapsible men of prominence" in a study of men overly dependent on very mothering wives (who themselves were compensating for their emotionally impoverished childhoods). These men collapsed psychologically when they felt their marriages were threatened.[19]

Dependency needs are among the most invisible. Managers, who must meet the dependency needs of others, must take special care that their own are met. People who are very powerful at work may not feel free to be dependent on anyone there. They must establish and maintain relationships elsewhere to meet these needs. Certainly the spouse is an obvious choice.

But it isn't good to be 100% dependent on your spouse, who after all may change, leave, die, or just get tired of holding you up. However good a marriage, it's better to have a range of dependencies—friends, colleagues, family. Ask yourself whom you could go to if you were in real trouble, whom you could tell something very embarrassing or incriminating. If there's only one person on earth, you're vulnerable.

What, You Again?

Some people always have a problem. They are always asking someone to help them with something or reassure them that everything is fine. Some of these people specialize in a certain kind of problem—physical complaints, social or family problems, or difficulties with work. These people can be very hard to take, especially if you're the one who's being asked to help for the ten thousandth time.

Psychiatrist Charles Ford, Vanderbilt U. School of Medicine, has an interesting idea about the relationship between hypochondriacs and physicians: they are very much alike, he says. They have certain similar characteristics—emotional inhibition, a tendency toward sexual and marital difficulties and drug abuse, a lack of close relationships with parents in childhood, and a childhood experience of serious illness or death in the family. This leaves them with a fear of illness and death, says Ford, which hypochondriacs handle by developing physical symptoms and physicians handle by learning all they can about treating physical symptoms. And Ford concludes that physicians dislike hypochondriacs because they recognize themselves (often unconsciously) in these patients.[20]

If Ford is correct, there may be a similar relationship between people who have other kinds of problems and the people who are asked for help. Having problems is one way of getting attention; solving problems can be a way to get attention, too. Everyone needs the expert's help. But some people ask for help too often—they don't really need help, they just need attention. And to the extent that experts recognize their own great need for attention in the person who persistently asks, they become irritated with that person. This is not to minimize the real frustration of repeated and apparently unnecessary interruptions.

Ford's suggestion for treating hypochondriacs could be adapted to management. He recommends periodic short visits to the physician during which the physician should first do "doctor-type things" to let the person know his or her health is being taken seriously, and then ask the patient about his or her feelings and family. "Give the patients a chance to talk. The doctor is really practicing medicine when sitting and listening to patients." Managers might do the same with people who chronically complain or ask for help. The manager is really practicing management when sitting and listening to subordinates.

Indulging In Savior Behavior

Firing people is always hard, but it's easier to fire people who have a modicum of competence. Those people can take care of themselves. However, the ones whose performance is so bad that they look like they can't fend for themselves can become psychological traps for managers. The manager fears that these people will actually become the "basket cases" they appear to be, should the manager fire them.

A manager who falls into this trap is participating in a rescue fantasy: a thought, wish, or action about saving somebody from what seems to be a fate worse than death. Rescue fantasies are not limited to subordinates, but can involve a parent, child, spouse, or friend. People who appear to need rescuing often actually survive by attaching themselves to rescuers. In other words, rescue fantasies work in both directions. There are people who cope by getting others to rescue them, as well as people who look for people to rescue. The rescuer unconsciously falls into the trap that is unconsciously set by the rescued: to assume responsibility for the rescued's life. The problem is, no one can live another's life.

Rescuing seldom works. The rescuer expects the other person to eventually stand on his or her own feet, or at least to appreciate what's done for him or her. Neither of these things is likely to happen, and in some cases that's part of the unconscious scheme. For example, when an alcoholic recovers, the spouse who has stayed and suffered for so many years often can't stand the reformed alcoholic. The spouse needed to suffer, and his or her rescue behavior grew out of a need for self-punishment.

The first step in escaping from a rescue fantasy is to recognize that you're indulging in one. If you are, one of these signs is likely to be present:
1. You are angry with the person for not improving or beginning to take responsibility for him or herself.
2. You feel hopeless about the person's ever becoming self-sufficient, and think of the person in terms like "basket case."
3. You find yourself speaking of saving the other person, or of being a savior.
4. You find it upsetting when the person doesn't need you any more. You find yourself being irritable, or you find the other person irritating to be around or think about. You wanted the person to need you, and now he or she doesn't.

If you find yourself in one of these situations, be suspicious of your motives. It's a good idea to talk to someone else and see if he or she can give you a different perspective on the situation. If talking to a colleague or friend seems inappropriate, speak to a professional.

No one can make another's life decisions for very long. We all have the right, and the responsibility, to run our own lives and to make our own mistakes.

You're The Only One Who Can Do It

If you hear yourself saying, "I could do so much if only someone would let me," or "They never give me a break," look at how you're getting in your own way. Many people think they are failures because their managers or organizations don't use them fully. These people frequently experience their work lives as a series of frustrated opportunities, largely because they expect so much of others. They want to move up, but they have such strong dependency needs that they wait for others to create opportunities for them. It is far better to act on your expectations as fully as possible. No one can live another's life or meet another's expectations. When sizing up your career, it's important to be frank about how much you hold others responsible for your lack of progress.

CASE STUDY 151: The Overly Dependent Boss

Who is involved?
Ken Alperin, 31, came to our department a year ago, after making an outstanding contribution in the field. The move was surprising because he had previously stated that he would never consider such a move. At any rate, he became my manager four months ago. Apparently the move was a reward for the project he developed, although it may be that he had threatened to leave the company if he were not promoted. As far as I know, Ken has no prior managerial experience.

What is the problem?
I feel that Ken's promotion should have been mine. My record is good; I have twice as many years of service with the company as he, and am ten years older. When my director told me this man would be my new manager I couldn't believe it. I expressed my disappointment and disbelief strongly, but to little avail. I was assured that I had been doing a great job, but this man needed to be rewarded. For the time being, my salary is higher than his, and I fear there may be some resentment on Ken's part.

What has been tried?
I congratulated my new manager and told him I was pleased that he had been promoted. I also told him that I was disappointed for myself, in view of my record, but that there was work to be done, so we should do it together. Well, it looks like Ken's idea of working together is that he concentrates on his specialty and leaves the managerial work to me.

Where do matters stand?
Ken just isn't holding up his end of the work. He's very unsure of himself and looks to me for guidance, direction, and implementation in everything except his one successful area. He is also very uncomfortable in social situations and handles them poorly. When traveling, he is hesitant about taking the responsibility for car rentals, paying for meals, and so on. Decisions he should make are finally turned over to me. He knows he isn't doing well, and keeps saying he doesn't see how he can do the job.

What change is sought?

I can't keep spending so much time and energy taking care of Ken and the work he doesn't do. He has to learn to stand on his own feet. Besides, I have my own future to consider. How can I get the recognition and promotion I want, if I spend all my time supporting Ken and making him look good through my efforts? On the other hand, if I let Ken fall flat on his face, as I think he would without my support, it would harm the company, not just Ken. Where does the good of the company end and self-interest and ambition begin?

ANALYSIS

Where is the pain?

The narrator is in pain because he didn't get the promotion he thought he deserved, and because he is now burdened with an incompetent boss. He sees Ken as a usurper of his rightful position. Ken is in pain, too; he apparently feels as inadequate and incompetent as the narrator paints him.

When did the problem begin?

The present situation resulted from Ken's promotion to manager. We don't know whether Ken has always been reluctant to take on responsibility and is characteristically uncomfortable in social situations. He may simply lack the experience this position requires.

How does the person handle affection?

Ken invests himself considerably in his own area of expertise, as evidenced by the outstanding contribution for which he is being rewarded.

How does the person handle aggression?

Ken has a rather inhibited way of handling aggression. He can't act straightforwardly and responsibly, and he is having trouble directing his aggression into learning the new aspects of his position. If this is typical for Ken, the narrator's resentment and low opinion of him are only exacerbating it. However, Ken may just be overwhelmed by his new job, and may gradually be able to take on more responsibility with appropriate support from his superiors and the narrator.

How does the person handle dependency?

Ken's constant need for reassurance indicates that he is quite dependent. He leans heavily on the narrator and others to help structure his activity. Perhaps he devoted himself so exclusively to his field that he never learned how to associate with people and how to manage. His dependency could be a product of the situation, but for a grown man to be acting this way seems to be more characterological.

What is the person's ego ideal?
The fact that Ken made an outstanding contribution indicates that his ego ideal involves doing well at his job. His area of specialization must also be very important to him, since he can't tear himself away from it to start learning other parts of his job.

Can this problem be solved?
The narrator's conflict about whether to help Ken and possibly under-cut himself or to let Ken down in the hope of getting that position for himself may not be a continuing problem. His superiors may know that giving Ken this spot is a mistake, but feel they have to give him a shot at it. If he continues this behavior they will become aware of it, so the situation is likely to be temporary. Meanwhile, the crucial issue for the narrator is his own reputation. He could make a terrible mistake by under-mining or not supporting Ken. That might indicate to his superiors that he can't distinguish between disappointment and defeat, and should not hold a higher level job. If he supports and builds up his manager, he will demonstrate his loyalty, conscientiousness, and ability to take things in stride. By accepting the fact that Ken's promotion is no reflection on him, the narrator can turn his present painful situation into an opportunity to demonstrate his managerial skills.

Ego Ideal: The Ideal Self

Each of us has an image of his or her perfect self. We may not be very conscious of this ideal, but it exists at some level of awareness. We are constantly striving to achieve this ideal, and we need to believe that we are approaching it, because the gap between the way we see ourselves (self-image) and our ego ideal defines our level of self-esteem. We tend to be unhappy when we are not working toward our ideal, and we tend to be angry with ourselves when we see the ways in which we don't live up to our ego ideal. This often-unreasonable pressure to be perfect now comes from our conscience, called the superego. We also tend to be angry with people who would point out to us or to the world our "inadequacies," our failures to match our image of the ideal. Or else we don't even hear what they say. That's how important it is to see ourselves as moving toward our ego ideal.

The ego ideal is a double-edged sword. It is the single most powerful motivator of behavior. We strive to like ourselves; the narrower the gap, the better we feel about ourselves. Offering a person an opportunity to move closer to his or her ego ideal is the best way to get good work from a person—both parties gain. But offering a person a challenge that is too great and ends in failure, thus pointing out that he is not who he thinks he is, can be devastating. The problem usually is a mismatch between what the person wants to become and the opportunities the job affords, which may result in boredom and dissatisfaction with the job and himself. For this reason obtaining "job fit" for yourself and your subordinates is a very important factor in managing a successful organization. Sometimes a good fit between person and job is not possible because the person's ego ideal is unobtainably high, and no amount of success will be sufficient. And for some unfortunate souls, success is psychologically proscribed: they don't know what they want and are chronically dissatisfied with whatever they've got; or they think they know what they want but prevent themselves from getting it or don't like it once they do; or they attain success and then self-destruct.

Take notice when descriptions of behavior indicate a consistent striving for a certain result (regardless of whether it's already been achieved), the person's satisfaction or disappointment with results of his or her efforts, or satisfaction or disappointment with opportunities offered. The behavior is a clue to the person's ego ideal.

Survival Of The Idealists

Concentration camp survivors didn't survive through guile, betrayal, or force—they survived because they lived for ideals that transcended their own lives. So says psychologist and camp survivor Bruno Bettelheim in *Surviving.*[21]

Few of us face such tests. But no one can survive the distress, failure, and grief we all inevitably encounter without ideals that transcend our day-to-day concerns. That's why everyone needs a clear understanding of his or her ego ideal. Namely: What were your parents' values? What is the first thing you recall doing that pleased them? Who are your models or heroes? What education and career choices have you made—and why? What were you doing the two or three times in your life when you were most elated? The answer to these questions will give you a microcosm of your ego ideal. Your values and behaviors are most likely much the same now as they've been in the past. True, your ego ideal will change somewhat over time as you mature and the emphases of your values shift. But the unfolding pattern of your life will remain consistent. If you can see the pattern, you will understand your ego ideal, and you'll be prepared to cope adequately with whatever life presents.

It's All My Fault

People with strong superegos and high ego ideals are prone to depression. When things go wrong we don't blame external forces or chance or fate—we blame ourselves. We want to control so much. We feel responsible for our work and our subordinates' work, for our feelings and our families' feelings. But life never goes smoothly; there are always ragged edges. When our marriages flourish, our work relationships may languish; when our careers are secure, our adolescent children are at a pitch of uncertainty. If we blame ourselves for not resolving all our problems, we can sink into debilitating depression. Better to see our limits and stop punishing ourselves for our human imperfections.

It Isn't As Easy As You Think

We often look at well-known people and, seeing the apparent effortlessness of their success, judge ourselves harshly for our mistakes and shortcomings. But most success is far from being as effortless as it looks. The problem is, we see only the finished product, not the struggle to achieve it. Sculptor Louise Nevelson puts it this way: "I had to run like hell to catch up with what I thought of myself—if someone went six, I'd go twelve, you know? I had to move, not to get frustrated; and I was frustrated enough."[22] Her ego ideal is so high, so impossible to reach, that she must constantly strive, harder and harder. She can never succeed at attaining it, even though the struggle brings her success in the eyes of the world. A similar discomfort is apparent in Walter Cronkite's description of himself at work: "I'm a very difficult boss. I'm also very impatient with myself. If I've dropped the ball, I start screaming and hollering at the entire production. I hate that in myself. I haven't been able to cure it."[23] His ego ideal is so demanding that a slip is practically intolerable. The anger at himself comes flooding out over anyone and everyone handy, despite all his efforts to control it.

Do you have a manager who yells at everyone in sight when she makes a mistake? If so, it's important, as a protection for your self-image, to recognize that the manager is really angry at herself. And if you find yourself being unreasonably angry, either at yourself or others, when you don't measure up to your own ideal of perfection, stop a minute. Remember that those above you in the organization, and famous and successful people, only *seem* to walk on water. If you scratch the surface, underneath you'll often find restless, driven people, whose faults loom large in their own eyes as they struggle to meet the demands of their impossibly high ego ideals.

Let's Go Fly A Kite

Dr. Lawrence Susser has an unusual treatment for workaholics: he takes them hiking. After a period of regular psychotherapy, he detaches his clients from their usual surroundings and the opportunity to work, and encourages them to take a look at the world around them. He counteracts the superego—the conscience—by providing lots of time but minimal tasks. When they run out of things to push themselves to accomplish, they begin to relax and enjoy the beauty of their surroundings. As

Dr. Susser's success in treating workaholics has become known, they have come to comprise almost one-third of his private psychiatric practice.[24]

This treatment isn't as strange as it sounds. Most workaholics are people with astronomically high ego ideals. The unconscious guilt of not living up to their expectations of themselves, or to their parents' expectations, or both, needs to be relieved. Workaholics drive themselves hard all the time in order to relieve this guilt. They can't give themselves permission to stop working, relax, and enjoy themselves. Dr. Susser's treatment provides the authoritative permission they need to do that, and he himself is a role model for doing so.

Managers can ease some of the internal pressures their subordinates feel by clearly defining the requirements of a situation—both what *is* required and what *is not*. This gives people permission from an authoritative, parental-type figure to work a little less hard. The manager will need to do this frequently, because it can only provide temporary relief. This is particularly necessary in ambiguous situations, as when people are evolving new products or techniques, or are on some other innovative frontier. Many managers take pride in driving themselves hard and want their people to do the same. But in fact they will probably get better quality work from their people if they help their subordinates ease up. The result will probably be more creative effort and less destructive pressure.

Others who may need permission to slow down are women and minority group members. These people are trying desperately to find a place for themselves and to prove that they are just as good as, if not better than, their white male counterparts. Again, this relief is temporary, but if permission to slow down is given often enough and by a powerful enough figure, it can ease some of the self-imposed pressure.

FOCUS ON . . . . Identifying Organizational Purpose

The Difference Between Objectives And Purpose

Every organization, from a three-member task force to a multinational corporation, was originally organized for a particular object—to make money, to market a product, to fight cancer. Once the organization is rolling, the apparent, conscious purpose begins to take on another dimension. Subtly, there arises what I call a transcendent purpose. The conscious purpose is an objective to be achieved. But the desire to achieve that objective is based on the unconscious striving of the founders toward their ideal selves—their ego ideals. That is their transcendent purpose.

An organization has both objectives and purpose, just as a song has both lyrics and melody. A song's lyrics are explicit, as are the objectives of an organization. The melody is not so direct, but often more expressive. Likewise, organizational purpose may not be clearly stated, but it is the more powerful motivating force. Lyrics and melody sometimes tell two different stories; so do objectives and purpose. Where they are different, hearing and acting on the lyrics alone can get the organization into trouble.

Can't Sing The Words Without A Tune

The founders of an organization are generally not aware of their transcendent purpose, their expectation of moving toward their ego ideals. It's not clear to them that they went into the venture for any reason beyond their expressed objective. So when the organization achieves its original objective, the leadership is at a loss as to where to go next. When polio was a major crippler of children, an organization was needed to raise money to fight the disease. Once the disease was controlled, the leadership didn't want to dismantle such a successful fund-raising organization. So they turned to fighting birth defects, duplicating others' efforts. Had they been clearly aware of their transcendent purpose—probably to achieve social and political power—they might have chosen quite a different course.

Often an organization is successful precisely because of the founders' transcendent purpose, without anyone ever knowing it. General Motors was successful for many years, largely because it established innovative controls; Alfred P. Sloan's ego ideal involved being a great control innovator. Not realizing the significance of his ideal, Sloan hired people who could carry out his controls, without worrying about whether they had the flexibility to evolve further methods. After he left, the company continued to benefit from his innovations, but adhered to them too rigidly to meet changing market demands.

When an organization is unaware of its transcendent purpose, all it can do is increase its efficiency in reaching objectives. It's taken for granted that what you're doing is what you ought to be doing, because it's what you've always done. Small units of large organizations are particularly prone to this attitude. The middle manager figures, my bosses must know what they're doing. Who am I to question their reasons? The unit strives for efficiency and becomes rigidified without knowing it. The mighty Roman Empire declined, according to sociologist Robert Antonio, U. Kans., because it functioned so efficiently that it took on a life of its own. It lost its original commitment to service, and efficiency and self-preservation became its only goals.[25]

The environment is always changing, and organizations must be able to adapt if they are to survive and grow. Without a transcendent purpose, there is nothing to guide the modification of objectives to meet new circumstances. The need for change is often denied until its effects become too drastic to ignore—as in the case of GM. Even then managers may simply try harder in the same old ineffective ways, and wonder why they fail despite their efforts. On the other hand, if an organization is aware of its purpose, it has a central theme to guide its activities at all levels, through both internal and external changes.

Are You On Track?
It's important for managers to step back from the daily routine and look at the way their units are functioning in relation to the larger organization, or how the organization is doing in relation to its environment. Are your expressed objectives consonant with what you are trying to become? Such a review is needed periodically to keep the unit or organization from inadvertently becoming inflexible.

When you find your unit or organization isn't doing as well as it should, what do you do? It's easy to get caught up in formal planning in the attempt to get back on track, as Tom Peters has noted.[26] With computers to handle masses of data, you can have statistics on almost anything you want, but statistics don't tell you much about the real world. You may know someone's vital statistics, but they don't tell you what that person looks like, much less what he or she thinks and feels. Instead of running to the computer, doing a survey, and getting bogged down in detailed plans, think first about what you're doing there.

If your company has identified and communicated its transcendent purpose, consider how your unit fits in. Using the organizational purpose as a guide, identify your own unit's purpose. If your company has not identified its purpose, it becomes even more important to identify that of your own unit. It will have to be based on the organization's objectives rather than its purpose; but you will need it to maintain your unit's flexibility in adapting to the changing organizational environment, regardless of what motivates those changes. And the more clearly you communicate your unit's theme to your subordinates, the more likely people are to identify with it, make it their own, and join you in working toward it.

Peters talks about "playing with lofty ideas, searching for an enduring theme." It's important to realize that the place to search is not "out there" in the world. The theme already exists, in the hearts and minds of the leaders of the organization. The place to look is inside.

Discovering The Melody
To begin, you need a simple statement of your own ego ideal, and the same from each of your subordinates. One way to arrive at that statement is to consider what you would like to leave behind when you leave your present job. Once you have stated your own desired legacy, ask your subordinates to do the same, and then share them with each other. Taken all together, what do they say? By combining the individual themes, you will evolve the theme of the group.

A business is like a play—it has a theme which directs the action. Once you have discovered your organizational theme, the plot will follow. An actor who forgets his lines still knows what his presence on stage is meant to accomplish and can improvise on that basis; a play can be written as a bare outline for improvisation. When people know what the theme of their organization is, detailed plans for every move are not necessary. What they need is an outline on which to improvise.

A play without a theme would be just a bunch of actions—there would be no way to make sense of what was happening. It would have no life. The same is true of an organization. The central theme is the spirit that gives life to the actions. It answers the perennial question, why are we doing this?

Basic Concepts

Here are a few other concepts that come up frequently—guilt, denial, *and* ambivalence.

The Unconscious Guilt Trip

Different people have different ideas about what guilt is, and whether it serves any useful purpose or is simply a painful feeling to be avoided or removed as quickly as possible. One reason for the variety and a certain amount of confusion is that there are two kinds of guilt. P. L. Travers, creator of Mary Poppins, says that guilt is valuable and should lead us to try for absolution instead of attempting to forget it.[27] She is talking about conscious guilt. When we "feel guilty," that's conscious guilt. It usually reflects a wish not to hurt another or regret for something we have said or done. It's an alarm signal that we're not living up to our own code of behavior, and that we should apologize or make some kind of reparation.

Unconscious guilt, on the other hand, usually shows up as a failure to take action, as in being unable to speak up or be straightforward with people or take charge. This reflects a general fear of hurting others, rather than a reaction to a specific instance of having hurt someone. This inhibition of behavior is usually not easily explained and not easy to change. Unconscious guilt can't be forgotten, because it isn't conscious to begin with. It's also very difficult to wipe out. Since it's irrational, one can't correct the cause, apologize, or make reparation. But if it gets in the way of appropriate behavior—that is, if you have trouble taking charge, giving directions, appraising performance, or standing up for yourself—you need to work toward some kind of change.

What can you do? First, recognize that the behavior you want to change is the result of unconscious guilt, and that unconscious guilt is irrational. Second, recognize the ways in which the inhibited behavior is actually hurtful, instead of preventing hurt as it is intended to do. A clear example is performance appraisal—people are hurt more by being told things are fine when they aren't than by being told what is not fine about their performance. In fact, being told what's wrong is helpful to them, once they get over their disappointment, because then they can move closer to being the way they would like to be. Finally, try out and practice behaving in ways that are appropriate and acceptable, such as standing up for yourself when you feel pushed around, putting yourself forward when you deserve recognition, and stopping yourself when you realize you're bending over backwards for someone when you would rather not. And in any situation where someone else would feel angry but you don't, see if you can find that anger in yourself. It's probably there, and that's OK.

One Cheer For Denial

We generally brand denial as a problem—an unproductive way of coping with unpleasant realities. But denial, like all psychological defense mechanisms, is neither good nor bad in itself. It is either appropriate or inappropriate for a given person in certain circumstances.

From an early age, we know that someday we will die. This should be terrifying. Yet most people are not living in fear of death. How do we do it? Denial: death is a fact, but we just don't think about it very often. The situation changes drastically when one is diagnosed with a terminal disease. Denial is no longer so easy and automatic. According to Drs. John E. O'Malley and Gerald Koocher of Sidney Farber Cancer Institute, Boston, who studied children with cancer and their families, "The central issue for these people is how they cope with uncertainty. . . . While denial has traditionally been considered a rather primitive, undesirable defense mechanism, in this study the best copers proved to be those who learned to deny in useful, therapeutic ways. . . . We don't know how to teach adaptive denial, though. We wish we did."[28]

Adaptive denial is adaptive *only* when there truly is nothing else to be done. In these cases, such as terminal diseases, the medical profession is realizing the importance of psychological adaptation, both for the dying patient—who may have years of life left to live—and for his or her family. If you or a member of your family are ever in this unfortunate bind, and if psychological information or counseling is not offered to you, ask about it. Even if you never need such help, it's wise to know that it's available, and where it is.

What Do Followers Really Feel?

We all have had mixed emotions about power figures such as our parents and our managers. These emotions are called *ambivalence,* a fundamental psychological experience in which two feelings are present simultaneously, one of which—usually the negative feeling—is unconscious. Ambivalence often makes the leadership role difficult. Leaders who have expected praise are often disappointed by the hostility, envy, and jealousy of their followers. Outstandingly competent leaders are likely to evoke such feelings. The reason is that subordinates want to follow such a leader and want to emulate him or her, but at the same time, followers have the feeling that they can never be as competent as the leader. This maximizes their feelings of inadequacy and of dependency on the leader. Followers react to those feelings (which are usually unconscious) by trying to shoot the leader down, by gossiping about him, criticizing him, attacking him verbally, and even by rejecting him. When the leader pulls back from this type of assault, the followers are likely to become frightened. They feel that without the leader, they cannot succeed. Followers need leaders as a target for their ambivalence. Through their interaction with the leader, their ambivalent feelings are worked out in a continuous process. This means that the leadership role is, in many ways, like a seesaw. It is fraught with crosscurrents of feelings on the part of followers. The leader, too, has mixed feelings about his followers.

Leaders who learn to understand ambivalence can manage it by keeping followers focused on the task to be accomplished. When followers bring up problems, the leader should ask, "What do you want to do about this?" This helps alleviate the followers' dependency feelings, and gives them an opportunity to demonstrate their own capabilities.

All people being trained for managerial and executive roles should understand the concept of ambivalence. Participants in executive training programs should have the opportunity to talk about the confusion leaders feel when they receive mixed messages from their followers so they can learn how to manage those feelings.

In Summary

1. *Unconscious feelings are, by definition, outside the person's awareness, but their presence can be inferred from behavior. Puzzling behavior is less puzzling when we see how it fits into the person's consistent patterns of behavior.*
2. *The way a person typically handles affection can be seen in the amount and kind of contact he or she has with others.*
3. *The way a person typically handles aggression can be seen in the amount and direction of energy invested in accomplishing tasks, and in the way the person acts when feeling angry.*
4. *The way a person typically handles dependency can be seen in the degree of willingness to take part in cooperative projects, and in the extent to which the person is willing and able to give and receive help.*
5. *A person's ego ideal can be inferred from the kinds of activity he or she chooses over time and the values implicit in the person's typical ways of handling affection, aggression, and dependency.*

Satisfying Work

To maintain their emotional health, people need satisfying work. That is, they need opportunities to have an effect on the world in ways that are consistent with their values, their imagined ideal selves, and their characteristic ways of handling affection, aggression, and dependency. They need to be able to commit themselves to their work, to invest themselves in tasks that they consider worthwhile. This is one of the things that gives meaning to people's lives.

Organizations don't *have* to consider the psychological meaning of work for their employees—and until recently, they didn't. But ignoring it is usually a tremendous waste, and destructive to the organization as well. People do their best work when their work fulfills some of their psychological needs. They do their worst work when their tasks run counter to those needs; in addition, their internal conflict over the situation may lead to destructive behavior toward themselves or others. These psychological realities should be taken into consideration when hiring and promoting people, when reviewing their performance, and when considering how to maximize productivity and creativity.

Job Fit

Now we can get down to the nitty-gritty of applying this psychological understanding to the working world. First, let's look at the job and organization as a whole. How do you figure out what sort of person a particular job requires? How do you tell whether a particular person will fit the bill? How can you define your own behavioral characteristics and ideals, so that you can find roles and organizations that will help you fulfill your own needs? What kinds of changes can be made in a job without throwing off the fit between person and role, and what kinds of changes are doomed from the start? What kinds of job dissatisfaction just won't go away, try as you will to make things better?

Fundamentals Of Job Fit

A job that suits you is likely to contribute to a long, healthy life. Or so says U. Pa. psychiatrist Dr. Peter Brill, who adds that our self-esteem and psychological health are closely bound up with our sense of competence.[1]

Satisfying work does contribute to our overall well-being, but not simply because competence contributes to self-esteem. The right fit between person and role satisfies our most fundamental and deeply rooted personality needs. The requirements for affection, aggression, and dependency that we establish in earliest infancy are gratified or frustrated in our work experiences and relationships. People with strong aggressive drives, for instance, can profit from jobs that require them to attack problems; without such jobs, they're likely to find less appropriate outlets for their aggression.

Work shapes our habits of thought and action to an extraordinary degree. Without it, we'd be overwhelmed with fantasies we'd rather keep at bay, or with great stretches of emptiness. But if the job doesn't interest us or feel right, then our lives are thrown off balance. The lesson for managers is clear: it's no favor to keep subordinates in slots that don't suit them. Next time you find yourself despairing over a subordinate who cannot or will not do what's required, remember that no one wants to be killed with misguided kindness.

The Wisdom To Know The Difference

Managers often find themselves wanting to change a subordinate's behavior because it hampers his or her performance. Before trying to get someone to change, assess carefully both the person's behavior and the behavior required by the job. You may be asking the impossible, and the consequences can be tragic.

One manager transferred a subordinate to another city in an attempt to change his behavior. The subordinate's characteristic behavior reflected his desire to please others, and that behavior fit his original role admirably. But his manager wanted him to be more aggressive. The man had been in the first city for nearly 20 years and was reluctant to transfer, but he was given no choice. He did poorly in the new role (which did require more aggressive attack), despite wanting very much to please his manager and do well. By now, it's an either/or situation. The manager is unhappy because the subordinate didn't shape up, though he had a good record before the move. The subordinate is unhappy because he is failing in his work and because he can't please his manager.

Since the new role required different behavior, the man's previous performance had no bearing on his ability to succeed in it. This man cannot be the aggressive attacker his manager wants him to be. During a performance review, he finally realized that he was up against the impossible. The manager reports that, "Halfway through the performance appraisal, his face changed." As the impossibility dawned on him, he felt overwhelmed and paralyzed. There was simply nothing he could do.

Never assume that one function is the same as another, even when they are very close in concept; the behavior required may be substantially different. What does that matter? People can adapt and change within certain limits, but they cannot adopt a completely different approach to the world, and sometimes that's what they are asked to do. *Take the consistency of behavior seriously.* Do not try to wrench people out of their consistent patterns and force them into others. Those patterns represent the person's method of maintaining his or her internal equilibrium, and meddling with them can have serious repercussions.

How do you evaluate the degree of fit between person and role? Analyze the behavior required by the role, just as we analyze the behavior of people in our cases. (See p. 30 for an example.) Ask, "How does this role require the incumbent to handle affection, aggression, and dependency, and if the function is performed well, what are the gratifications?" For instance: If a person does the job well, where will his or her kicks come from? Does the job require one to please a lot of people? If so, primarily upwards, or downwards? How much response does the job situation provide from above, or below, and how quickly will it come? What must be attacked and by what means? Is a vigorous intellectual attack called for, as in a lawyer's brief, or faultless control of many small elements, as with an accounting ledger? Does the job require supporting and developing others? Who has to lean on whom, and for what? What kinds of expectations, problems, conflicts, and rivalries will arise? Once the job is defined in psychological terms, the candidates should be assessed in the same way.

My Kind Of Business

Different types of leaders are needed for different phases of an organization's life cycle.[2] By the same token, a particular manager is likely to enjoy a particular phase of the organizational life cycle, and do his or her best work in an organization which is at that stage. Apparently John Sculley recognized this when he resigned as president of Pepsi-Cola Co. to become president and CEO of Apple Computer, Inc. In making the move, he gave up a good shot at becoming the head of PepsiCo Inc., Pepsi-Cola's parent company. But he had no regrets. "I see the computer business where the soft-drink business was 10 years ago," said Sculley. "It's a high-growth business, and competitors are still being formed." The soft-drink business, on the other hand, has reached a slow-growth phase, "and we're all fighting to gain half a share point. It's not as exciting as it was."[3]

There are risks in moving into such a different business, and it is far from assured that Sculley will repeat his previous success. But he recognized an important facet of his personality—the need for the excitement of a competitive, high-growth situation.

Stressing The Essence Of Stress

Unskilled laborers, clinical lab technicians, and house painters have highly stressful jobs, reports *Parade* magazine; garment workers, child care employees, and heavy equipment operators have among the least stressful jobs.[4]

There's a lot of nonsensical talk these days about what work is stressful and what isn't. Most of it shows little understanding of the psychology of stress. Imbalanced personality functions cause stress. For instance, superego conflicts, as when employees are asked to produce inferior work or support policies that run counter to their own principles, create stress. Growing older and becoming outdated on the job can create stress. People also experience stress when they can't measure up to the requirements and expectations of their jobs, or when the requirements of their jobs are ambiguous and contradictory. And when people work without the approval of others, or without relationships that satisfy their dependency needs, they often feel stress.

Most discussions of job stress ignore or slight the dynamic relationship of person and role. Any job can be stressful if the wrong person fills it; any person can feel stress if job demands, life changes, or emotional conflicts upset the personality balances he or she has evolved since earliest childhood.

If you're suffering from stress, ask yourself, perhaps with the help of a professional therapist, what your ego ideal is and how you've fallen short of it. You may be able to change directions, work habits, or leisure activities in ways that bring you closer to your ideal. You may be able to scale down perfectionistic expectations. But until you know what's causing the stress, you won't know how to counteract it.

Hiring

It's one thing to analyze the behavior patterns of a person whose work you know, and whom you see every day and have known perhaps for years. It's quite another to meet someone briefly through a resume, an interview, and perhaps a few phone calls to people who have worked with her or him. What sorts of clues should you be watching for? How much can you really tell about a person's characteristic behavior from such a small amount of information? What kinds of questions are worth asking in an interview— and how do you take the answers? Does it make sense to use tools such as lie detectors, handwriting analysis, psychological tests, and assessment centers? And if you do, how do you interpret the results?

Just A Little Bit

"When we hired this executive," said his boss over the telephone, "we thought we saw a little bit more authoritarian behavior than was optimum, but it was just a little and we didn't think it would get in his way. It has. Where can we send him for help?"

This kind of call comes in frequently. Interviewers often note an aspect of behavior that waves a red flag, but in the interview that behavior is minimal. So the interviewer discards the observation and hires the candidate. The upshot is predictable. If there is a small flaw in the interview, or if references describe the negative aspects of someone's behavior as being minor, it would pay to think of those characteristics as magnified a number of times. People are on their best behavior in an interview. In the day-to-day struggle, personality features that were fleeting impressions are likely to assume their true proportions. Don't discard those impressions. Explore them in greater depth; anticipate that what looks like a little problem will be a big problem before you get done with it. It's no fun, having to tell a recently hired executive that he'd better get professional help or start looking for another job—and it's not fair.

Washington Didn't Lie About The Tree

Many executives fail to become CEOs when they overrate themselves in interviews. This is one finding of Business Careers, Inc., a recruiting firm that analyzed the performance of 250 candidates for 16 CEO positions. Many unsuccessful candidates were not objective about their own strengths and weaknesses, glossed over their past failures, and passed the buck to others in their organizations.[5]

It's easy to assume that nothing succeeds like success, and that any failure or weakness can cost us the promotions we want. Or if we're interviewing others, we can be dazzled by the candidate who seems to have the Midas touch. But no one is perfect, no record is unblemished. An applicant who brags unduly, especially at the expense of others, is arrogant and narrow-minded, not superior. This behavior shows a person who doesn't respond well to pressure. A good leader, and a good bet for promotion, is someone who has learned from past experiences, and can assess himself or herself objectively. Don't let a slick candidate sell you a bill of goods. Ask candidates for promotion what their worst mistakes were, how they handled them at the time, and how they'd handle them today. You'll learn a lot about their business sense and character. The person who has blundered and recovered often has more strength and shrewdness than the person who has performed without a hitch and hasn't yet been tested by failure.

Computerized Psychological Testing

Psychological test reports are not necessarily what they seem. Business executives don't realize that frequently they are being presented with pasteups of computer printouts, rather than the considered opinion of a well-trained psychological professional. It's not the executives' area of expertise, of course, but it's also very easy for an insufficiently trained person to make a valid-sounding "personality assessment" by throwing together a bunch of statements reflecting common human experience. This was demonstrated in 1948 by Bertram Forer, who gave his students a personality test, then asked them to rate the accuracy of the "results." They didn't know that he gave them all the same description, which included the following statements:

"Some of your aspirations tend to be pretty unrealistic. . . . You pride yourself on being an independent thinker and do not accept others' opinions without satisfactory proof. You prefer a certain amount of change and variety, and become dissatisfied when hemmed in by restrictions and limitations. . . . Your sexual adjustment has presented some problems for you. While you have some personality weaknesses, you are generally able to compensate for them. . . . You have a tendency to be critical of yourself. You have a strong need for other people to like you and for them to admire you."

Most of those statements were gleaned from an astrology book. On a scale of 0 (poor) to 5 (perfect), 34 out of 39 students rated the description 4 or 5, and none rated it below 2. Over the years, other students have given it similar ratings.[6]

Those statements probably are true for many people. They are so general that they don't really say much anyway. But people are so much under the gun of their superegos, so unsure of themselves, and want so badly to know more about themselves, that they are willing to believe those statements are uniquely about themselves. They also find greater or more specific incidents that are evidence *for* those statements, and tend to ignore the fact that there is much evidence *against* them, too.

So the results of computerized psychological tests can be entirely believable, without being the least bit valid. We know that the validity of most paper-and-pencil psychological tests is low. That's why the competence of the tester is so important. Replace the tester with a computer, and you lose whatever added strength professional judgment can give the test results. The American Psychological Association Code of Ethics says that the tester must *see* the person he or she is testing; that otherwise it is unethical to interpret the results of a paper-and-pencil test.

Tests like the Rorschach inkblot test and the TAT (Thematic Apperception Test, in which subjects make up stories based on a situation in a photograph) don't hold up well in validity studies, either, because the objective measurements or scores are beside the point. It's like measuring a cloud. You can take the length and the width, but that doesn't tell you much about the shape of it. And with psychological tests, it's the shape of the cloud we're interested in—the dynamic interrelation of many factors. It is the skill of the psychologist that makes sense or nonsense out of psychological test results.

The Truth About Polygraphs

Do polygraphs lie? Not exactly, but neither can they detect the truth, as so many people believe. For instance, researchers say that polygraphs haven't unearthed much accurate information about employees for the many companies that use them. The tests aren't even much good at screening suspects of a particular theft.[7]

Despite their name, lie detectors can only monitor skin temperature and blood pressure—they can't detect lies. Someone must interpret what the blips on the machine mean, including whether they reflect a fantasy or anxiety or a real situation. Conversely, those who don't feel guilt don't activate the machines; it may also be possible for people to learn to fool the machines. But too often the people using polygraphs aren't sophisticated enough to understand the variables, much less interpret them sensitively. Although in some instances, when used by highly skilled and experienced professionals, polygraphs can be of some value, for most companies they're just not worth it. They don't generate hard data; but using them often generates hard feelings.

Shrewd: Sagacious, Perspicacious, Astute

In working with executives on selecting managers and discussing who are good managers and who will be most successful, I am struck by the absence of the word *shrewd*. Nobody speaks of the shrewdness of the candidate: the person's ability to see angles that other people do not see, or to pick needles out of haystacks, or to devise competitive methods when other people have given up, or to construct financial packages that show great imagination. Shrewdness seems to have acquired a bad name. And although it apparently is fine for an entrepreneur to be shrewd, it's not all right for a manager.

Dreamers And Doers

Recruiters often look for "he-men" when they're filling executive positions. They want competitive and aggressive, dominant and self-confident leaders, and they think he-men can control others and express themselves openly. But research by my colleague Dr. Kenneth D. Stein of Berkeley disputes these assumptions. The action-oriented male, says Stein, has low tolerance for complexity and little independence of judgment. He also lacks self-control, sensitivity to others, and an ability to abstract. Research by David Loye, UCLA, corroborates Stein's findings. Aggressive people are likely to be low fantasizers, Loye found, because they act impulsively and don't seek other outlets for their emotions.[8]

Is the best executive someone who can take charge? Yes, but that's not enough. The best executive must also be able to entertain fantasies and evolve creative solutions to problems. When examining people for executive roles, look at how freely they can express fantasy lives. Ask what novels, plays, music, and art they enjoy. People who have creative interest *and* the ability to take charge are likely to be innovative and comfortable with their aggression. They're good bets for leadership roles.

Performance Appraisal

Performance appraisal is one of the most universally required managerial tasks—and probably the most universally avoided as well. The reasons for this avoidance are explored in this section, along with some antidotes to it. Better yet, it turns out that performance appraisal can work to the appraiser's advantage.

Most people sustain their enthusiasm for a task best when their efforts are acknowledged and evaluated through regular feedback and performance appraisal, even when the task is one they find personally engaging. People need, at the least, confirmation of their own appraisal of their performance. Sometimes they need to be told how much better they are doing than they think they are, if they tend to judge themselves harshly. Sometimes, unfortunately, they must be told that they are not doing as well as they think, and must improve in certain ways or look for other work they can do better. Although that's the hardest appraisal to give, it can be the most satisfying in the long run, because it opens the way to positive change.

Measuring The Unmeasurable

If you asked, "How's the weather?" and the reply was, "Oh, about 87%," you'd probably think the person was crazy. It's just as crazy and pointless to talk about performance that way, yet people persist in doing so. *Measuring* performance means reducing complex human behavior to numbers, and you just can't do that.

There are a few types of measurement in the behavioral sciences, but their usefulness is rather limited. For instance, you could use rank order, listing people in order of how well they do their jobs—but what do you do with Jack, who does a great job whenever he's not busy feuding with Sue? Does he go at the top of the list for quality, at the bottom for productivity, or in the middle as some sort of average? You could use a rating scale, giving people points from 0 to 10—but you really can't say the distance between 1 and 2 is the same as the distance between 7 and 8, as my colleague Dr. Fred Glixman points out. It's just not the same as measuring inches on a ruler. You could use a curve of normal distribution, and say this person is in the upper 10% or that one is in the lower 40%—but that's still vague and there's always a degree of error. Clearly none of these are objective measures; they all depend on assigning a number to a subjective opinion.

So what can you measure about performance? How many dollars a person earned for the company, how many units someone produced, how many complaints an individual handled? None of the things you can measure tell you much about how a person manages a department and whether he or she could do it better. If you try to measure performance, you may find yourself ignoring the most important aspects of a job, merely because they can't be measured. Would you measure an airline pilot's performance by the number of miles flown without a crash? You'd never know that he or she took dangerous chances in flight until there was a crash. It's the *how* of how a person works that counts, but that's what tends to get lost in performance appraisal. The quality of a manager's continuing relationships with people is unmeasurable, yet fundamental to his or her performance. It's not that measurement is bad; in some cases it just doesn't apply.

Making Your Signals Clear

What do you do when you're disappointed in a subordinate's performance? If you're like many managers I see, you avoid the issue. After all, it's painful to tell an old and loyal employee, or someone who came highly praised, or someone you selected yourself, that he or she isn't making the grade. In such cases many managers feel they can't criticize the subordinate because they share the responsibility for the failure. But managers who procrastinate hurt all concerned—the subordinates, themselves, and their organizations.

Managing by guilt, rather than by sound judgment, is one of the cardinal sins of management. It creates the following problems:

1. It denies subordinates the opportunity to develop their skills and adapt their behaviors to the real requirements of the workplace.
2. It permits problems to drag. By keeping people in the dark about their inadequacies, it perpetuates failure.
3. It undermines the relationship between managers and subordinates by allowing the managers' unacknowledged anger to build and spill out in thinly veiled, inappropriate ways. And the subordinates are caught in a double bind: on the one hand, they're told everything is fine, but on the other, they're never really permitted to savor success. They can't read the managers' clouded signals, so they're deluded or paralyzed.

Some managers think they have to string inadequate subordinates along or palm them off on unsuspecting peers. Not true. Many times people can change when their managers tell them directly what's wrong with their performance. And when people are dead wrong for their jobs, managers can often help them find appropriate positions by talking with them (and with managers who might take them on) about the conditions in which they thrive or stumble. Managers who call the plays as they see them find they win the respect of others. And they respect themselves for managing with fairness, not managing by guilt.

On The Firing Line

After Ed McGrath got a midnight phone call one Sunday telling him that he was fired from his executive position, he decided to act. He eventually sued the company, and won two million dollars in damages. The heart of his argument: he knew he could be fired for performing poorly, but had never been given any prior indication that his manager was unhappy with his work.[9]

People aren't "No Deposit, No Return" containers. And managers who use people and toss them carelessly aside will find more like McGrath who stand up and assert themselves at great cost to their old companies. This settlement makes the most resounding argument to date for the significant incident method of performance appraisal (see next item and p. 54).

Performance appraisal is more than a matter of rating people. It's a matter of evaluating *how* they're getting to the goals set by their jobs. And that entails the collection, recording, and feedback of specific information about how they behave on the job. Does someone make profits but fail to develop people? Does a manager delegate or run the whole show? With the significant incident method, people know where they stand and where they need to improve. And managers feel less guilt about judging people when they have clear standards and factual data to work with. With this method, there's no need for midnight firings or costly settlements—everyone is less vulnerable. Neither common decency nor consideration for employees' feelings and career plans have inspired many organizations to revamp antiquated performance appraisal methods. More may change now that the need for appraisal data that can stand up in court becomes obvious.

What Is A Significant Incident?

If you want to use the appraisal method I've been advocating, you'll need to help managers learn to recognize, define, and write up significant incidents. What is a significant incident? Defining one is not as hard a task as many people think.

First, what is significant? Any piece of behavior which you as the boss consider important. A good way to gauge importance is to look at the intensity of your feelings, whether positive or negative. If something in a subordinate's job performance makes you angry or upset, that's a negative significant incident. A positive significant incident is likely to leave you feeling elated. When you don't have strong feelings one way or the other about an aspect of a subordinate's performance, the behavior isn't significant. You are the ultimate judge of what is to be considered significant.

Second, what's an incident? It is a piece of behavior—*not* an interpretation of behavior. For example, if a subordinate is abusive with a customer, the manager should record the significant incident by noting specifically what was said: "Frank Simon told customer Arnold Handler, 'Shut up or take your business elsewhere.' " (You might also include the provocation, if you thought it was relevant.) If the manager instead records simply that "Frank Simon got mad at customer Arnold Handler," then no one will know later what he actually did. But if managers accumulate a record of specific behaviors, then later they or other managers can see and interpret the subordinate's characteristic patterns of behavior.

People are less defensive when managers confront them with actual behaviors instead of personal interpretations. It's usually easier for people to talk about their behavior when they don't feel their managers have already "tried and convicted" them.

Attention Must Be Paid

The key question that superiors should ask of their subordinates is: "What are your people up against?" This calls attention to what subordinates need at every level within the organization, and what they need from the organization to help them to do their jobs more effectively. It also calls attention to the realities all subordinates have to face, which may not be fully appreciated by their superiors. This is a question that should be asked repeatedly by the superior each time a subordinate reports to him about her work. It should be included in the performance appraisal form to discover how much a subordinate knows about her own people and how sensitive she is to their needs. This focus on what subordinates face will increase the requirement for managers to listen to their people—to hear their concerns. Most performance appraisals fail to take these issues into account, resulting in a great deal of upward attention, but inadequate downward attention. Keep asking the people who report to you: "What are your people up against?"

Appraisal Avoidance

When managers are told to appraise subordinates face to face, formally, and in detail, many avoid the task. They feel guilty about judging others, and uncomfortable about being straightforward. Managers' superiors should be on the lookout for the following forms of managerial avoidance:

1. My subordinates know where they stand because they've worked with me for a long time.
2. I review my subordinates' projects and comment on their approaches and progress. That's enough appraisal.
3. We have a lot of give and take in my department that will be threatened by formalized procedures.
4. I have several older managers who aren't going anywhere and will only be hurt by detailed appraisals they can't respond to.
5. I have to be free to relate in my own way to my subordinates.
6. It's too much trouble to keep written records.

All these assertions are evasions. People who supposedly know where they stand usually do not. I have encountered hundreds of people, supposedly appraised by their managers, who actually had been left in the dark. These people needed to know how they were performing and how they might get ahead. Instead they got only piecemeal comments, tempered by the managers' guilt and good will. If they were in trouble, they often couldn't read between the lines and do something about it. Plateaued subordinates, protected for many years from poor performance appraisals, are especially stunned when the ax falls. And it's too late for them to change by the time they're appraised honestly.

In theory it's fine for managers to relate to subordinates in their own way, but in practice that's often an excuse to pussyfoot at appraisal time. People are entitled to direct information from their managers on where they stand and how they're doing. That's why it behooves all organizations to recognize these evasions for what they are, and to help managers confront the guilt that creates such avoidance. Managers who can't accept the responsibility of appraisals have no business being managers. They're misleading the people they're supposed to lead.

The Painful Truth

Sometimes managers must create pain. This is a difficult issue that I raise from time to time, and it often makes managers recoil. But there's a strict logic behind it: where there's no pain, there's no sense of a problem. And where there's no problem, there's no attempt at a solution. No one will be motivated to change behavior unless and until he or she feels pain.

Managers who don't want to create pain are confusing pain with harm. Harm implies destruction. But pain is a motivator. It's like a tack in your shoe, calling attention to something wrong that needs correction. People must be confronted when their behavior causes others pain. Until they too feel pain, they just won't have any reason to change.

I'm not saying, of course, that managers should discharge a barrage of negative criticism. That makes people feel helpless, and can indeed cause harm. But causing pain need not harm anyone. Managers who fear that words which create pain will destroy people are caught up in primary-process or magical thinking—they're confusing thoughts and words with extreme actions. Anyone who supervises, appraises, teaches, or mobilizes others must be able to distinguish pain from harm. Harm is never constructive. And though confronting people with reality may cause pain, it rarely causes harm.

The Universal Stumbling Block To Accurate Appraisal

People need abundant permission to speak up about how they feel. Attention to feelings has been programmed out of many people in our society, and feelings have been so covered over with habits of thought that they are easily overlooked. When a person expresses negative feelings about somebody or about a situation that he's in, he often acts as if he is revealing some terrible hostility. Yet once on the table, the issue doesn't look so remarkable at all.

Everybody is uncomfortable about negative feelings to some degree. This is because everyone experienced, in the dim, dark reaches of childhood, the feeling that words are the same as actions: that angry words or thoughts can kill. That feeling can hang around despite the rational knowledge that it just isn't so. This means people feel guilty for just feeling, let alone expressing, anything negative. Sensitive people bend over backwards not to say "bad" things, or if they absolutely must, they do it so obliquely that the message can't be understood. As a result, communication breaks down.

The fear and avoidance of directly expressing negative reactions is always getting in the way of managerial tasks. It cripples appraisal and supervision especially. That is why the best recipes for doing good evaluations still come out hollow in practice. What people need is a chance to rehearse the process:

1. Get managers together to share their feelings about appraising subordinates, and to discuss the problems of performance appraisal in general. The group should be no larger than seven or eight, and the managers should be at the same level in the organization.
2. Discuss the specific problems expected with certain difficult-to-appraise people. To the extent possible, members of the group should offer concrete suggestions for handling these situations and help the manager evaluate these suggestions.
3. Practice for the appraisal interviews by role-playing them. Such rehearsals increase the appraiser's sense of familiarity with the process and the material, and ease his anxiety about handling the individual's reactions.
4. Do the actual appraisal interviews.
5. Review what happened. Discuss the outcomes of anticipated problems, as well as unanticipated ones. What lessons were learned? What needs for further skills surfaced?

This procedure should be helpful each year, regardless of changes or lack of changes in the system in use. Guilt is not eliminated once and for all, but is present in every appraisal situation and must be dealt with repeatedly.

First Over The Barricades

People sometimes say I am unrealistic about performance appraisal. Can't I offer some help, they ask, to managers who are faced with doing performance appraisals as they exist today? It's true that I come down hard on the methods in general use, but I *insist* that performance be appraised continuously on the basis of significant incidents. Managers whose companies require a particular annual performance appraisal ritual should simply do it. There's no harm in it, as long as you supplement it with immediate feedback on significant incidents. Filling out a required form each year doesn't stop you from recording incidents as they happen, and periodically summarizing and discussing them with subordinates. Using the significant incident method throughout the year should make filling out the forms that much easier; you won't have to rely on your memory, and end up giving excessive weight to the last six weeks.

Annual appraisals are contaminated by the inability to present factual behavioral information; you can choose to provide that information on the side. They are also contaminated by the subordinate's experience of being "indicted" once a year; you can mitigate that by providing regular feedback, along with support and guidance in improving performance. Finally, they are contaminated by being combined with salary reviews, leaving the subordinate too preoccupied with the money aspect to hear the performance information. That's why it's important to provide performance information at other times as well.

As for guilt, it will always be there, but saving up all the criticism for one meeting makes the guilt that much greater. Immediate feedback has a greater chance of being constructive. In addition, you can get together with peers, whether the organization facilitates it or not, and talk about your feelings, get some support, increase your objectivity about your subordinates, and practice saying what you know you ought to say. You don't have to wait for the revolution to start doing things differently. And if enough managers use the method of appraisal I suggest, personnel will have to recognize it.

Speaking To Deaf Ears

From time to time managers find themselves trying to get through to subordinates who are overly enamored of their own worth. Such people cannot and will not hear any wrong spoken of themselves, and consequently never see any need for self-improvement. The greater their illusions of grandeur, the less likely such people are to hear what their managers say. So there's no point in talking yourself blue in the face. If you've been confronting such a person repeatedly without success, face the fact that you're not going to get through. And then decide what you must do for the good of your whole unit.

Dangerous Denial

How do you respond to negative criticism? If you deny the problem, blame it on your manager, or attribute it to malice on someone else's part, it's time to ask yourself why you can't face the problem. What is it about the way you operate that obscures whatever is getting you into trouble? If you can't see your own behavior objectively, it may be time to talk with a professional for a better understanding of how your behavior gets in your way. A good therapist can help you step outside yourself for a more objective view.

Denying significant problems is dangerous and self-defeating. It may not get you fired—but you probably will be held back. It's far better to deal with a problem and get it out of the way than to pretend it isn't there until it has grown into an insurmountable obstacle.

Promoting

Most promotion decisions fall into the "a little knowledge is a dangerous thing" category. You think you know the person, you're familiar with her work, everybody's sure the move is going to be a great thing, and then the person falls flat on her face. What happened?!

And what do you say to the people who didn't *get the promotion? Would you believe me if I told you it can be a highly motivating experience if you handle it properly? Disappointment and all. Then there are those mysterious—or are they insufferable?—people who say "No" to a promotion. If you look for the psychological consistency of their behavior, you'll probably find it, and the mystery—and perhaps your anger along with it—will begin to fade.*

Promoting Behavioral Job Descriptions

Most performance appraisal forms ask whether the person is promotable. Everyone wants the label badly. But the question is unanswerable unless the kinds of positions to which the person is promotable are *specifically* designated. No one is equally able to perform all jobs; a person may succeed brilliantly in one position and fail miserably in another. And if the person's promotable qualities aren't specifically described in appraisals, he or she may get the first promotion that comes along and live to regret it.

Hollow Appointments

When managers have to choose one person over another for an assignment or promotion, they often feel badly about the effect on the person not chosen. Frequently they try to appease their guilt by giving that person a new title and exaggerating the opportunities that are likely to go with it. Unaware of being toyed with, the person expects to take action and be effective in the new role. When he is bypassed or not involved in what he regards as legitimate functions of that role, he may kick up in embarrassing circumstances. Of course, this will anger those who are subject to his attack, as well as the appointing authority, who was only trying to be kind. It's easy to land on the person for that behavior. But, without excusing the behavior, it's important to realize where it came from.

When you make a hollow appointment, you're asking for trouble. Better to face up to the situation in the first place. Tell the person directly that he is not going to be promoted, and give the reasons why. If this is the end of the road, *tell* him, and tell him why, so he can learn to live with that fact. If it's simply a matter of too many qualified people, say so. If it's a matter of waiting for a more appropriate opening, explain why this assignment is less suitable, and what would make another more so.

The main thing is to let the person know where he or she stands. That may be difficult at the time, but the alternative is a time bomb. It could explode when you least expect it.

The Ends And The Means

When you're thinking about promoting someone, it's not enough to look at what the person achieves. No one takes bottom-line results to the new job. But all promoted people take their typical ways of achieving results into the new positions. Managers who promote people who achieve good results by dubious or undesirable methods run significant risks.

Some people, for instance, always get a good bottom line by controlling their whole operation single-handedly. Such managers are often bright, quick, and technically gifted. But they're failing as managers if they're not developing people and delegating responsibilities. No matter what they achieve, such managers strip their people of responsibility, undermining morale and motivation. Their managerial failures show up after they leave, for their units usually fall into disarray. And though the successors are usually blamed for the failure—"Hank sure couldn't fill Paul's shoes"—the truth is that the higher level managers swapped short-term gain for long-term vitality. It's a narrow-minded and self-serving trade, especially when someone else is left holding the bag.

Clotheshorse Sense

Managers sometimes ask how to handle subordinates who want promotions but don't dress for the role. These people are often competent and sometimes highly skilled. But they're unkempt, flamboyant, or overly casual. Their managers know these subordinates could handle more responsibility, but they don't like the idea of their representing the company at high levels. And the managers don't want to make personal or inappropriate criticisms. They feel stuck.

Managers don't have to—and rarely should—spell out specific dress codes. But it is entirely appropriate to tell a subordinate what *image* his or her dress conveys and why that image creates a problem. A brilliant engineer who favors loud Hawaiian shirts may think his performance alone will earn him a promotion to unit head. If that's not the case, he needs to be told. That promotion may entail political contacts that require a more solid, conservative appearance. In this case the engineer may opt against the promotion. But he'll be making a choice based on the facts of the matter.

Our clothes speak volumes about our self-images. Unkempt people often have low self-esteem; overly casual people are often highly independent or rebellious. But many people are unaware of how they look or the impression they make. A forthright manager can help a subordinate see herself better than any mirror could. A case in point: one manager reports that a young woman in his unit complained that no one took her seriously enough. He suggested that she stop dressing "like a little girl." When she abandoned her college denims for a working woman's wardrobe, people listened more closely to her ideas and treated her with more respect. This manager did the young woman a favor by telling her bluntly what the problem was. But note that he didn't tell her *how* to dress. He told her *why* she made a given impression on people.

The Critical Test

The higher people move in an organization, the less opportunity they have for "hands-on" control of what's going on—and the more they are compelled to deal with ambiguity and high-level bargaining. This is one of the major changes in the managerial role. And it's the point at which those who are so heavily oriented to control have the greatest difficulty. They become terribly impatient with the extended negotiations that have to go on inter-organizationally (with respect to the government and other agencies) or intra-organizationally.

As people move up into higher levels, this capacity for tolerating anxiety and less control of a situation needs to be tested. People should be put into situations where they are compelled to engage in negotiations, particularly difficult and protracted ones, to see how well they can sustain that tension. If they can't handle the gradual development of relationships that makes it possible to hammer out a bargain, they probably shouldn't move much higher in the organization.

Which Way Is Up?

Here are some important qualities to look for in people coming up for promotion:
1. Their pursuit of managerial roles should arise from identification and not compensation. That is, they should be building on skills and models to demonstrate their competence. They should *not* be seeking power to make up for a real or fancied deficiency. First-born

children often identify best with authority figures, and are most comfortable in authoritative roles. Having been successfully mentored would be one indication of this quality.

2. They should be able to manage change successfully—to anticipate it, to alleviate its stresses, and to ameliorate its negative effects by supporting their people and involving them in resolving problems.
3. They should be able to tolerate tension. They should be able to work for months without direction from their superiors. Not that they shouldn't be getting work done and demanding results, but that they can tolerate ambiguity because they trust their demonstrated competence.
4. They should be able to absorb hostility and deflect it into problem solving. There will always be hostile events to turn to managerial advantage.
5. They should be able to resolve the crises of normal adult development—for example that of middle age, with its attendant boredom and rethinking of goals. They should also be able to resolve the critical family problems that arise at such times.
6. They should be able to demonstrate their competence, especially in a downturn. They need to have been in their present roles long enough for their actions to be visible.
7. Their performance appraisals should have many consistent significant incidents noted by a range of bosses.

Successive Successors

When thinking about who to promote, most managers look for the best-qualified person, unless there are political considerations. That's a limited way of looking at things. When you promote a person, you are also opening doors to the people that person judges to be important. That is, the person has a social network, and will bring those people along if and when the opportunity presents itself. It's like what happens when you get married. You marry into the spouse's family, and will have to live with them and cope with them on some level, depending on where you live and your spouse's relationship to them. It's important to realize in advance what those connections are going to be like.

The same is true when you promote managers. Ask yourself: On whom are they heavily dependent? Who are their allies and supporters? Who are the people they regard highly? Because inevitably you're tying into a network.

Next, watch out for the implicit psychological contracts that are created with the members of that network. The people behind the person you promote may expect that they are in line for the next steps. But you may not want those people to move up. They may not be adequate or suitable. So it's important to assess not only the person you want to promote, but also the people that person regards as valuable and important. Who does he or she recommend as a successor? And what situations might that pose for you two, three, five years down the line?

Why People Stay Where They Are

The only possible reason a person wouldn't want to be promoted is because he or she is unmotivated. Right? Wrong. There may be many different reasons. Often people are frightened of larger responsibility. People who characteristically have extremely high standards may fear that they will not be able to meet them. Others tend to lean heavily on superiors, having been taught over a lifetime to be more dependent. They feel they have no right to stand on their own feet or to make decisions independently. In either of these two situations, the person lacks self-confidence. Such people can often be helped to increase their confidence in slow, step-by-step increments.

Then there are those whose basic interests are somewhere else. They have little investment in the organization and want to comply with it minimally. Some people learn this attitude through experience. I think, for example, of the new dean of a business school who tried to get his faculty to commit themselves to his leadership. They balked, saying they had been through several deans, each of whom expected the same thing, but all of whom left to go elsewhere. Therefore, they said, "Just leave us alone to do our teaching and don't expect more from us." With diligent effort he persuaded them to commit themselves to him. Within two years he had resigned. Once again, they had discovered that it doesn't pay to commit yourself to a boss; he is always transient.

Others turn elsewhere because they have discovered that they are not going to move in the organization, or that the organization is not going to provide the gratification they seek. As they move into a different stage of adult development, they shift the emphasis of their values. Such people are usually better left alone.

There are many other reasons why people may not want to be promoted. They should be explored case by case. Otherwise management runs the risk of condemning whole groups of people, thereby undermining morale and motivation.

Firing

There's no way to make firing someone an easy task. Calling it by cool, impersonal names—dismissal, termination—doesn't stop it from being a hot emotional issue. But when it has to be done, nothing less will suffice. And the longer you wait the harder it gets, on you and on the one being fired. Firing a person is inevitably painful, but it doesn't have to be a disaster. And it's in your power to make the difference.

Jobs As Property

It is becoming increasingly difficult and expensive to fire nonunion employees. There is a growing tendency for the courts to view a job as property, and to require employers to show just cause for firing people, especially those who have been with the company a number of years.[10] This is another step toward the practical recognition of the psychological contract.[11] That is, there are implicit expectations on the part of both employee and organization, which take on the force of a contract. People's feelings about these unspoken expectations are as strong as if they were explicitly stated and written in blood. The courts have ordered large settlements for some employees who were fired arbitrarily and the reinstatement of others. This is just the beginning. Organizations have to look much more carefully at what their psychological contracts are. What unconscious expectations do people bring to the organization, and what expectations does the organization have of its people? These expectations grow out of the psychological needs of the individuals, the traditions of the organization, standard practices, and the organization's reputation. The unconscious aspects are particularly important because many people have applied the phrase "psychological contract" to conscious expectations alone. Those are part of the contract, but the underlying issues are more powerful. And organizations ignore them at their peril.

Problems Don't Reorganize Away

Organizations sometimes get themselves into hot water by reorganizing around incompetent people instead of replacing them outright. Sometimes the manager doesn't want to fire "good old Joe" who's given his life to the company; sometimes the manager fears a firing will unleash a political storm. And she's often right. But the alternatives are usually worse. If someone's wrong for the job he holds—and is blocking the organization by being in the slot—then it's best to face the issue in those terms.

What happens when you reorganize around such a person? First, he is likely to feel attacked without reason. If no one complains of incompetence, why should he be left out in the cold? The manager who wanted to avoid a scene may therefore have a battle—including lawsuits—on her hands. Second, people within the organization are likely to see the whole reorganization as a sham. The leadership looks evasive and manipulative, and people lose trust. Then the reorganization doesn't take hold as it should—and the real issue gets lost in the shuffle.

When you take a circuitous action to avoid pain, you're likely to create more pain in the long run. That's what happens when managers can't criticize people honestly in performance appraisals, when they can't fire people who aren't functioning and are making their coworkers miserable. It's just a way for managers to continue avoiding their problems, and they shouldn't allow themselves to get away with it.

The Work Must Be Done

What do you do when a competent, hard-working subordinate is chronically late or absent for legitimate reasons, such as illness? It's hard to let go of a good worker, and hard to feel right about "punishing" someone for something he or she can't really control. But the fact is, the job must be done. Sometimes that can be accomplished, short of dismissing the person. Here are three possibilities:

1. You can move people in and out of roles, if you have enough flexibility in the operation and in personnel to do so.
2. You can train others to take over the subordinate's function when he or she is not there.
3. If cross-training or job rotation is not possible in the person's present role, you can move him or her into a role where that is possible, or where several people share the work load so that others could pick up the slack.

In managerial ranks, there usually isn't much choice. Someone has to manage the function, and there usually isn't anyone who can step in for a while and then go back to his or her own role, without having both functions suffer. The manager who must make the final decision to dismiss a frequently absent subordinate is likely to experience considerable guilt, imagine himself or herself in the other person's shoes, and so on. Some of the guilt can be assuaged by assisting the person in finding another position. But if the person can't be there often enough to do the work that must be done, he or she must be replaced. Reality demands it.

Terminating Without Guilt

People who must be discharged, whether for performance or economic reasons, need careful management. Severance pay and help in finding a job are not enough. Companies often assert that they have no responsibilities for people's social lives. But when they talk about an organizational family and when they encourage social interaction through consistent cooperation on the job, company publications, and so forth, they are creating the conditions of psychological investment. Therefore they have a responsibility for what happens when people are compelled to uproot that investment. People who are terminated lose not only their occupational identity and a predictable life course, but also their whole network of on-the-job social interaction. Many have taken this social system for granted. They have had no experience in building one on their own. For people in middle age or beyond and for those who have "married" their organizations, this is a crucial issue. To help them avoid profound loneliness and depression, organizations should group them so that they can regularly talk over their job-finding activities and difficulties. The mutual support will help them partially counteract the universal tendency to delay facing and coping with the realities.

All people facing termination should be made aware that layoffs inevitably induce family stresses. They will need to spend a good deal of time talking with their spouses and children about what the implications are for each one of them. Families, too, need to be educated about the deep emotional ramifications of major changes and loss. Those who don't strengthen the family bond in the face of such stresses risk adding a family breakup to their troubles. The search for a new job increases the need for a safe place to talk about frustrations and renew self-confidence and courage.

Human resources departments can help in the usual ways—by teaching people how to prepare resumes and summarize performance appraisal statements, and by checking into potential local employment opportunities. But more, they can encourage people to reevaluate their skills and talents and review all experiences they have found especially enjoyable. Many will have to find work in new areas. Practice in breaking away from habitual categories of thinking can prepare them to seize new opportunities.

Revenge!

Many managers fear that firing people on Monday instead of Friday will make them a target for revenge. They fear that a person who is allowed to stay around will angrily sabotage computer programs and machinery, steal property or information, or sow dissent among other employees. My experience is that this rarely happens. When people are treated well, they tend to return the courtesy. Certainly a person who loses his or her job will be angry and disappointed. But there's a difference between anger and outrage. It's the sense of outrage at being treated unfairly or inconsiderately that leads to revenge.

Occasionally, people are dismissed for being hostile; they may indeed be destructive if allowed to return to their offices. Sometimes there are security concerns. One man went back to his office, collected all the data he could lay his hands on, and tried to sell it to competitors. But unless the person is himself vengeful, I wouldn't worry too much about that, as long as the dismissal is handled well.

The basics of handling termination well are to give the person: 1) time to let reality sink in; 2) straight information about why he or she is being dismissed; 3) time to say good-bye to friends and colleagues, the place, and the work; and 4) help in finding a new job.

The manner in which one person is fired is a message to the rest of the organization. If people see that the organization is trying to be eminently fair and reasonable, they respect their superiors. If they see someone dealt with summarily, they can imagine being in that person's shoes. Then they are likely to be angry and hostile. An atmosphere of fear and distrust develops; people go to great lengths to cover themselves, and to even greater lengths to get even with the organization for its arbitrary way of handling things.

Word gets around about the way organizations treat people. A reputation for treating people unfairly or inconsiderately when they are leaving—hitting them when they're down, you might say—makes it harder to bring people into the organization and even harder to foster commitment once you do.

So, from every angle—people inside as well as outside the organization, the person leaving, and the conscience of the person who does the firing—the practice of firing people on Friday, or handing them the contents of their desks and telling them not to go back to their offices, is reprehensible. It would take extreme circumstances, such as irately destructive and threatening behavior, to justify such action.

In Summary

1. *Work is most satisfying when it enables the person to move toward his or her ego ideal. A job that fits well also allows the person to behave consistently with his or her characteristic ways of handling affection, aggression, and dependency. Ideally, the job helps the person cope with these basic feelings.*
2. *When hiring, do not disregard "minor flaws" in the interview; what you see is likely to be the tip of the iceberg.*
3. *People need continuous appraisal of their performance, based on written records of specific behavior that the supervising manager considers significant. Those who are not performing up to standards should be informed immediately, so they have the opportunity to improve or to move on rather than waste time in an inappropriate position.*
4. *Unconscious guilt is the universal stumbling block to adequate performance appraisal. Managers who appraise others need permission, support, and rehearsal for giving negative feedback, and an opportunity to share their feelings with peers after doing so.*

5. *No one is "promotable." People are promotable* to certain positions *which require the behavior they have demonstrated.*
6. *Being fired doesn't have to be devastating. It can't help but be painful, but if handled well it is not only a failure but also a new opportunity to be successful.*

Releasing Energy For Work

The willingness to work is there in most people, but in many cases it has been buried under resentments. You've heard them all before—pay, how people are treated by superiors, being blamed for situations they can't change or about which they have made suggestions that are ignored, having suggestions taken along with the credit for them—the list goes on.

Restoring people's natural willingness to work is largely a matter of fair pay, an organizational structure that is consistent with expressed organizational objectives and purposes, and a willingness on the part of managers to appreciate the efforts made and obstacles faced by subordinates. When managers also understand their subordinates' ego ideals and provide opportunities for people to work toward their ideals, then they will release the psychological energy that is the key to improved motivation and increased productivity.

Compensation

People work for pay. They work for other things as well, but if they don't feel they are being paid fairly, they will be dissatisfied. The work of Elliott Jaques demonstrates that "felt-fair pay" is consistent and predictable. This concept can be used as a basis for compensation. In addition, organizations can affect the amount and kind of attention people give to various tasks and issues by relating pay to valid performance appraisals.

This Isn't What I Ordered

You get what you ask for, but in organizations, the real asking is done with money and position, not words. My old friend Dr. Nevitt Sanford, president emeritus, Wright Institute, says of American higher education: "At distinguished institutions teachers are oriented not to their undergraduate students but to their disciplines. . . . They want to present their subject matter rather than to influence the development of students."[1] When this happens, it's not because professors are perverse, but because universities compensate their faculties far more for putting out books and papers and bringing in grants and prizes than for engaging and stimulating students. So they get what they ask for: prolific scholars who may or may not be good teachers, and whose scholarship is often trivial.

The same happens in business. Too many organizations ask for people-oriented management with words, while asking for management of systems, ledgers, and organizational pyramids with money and advancement. If universities really want excellent teachers, they should appraise professors' classroom performance and attention to students, and get the students' reactions. If businesses really want managers who can build organizations that will last, by developing strong subordinates and sound succession, they must appraise for these qualities and compensate for them when they appear.

Let Compensation Fit The Time

Being mechanistic about compensation with little or no concern for the consequences to those involved solves nothing and may undermine morale. This often occurs with a "merit system" that turns out to be nothing more than regular salary increases. Merit systems and performance evaluations are crippled under these circumstances since people who are doing well cannot be promoted because they have reached the end of a given salary range. I suggest looking into the works of Elliott Jaques, particularly his book, *A General Theory of Bureaucracy.*[2] Jaques advances a concept of compensation based on "time-span of responsibility." He recommends that people be paid according to the length of time they can go without supervision or, conversely, how long they carry discretion for their work by themselves. This is a psychologically based concept which avoids many of the problems of wages and salaries based on inadequate job descriptions and evaluations. According to research by Jaques and others, the time-span concept reflects an internal sense of fairness that people experience. People seem to judge the value of their work in terms of the psychological responsibility they carry for the decisions they have to make.

A Forecast

A successful garage operator, who has a number of mechanics working for him, is asked who among them are better and who are less good. He points out the better people. When asked why those people are ranked higher than the others, he says the better ones know what to do in the face of ambiguity. They are able to handle things when it's not merely a matter of an oil change or some specified task clearly described or defined in advance.

A Montessori teacher, working with preschoolers, says she can easily divide her pupils into categories. Her categories have to do with how long they can focus their attention on a given task or play activity.

These examples, offered by consultant Dr. Howard Williams, are simple, everyday illustrations of Elliott Jaques' time-span concept. The more one looks around, the more it fits everyday activities. It will become an increasingly important part of the organizational psychology literature and practice.

For Services Rendered

Equitable compensation has always been an important goal as a matter of morale. But the time is fast approaching when it will be as much a matter of law as equitable hiring practices. The question, as I see it, is, "How do you establish the relative value of disparate contributions?" Most of the systems currently available assign point values to certain activities, and are based largely on production results and the number of people the individual supervises. But staff accountants, data processors, and secretaries may provide vital information and services to the company without supervising anyone at all. Organizations must develop compensation systems that pay such people for their contributions as well as managers are paid for theirs—or suffer the continual disaffection of nonmanagerial people.

Lump It Or Leave It

It's quite common for engineers to find themselves stuck in a rut at mid-career. "Engineers are viewed as failures if they don't become managers.

Anyone who is bright and aggressive must want to move up through management ranks, says the conventional wisdom; therefore, anyone who hasn't become a manager after 10 or 15 years must not be bright and aggressive."[3] Or, as Lotte Bailyn of MIT's Sloan School of Management put it, "To be successful in engineering means to leave it."

This attitude makes for a lot of deadwood. Not all engineers are capable of being good managers, and many of them know it. If they had wanted to be managers, they would have gone into management in the first place. But the parallel pay ladders come to an abrupt halt at a certain point. Then one still has to move over to management in order to keep going. Here again it would be helpful to use Jaques' time-span concept as a basis for compensation.

Not Everyone Likes Carrots

When Digital Equipment Co., the computer manufacturer, wanted to motivate its salesforce and lower the rate of turnover, it didn't raise commissions or offer special prizes. It put the salesforce on straight salary. Sales held steady, and the rate of turnover dropped significantly.[4]

Before you jump to institute this or any other incentive or compensation program, look hard at the values, ego ideals, and self-images of the people involved. If you assume you know what motivates them, you may find your new program is a dud. People's motivations vary. Not all salespeople, for instance, are motivated mostly by money. Some, like those at Digital, aspire to professional competence. They pride themselves on technical knowledge and expertise; they want to build long-term client relationships through a record of high-quality service. Professionally prepared questionnaires can help you assess the different values of various groups of employees. And some standard scales have proved useful in this regard.[5]

Return On Investment

No one complains about getting a bonus, but I still don't think much of the bonus as a management tool. That's because, however generous the motive, a bonus is a unilateral action taken by management. In other words, it's still a carrot; the stick would be withholding or decreasing an expected bonus, which management is always free to do.

I suggest the following system, which relates extra pay more palpably to extra effort:

1. Pay people strictly what they are worth to the company, based on time span of discretion, acceptable performance, and the job market.
2. When a group performs well, pay the members a pro rata share of the profits generated by their combined efforts, according to whatever criteria seem appropriate.

3. When a whole plant, a whole unit, or the whole organization performs well, pay people a pro rata share of the results of that effort. But this must still be limited to those people who actually had an effect on the overall performance, and can see the effect they had. When extra money goes to employees for results they can't feel they helped create, it's only an abstract reward, not true compensation.

These policies are more likely to foster identification with the organization. Employees know that the extra money they receive is directly tied to the extra performance they give, and not to the good or ill will of management. The company's profits come back to them as a fair return on their investment of themselves.

The Psychology Of Benefits

Cafeteria-style benefit plans are going to get organizations in trouble if they aren't managed carefully. Why? Because in many cases they're not really benefits at all; they're salary additions. (Some companies have recognized this and dropped the term "benefits." Now they call it flexible compensation.) This is a psychologically important change, and it's a mistake. Benefits were instituted for a purpose, separate from compensation. A cafeteria-style plan, or flexible compensation, doesn't do what benefits are supposed to do.

Benefits are supposed to be a product of the institution, something protective that the institution does for its members that they can't do for themselves. Pension plans, life insurance, health insurance—these are ways of providing for the future, or for when one is no longer able to provide for one's family, or for emergencies. Dental insurance, prepaid legal service, child care—valuable as these things are—don't serve those essential or emergency functions of caring for the employee and his or her family when they cannot care for themselves. Everything beyond emergency survival protection is actually a perk, not a benefit. There's nothing wrong with perks, and if top managers are going to get them, it's nice that lower level people can get some, too. But they serve a different purpose than benefits, and should not be confused with them.

Given a choice, most people will take what is of greatest immediate use to them and worry about the future later. But when later arrives, they'll be mad at the company for not taking care of them, instead of being mad at themselves for the choices they made.

Compensation, benefits, and perks are three separate kinds of payment, with three different psychological meanings and three different functions in employees' lives. Compensation should relate to the value of the work done by the employee; it should be a fair return on investment. Benefits should be the company's way of offering the employee and his or her family protection against loss of health, life, and earnings; they respond to dependency needs. Perks should be the company's way of expressing affection and appreciation to employees, independent of their minimal survival needs and the value of their work. Confusing the three, and especially offering perks in lieu of benefits, is dangerous.

The Organization And Structure Of Work

The Quality of Work Life movement was a recognition of the fact that the way work is organized affects the emotional health and happiness of workers, which in turn affects the amount and quality of work that gets done. Flextime, quality circles, decentralization, matrix management— what's worth trying and how can you tell? Is it possible to try things without courting disaster? To what extent are the psychological effects of various structures and processes predictable? To what extent do they depend on the psychology of the individuals involved? How do you figure out what suits your *organization and* your *people?*

Synchronize Structure, Processes, And People

A company's best efforts to motivate its people can be wiped out because everyday organizational structure or organizational processes, such as appraisal or compensation, run counter to them. Nobody will cooperate with others for very long when he or she is really being paid to compete. Motivational efforts, structure, and ways of going about things have to be of one piece to be effective.

If one assumes continuous adaptation to a changing environment as the fundamental task of an organization, then organizational structure can be seen as a set of role definitions expressing how people in this organization will interact among themselves and with the environment. After sizing up its primary aim in the marketplace, a company has to formulate appropriate strategies for getting and keeping a share of the market. There can be no single ideal way to structure the organization, because strategies and tactics, and therefore the nature of the corresponding tasks and roles inside the organization, will differ markedly. If you can define those tasks and roles in terms of the typical *behavior* they require and match them to *behavioral* descriptions of people (see p. 42), then you are in a position to design support structures that provide just the right amount of rigidity or flexibility for each identifiable group. As the components of the organization become increasingly differentiated in this way, the need for people to fill integrative roles will arise. Ideally, those with managerial responsibility for any given two groups should fill this role, but if this is not possible, another person who is thoroughly respected in both camps can substitute.

Organizational structure needs to be amenable to change at the point of contact with the environment—where shifts in the marketplace may at any time dictate changes of strategy, which in turn will necessitate reformulating internal tasks and roles, which in turn will affect how people feel about themselves as they work. That is, structure must suit the *people* being asked to do the work.

How Is A Business Organization Like A Soccer Team?

Have you noticed the profusion of town soccer team bumper stickers lately? Americans are beginning to take a real interest in the world's most popular sport. And it's a popular sport for good reason. It requires both individual initiative and team effort; it requires flexibility and fast action, both mentally and physically; and it is accessible to anyone who wants to learn because there is no inherent advantage in being tall, big, strong, or fast. Success depends less on what you start with and more on how you use it.

Soccer is also gaining popularity as a strategic model for the U.S. military and for big business. That's because the rules of competition are changing. We've reached the limits of what can be done with sheer size, strength, or power, both militarily and business-wise. If a unit of 1800 soldiers can be wiped out with one tactical nuclear weapon, it's hard to imagine how many troops would be needed to win an encounter on the basis of strength. A whole different style must be developed. The trend must be toward smaller units which can work together as a team, yet act on their own initiative; react quickly and flexibly to the particular circumstances with which they are confronted; and make the most of the various human characteristics available to them, rather than expecting everyone to have similar strengths.

Organizational Generation Gap

The American Revolution was a reflection of changing attitudes toward authority, according to Jay Fliegelman, professor of English at Stanford U. The ideal of the parent-child relationship was changing, moving away from strict enforcement of authority and toward more voluntary obedience based on love and respect. As the parent-child relationship changed, adult relationships with authority changed as well. The colonists came to see Great Britain's attempts to assert authority over them as illegitimate, and split off from the British Empire.[6] This can happen in decentralized organizations where identification with headquarters or the parent company isn't strong enough to legitimize the central authority. The same can be true within organizations or units where there is considerable employee participation in management. If the parts develop autonomously and fail to see their connection to the whole, they may reject the central authority and even attempt to split off. Identification keeps the authority from becoming the enemy.

Systems Don't Solve Problems—People Do

Ever see Charlie Chaplin's movie "Modern Times"? A man invents a machine that will feed factory workers while they work, eliminating the wasteful lunch break. The machine is perfectly designed to feed a person. But what person is designed to eat lunch perfectly?

Companies often base their strategies for attacking problems entirely on the problems to be solved. They ignore the fact that people will have to put those strategies into practice. If the systems are not geared to the people who are going to make them work, chances are they'll flounder. Many organizations have difficulty implementing strategies without ever knowing why. If your company is planning a new mode of attack on some problem, the first step is to look at the characteristic behavior of your subordinates (see p. 42). Who are they, and what can they do? Then, when you consider solutions and strategies, it will be on the basis of whether they will work *in your organization*, as well as whether they will handle the problem.

The Art Of Choosing And Using A Consultant

If you are considering using an organizational consultant of some kind, start with someone who can function as a diagnostician. Diagnosing your own illness can be risky, and that's what you do when you choose your own specialist. The first task of a good consultant is to clarify what you need and why. For that reason, the relationship should be established on a strictly experimental basis. If the association can't produce useful results, there's no point continuing. Be wary of consultants who offer the same methods for all problems.

Second, your consultant should be someone you like. She does not sell you a commodity; she teaches you. Your dependence on her should decrease gradually as you go along. Occasionally an organizational problem will be like a cut finger in that you will only have to wait for the natural healing process. But more often problems are complex. Learning something about controlling or managing an ongoing situation will be necessary. A good consultant increases your internal capacity to cope with the problems in her area, whether in the form of additional staff resources, or simply insights, perspectives, and skills. She should leave something that will last.

If a consultant can't do you any good, at least she shouldn't do you harm. The Hippocratic oath holds good for organizational intervention, too. You should beware of consultants who can't resist meddling. Those who have to do something—anything—to prove their usefulness may be impressive in the short run. But if your people feel manipulated, management will have to take the blame, and that consultant has merely left you with a new problem.

Faith And Knowledge

Dr. Rene Dubos, Rockefeller U., a widely respected medical leader, notes that an important aspect of recovery is faith: "Faith in the gods or in the saints, cures one; faith in little pills, another; hypnotic suggestion, a third; faith in a common doctor, a fourth."[7] I might add that much of what we are seeing in the literature in the form of success with organizational development activity parallels Dubos' observations: the power of suggestion combined with faith in the consultant brings immediate, but not necessarily long-term results. That is why any new fad which comes down the pike gains nearly immediate adherence—and why many don't work after awhile.

Now You See It . . .

People are gullible because they wish unbelievable stories and events to be true. Scientists can be especially gullible, says Martin Gardiner, as a result of arrogance. They are trained observers, and some are too confident of their abilities. Thus magicians and con artists are able to take in physicists who know nothing of magic but who are sure they know what they see.[8]

Managements, too, are frequently taken in by "magicians" who promise to deliver economies and solutions to problems, but whose products, on closer examination, turn out to be sleight-of-hand maneuvers. I often wonder why otherwise intelligent people are willing to accept extravagant promises and guarantees from consultants without question, when a check with some of the people who have used those services would reveal that either the recommendations could never be put into practice, or that the organization was disrupted when they were.

When something sounds too good to be true, it probably is. It's certainly worth some serious investigation before buying. There are reasons why the individual consumer may be taken in. It's harder to understand why the corporation, with all its resources for checking, making judgments, and seeking out background, would be taken in. But I'm afraid many continue to be.

FOCUS ON . . . . Participation

Participation is very much in the news, as organizations try all manner of programs to improve productivity. Many programs have been in place long enough to draw conclusions, and the results are highly mixed. What works in one place doesn't work in another. How can you know what is worth trying in your own organization? What can we learn from all the disparate experiences and points of view?

Who's In Charge?
The fundamental issue is power: who has it, who wants it, how it's used, and how everyone feels about all of those things. Power is something people don't like to talk about wanting, having, or using. In our purportedly egalitarian culture, it's not nice to want power, especially power that gives you control over other people. At the same time, our culture implicitly fosters a macho image of power and encourages people to seek power in organizations: those who are not climbers are losers. As long as people sidestep the issue of power, discussions and programs will get nowhere.

The whole point of quality circles, participative management, or whatever you want to call those activities, is to give people a sense of control over their work. When people have some control over their environment, they feel better about themselves, and they usually do more and better work. But you can't give people a sense of control without giving them some actual control. They know the difference, and they become angry at attempted manipulation. You're worse off than if you had done nothing. On the other hand, managers generally feel that giving subordinates any control over their work means giving up some of their own power. Furthermore, individual achievement is encouraged and rewarded through incentive and bonus systems, while group achievement goes largely unrecognized.

Pitting these two orientations—the desire for individual power and the effort to evolve contributing work groups—against each other is bound to result in a clash in which neither side can win, because the other side can always effectively sabotage results. In order for participation to work, there must be greater commitment to and identification with the group itself and its achievements, and less emphasis on individual identity and achievement. And if individuals who are looking for independent recognition can simply move to another organization to find it, it may be difficult to foster that group commitment in middle managers.

Power-Structure Fit
Some efforts at participation do work, as we can see from the experience of some Japanese companies that have set up plants in the U.S. But in some places Japanese-style management works, and in others it doesn't. The difference is in the behavioral styles of the workers they employ. Japanese management grows out of a culture that values adherence to group norms in the interest of harmony more than it values individual achievement, a culture in which roles and obligations are defined and not questioned. Sony's plant in San Diego employed Chicanos, whose culture

is group-oriented, and lower-class women, who are necessarily dependent and therefore more comfortable with a paternalistic orientation. Another plant, in the mid-South, employed men who held to the independent, "What's in it for me?" orientation of mainstream American culture. They did not want to be treated paternalistically.

Not all participative systems are paternalistic. In one plant, management abolished the foreman level so that there would be no "master-servant relationships." The employees were men from a subculture which valued independence and authoritativeness. They couldn't respect their bosses as mere chairmen of meetings. In addition, these men were not accustomed to expressing themselves verbally so they didn't say much in meetings. It's not surprising, then, that they expressed themselves by going on strike—although the plant management certainly was astonished.

The way people feel about power, independence, and authority matters more than the particular allocation of power. Just as an individual's characteristic behavior must fit the behavioral requirements of a job, the power structure of an organization must match the typical attitudes and expectations of its employees.

It should be clear by now that the first step in any effort to improve quality of work life is diagnosis. You must understand people's attitudes about power and authority at all levels of the organization. And you must understand their actual attitudes, not just the ones they are willing to express. The two are not necessarily the same. (See my book *Psychological Man*,[5] pp. 112-116, on values and measurement of values.) Once you know what people in various parts of the organization want and how flexible they are about it, you can begin to consider whether some increase in participation will make matters better, and if so, what form it might take.

Making It Stick

People often ask me whether a particular technique is any good. My response is always, "No." Some techniques are appropriate in some situations, but no technique is good in and of itself. All too often managers use the latest program the way some parents use Dr. Spock. They go by the book, disregarding their own experience and knowledge.

Having the right technique for the organization and its people is not the only consideration. Much depends on who instigates the change. That person must have the power to make it happen, or it will all come to nothing. In one organization, a high-level manager asserts that the work arena is now to be the shared responsibility of management and workers, and he is working hard to make it so. He notes that workers in his organization have a powerful wish to share in managing their work. I know that organization. He's right. However, the organization is headed by an overcontrolling entrepreneur. Before long there will be a clash between the employees, who think they are sharing the management, and the owner, who knows darn well that they aren't and what's more they aren't going to. At that point the whole thing will fall apart and there will be great disillusionment among the employees. A similar thing will happen in large organizations where top managers instruct middle managers to increase opportunities for participation at lower levels, but fail to provide the necessary motivating factors. Many experiments over the years show that when a boss wants something to happen, it happens. As soon as the boss loses interest, it no longer happens—unless the whole process is institutionalized. By that I mean:

1. The structure of the organization is reformed to support the processes that are set in motion (form following function).
2. The performance appraisal system holds managers accountable for instituting participation in their areas.
3. The compensation system is based on appraisal. If people are evaluated, promoted, and compensated on the basis of statistical measures, why should they allow others to participate in decisions—especially ones that may affect the statistics?
4. People must be able to trust the organization sufficiently to commit themselves to its fortunes. In most contemporary organizations that is not the case.[9]

In none of the cases I know, either firsthand or from the literature, has anybody thought seriously about these four issues.

It may seem that I oppose quality of work life efforts. Not at all. I do oppose throwing techniques at problems without comprehensive diagnosis and selection of appropriate activities. In doing so, you risk severe and costly disappointment.

Motivation And Productivity

Everybody's talking about motivation and productivity. Much of the talk is based on behavioral psychology, which dictates rewards for desirable behavior and punishment for undesirable behavior. But if you call up a mental image of a carrot (reward) and stick (punishment), what animal do you see between them? For many people, it's a jackass. And most people don't want to be put in the position of a jackass—it's hard on their self-esteem. The notion that techniques based on such a psychology can work is what I call The Great Jackass Fallacy.[10] People are motivated by the opportunity to think well of themselves. They need opportunities to use their skills to master their world, to take part in enterprises they find worthy of the effort, and not to be expected to behave in ways that are inconsistent with their values or their characteristic manner of handling affection, dependency, and aggression.

World Enough And Time

Alexander the Great wanted to be as great as Achilles. It is said that he read the *Iliad* over and over, and slept with it under his pillow. Nevertheless, he knew when to put the book down and strike out on his own. When Ray Bradbury was a boy, he wanted to write science fiction as well as Jules Verne and Edgar Rice Burroughs. His earliest stories were poor by comparison. Had he let that stop him, he never would have gone on to completely surpass his heroes, and even his own expectations.

If you've got a difficult problem to solve, or a large ambition to fulfill, you could study and plan from now till doomsday. But at some point you've got to stop preparing and start producing. And that's when it gets frustrating. Thrilling ideas start to stumble over reality. Your actions seem so small in comparison to your goals. But this is a frustration that has to be faced—there's no useful way around it.

One of the detours managers often take is elaborate feasibility studies, attitude surveys, and so on. These have their uses, but not as often as they are used. I think of the several times I pointed out a common problem to the management of a company. They responded by doing several attitude surveys to see if it was so, when repeated surveys had already made that quite clear. Not only is this procrastination, but it makes people mad to keep answering the same questions. The longer such nonsense goes on, the less people will trust whatever changes do finally come.

Fostering Creativity

If you wish to encourage creativity in yourself or your subordinates, you must first understand the three ways the process is stimulated:

1. Internal compulsion. Some people are driven to create by an intense inner need to express deep-seated, often unconscious feelings. We all carry within us the pressure of unresolved psychological conflicts. Some gifted people sublimate these feelings into creative acts, while others work them out through more common defenses like repression and reaction formation.

2. External pressure. Some people are sparked to write, think, or perform creatively when they bump up against a problem. Though such people may have worked without initiative before, a marketing problem, inefficient machine, or unsatisfied need suddenly challenges them and inspires a creative burst.

3. Stimulating leadership. Good leaders can create conditions that stimulate the creative thoughts and fantasies of others. Managers who ask subordinates to brainstorm freely, teachers who ask students to write poems or stories, and parents who encourage children to dream and fantasize all create conditions that encourage

creativity—especially when they discourage the tendency toward self-criticism.

Many managers who say they want more creative initiatives discourage them by coming down too hard and too often on people who don't get immediate results. If you want creativity, don't always demand action. Instead take time to nurture fantasies and free-floating ideas in a spirit of curiosity and pleasure.

People Catch On Slowly

In 1601, James Lancaster added a daily supplement of lemon juice to the diet of sailors on one of four ships under his command, and found that most of the men who died of scurvy came from the other three ships. With as much as half the crew dying of scurvy on long voyages, you'd think this little experiment would have had shipmasters falling all over each other to buy lemons. But it was another 194 years before the British Navy officially adopted the preventive measure, and it took the mercantile marine 264 years.[11] This incident was related by Harvard U. biostatistician Frederick Mosteller to illustrate how long it can take for new ideas to be accepted.

What takes people so long? Some have the "not invented here" syndrome: they envy the accomplishment, and devalue it to preserve their own self-images. Others are afraid because they don't, or feel they won't, understand it. Still others may not yet have recognized the problem when the explanation or solution is offered. When I wrote *Emotional Health In The World Of Work*[12] in 1964, few people were talking about managerial stress; now, of course, it's a common topic. So if you're developing new concepts, be prepared for acceptance to be a long time coming.

Successful innovators, Mosteller says, understand the needs of the user better than unsuccessful ones. They pay more attention to marketing; they develop more efficiently, though not necessarily faster; and they make better use of outside technology and advice. Of course, not every successful innovator has these qualities—but the statistics favor them!

Cooling Competitiveness May Increase Productivity

Intense rivalry can drain energy that should be going into work. The key factor in rivalry is the behavior of the superior. The more intense the downward pressure, the greater the rivalry. The result of this kind of pressure from their manager is that people will be less able to cooperate with each other. If, in addition, the manager either wittingly or unwittingly plays favorites, then the intensity of the rivalry will increase. A woman manager, with women subordinates, may experience considerable rivalry in her role when the women working under her unconsciously cast her in a mother role, reawakening the rivalry daughters feel towards their mothers when they vie for the approval of their fathers.

Every manager should look at his or her own behavior before trying to assess the behavior of a subordinate. Talking to him or her about over-competitiveness will be of little help if the manager's behavior is simultaneously fanning the flames of rivalry.

Learning From Crises

Many organizations fumble along in a hit-or-miss fashion until a crisis hits. Then suddenly everyone's creative energies are mobilized, and the organization pulls through with aplomb. Afterwards people wonder why they can't work that well all the time. As one presidential aide in the Carter Administration said, "We always react better to a crisis. I wish we knew how to bottle it and use it."[13]

It can be a highly satisfying experience to give your all to pull through a crisis. It's gratifying to work hard toward a specific goal with intense mutual cooperation. Crises are often opportunities for people to see immediate results, the proof of their own competence. But the positive responses quickly pall when people try to "bottle" them for regular use. Then you see organizations frantically spinning their wheels in a constantly tense atmosphere. But when there's no real crisis, there's no real resolution. People are expected to work as hard and as long as if there were a real crisis, but their frenetic activity becomes an end and a value in itself. As a result, people become burned out, cynical, and discouraged. They give their all, and get nothing. The best leave, and the worst stay on, churning out busywork.

If your group has pulled through a crisis with flying colors, meet with your people to discuss how they view the experience. What were their satisfactions? Frustrations? What would they do differently next time? Could the whole crisis have been avoided—and how? Wise managers can then develop these sessions into projective discussions of where the unit is headed and how it is getting along. That is, you can come out of a crisis feeling energized and newly able to predict and control circumstances—and able to weather the crises that take you by surprise. Healthy organizations come down from the intensity of a crisis, but without falling back into the lassitude of aimless management.

Don't Undercut Motivation

Discussions about productivity often center on motivation: people just don't put their hearts into their work. Why not? One reason is that they often can't be proud of their work. A contractor may complain that carpenters don't take pains with their work, but the carpenters know the contractor wants the building constructed at the lowest possible cost. The same thing happens in manufacturing. When my 20-year-old washing machine conked out, my repairman told me I can only expect the one that replaces it to last 10 years. Well, I had to buy one anyway. Then an interesting thing happened—I couldn't plug it in. The cord isn't as long as the one on the old machine. The manufacturer saved a few bucks, and I'm irritated because I had to go out and get an extension cord. But what does this say to the employee? It says, cut back. Give only what you have to. It undercuts motivation.

Now, managers are going to say, we're in a competitive situation, we have to keep costs to a minimum. Fine. Our economic system is built on the concept of profitability. But a better way of cutting costs is to talk with your people about how that might be done. Discuss the competition, how to sustain quality while reducing costs, and whether trade-offs have to be made. The decision may be painful, and the choice may be to do exactly what you would have imposed. But the decision will be accepted with more grace and commitment. The momentum of the work group will not be sapped. In fact, it may be stronger for having vanquished the problem together.

If you cut the washing machine cord, people know it, and they feel you've cheated the customer. How will they expect you to treat them? And how will that make them feel about the company and themselves? It's important to consider what your actions communicate to people, and in turn, what the effect will be on morale and motivation, and on interest and trust in the organization itself.

Give A Listen

Managers who really want to do something about low morale and productivity don't use questionnaires. They interview people.

It has been known for a long time that you learn more from an interview than from a questionnaire. But more than that, interviews can help both the interviewer and the interviewee, according to Dr. Nevitt Sanford, president emeritus, Wright Institute. Students who were interviewed for research purposes found it a valuable part of their undergraduate experience. Subsequently, faculty were interviewed as a means of relaxing the rigid boundaries between faculty and students, faculty and administration, faculty of different departments, and so on. Interviews make a difference because the interview gives the person "a chance to say things for which there had not previously been an acceptable audience," says Sanford. And the interviewer's attention and interest in the person's ideas raises self-esteem. This, in turn, makes the person more open to others' ideas.[14]

Improving morale and productivity is often a matter of changing organizational culture. And one way to start changing the culture, as Sanford's work implies, is to conduct interviews. If the way to prepare faculty to listen to students is to interview the faculty, then the way to prepare supervisors to listen to subordinates is to interview *them*. The higher in the organization this can start, the better. But the best place to begin is where you are.

How do you conduct an interview? You start by putting yourself into a curious and nonjudgmental frame of mind, and continue by letting your curiosity and acceptance show as you question and listen. That doesn't mean agreeing with everything the person says, or even keeping your opinions to yourself. It *does* mean believing, at least for the time being, that it's OK to have differing opinions, and neither is necessarily better or more correct.

You may be surprised to find that people you considered dull and uninteresting have an interesting story to tell when you truly want to hear it. Sanford makes this important distinction between just letting people talk without listening, and caring enough about what people are saying to really hear them. You know from your own experience that there is a difference. Your subordinates know the difference, too.

Live And Celebrate!

"The essence of work, or of mere work, is, and always has been, repetition," Stuart Hampshire observes. "But over most of known history the repetitions have been given significance by recurring celebrations of seasons and of work done, in feast, ceremonies, enactments of myths and history, dramatic and musical performances, public manifestations of all kinds. If the repetitions of work are not given any kind of seasonal rhythm or pattern, because the beliefs, principally religious, associated with such rhythms have largely disappeared, then they remain mere repetitions, leaving a blank, an empty aging, an undifferentiated stretch of days and months, as in a prison before death."[15]

We have not yet invented ceremonials more suited to a mechanical and electronic age. We now need something more than agricultural observances. It would be well for all organizations to establish traditions and ceremonies having to do with cycles of work, achievement, recognition for commitment, dedication, and service and promotion. Some organizations do have activities for retirement and retirees but generally we don't have enough celebration. One of my former students, now a management consultant, invited his clients and friends to celebrate the end of the tax season and the beginning of spring. That is a fitting example of what I have in mind. We shouldn't stop at Christmas parties.

If You Haven't Got It, By All Means, Get It!

What is morale? How do you know when you've got it?

You know you have good morale when the people in your organization want to come to work, enjoy being at work, and would rather work in your organization than anyplace else.

You know you have good morale when you have credibility with your people—they feel they can trust the information they're getting and the people who give it to them.

You know you have good morale when people have an effect on what's happening to them rather than simply being subject to manipulation and to arbitrary and unpredictable events that make them feel victimized.

You know you have good morale when people are identified with their leadership—when they have confidence that the leadership knows where it's going and has a reasonably reliable and successful method for getting there; when they can touch the leadership either in person or in spirit and have a sense of being related to it; and when they feel their leaders are concerned about them and the organization.

A Pithy Truth

"Morale is self-esteem in action." So says Dr. Avery Weisman, a Boston psychiatrist and psychoanalyst. That's one of the major reasons why managers must be concerned with their people's self-esteem and capacities for action.

In Summary

1. *People have a sense of what is fair pay for the work they do, which is quite consistent and correlates highly with their time span of responsibility.*
2. *Compensation should be a fair return on the person's investment of himself or herself in the organization's tasks.*
3. *Benefits and perks relate to dependency and affection, respectively, and should not be confused with each other or with compensation.*
4. *All organizational structures and processes (especially compensation and performance appraisal) should be designed to support rather than undermine the values, objectives, and purposes of the organization.*
5. *The key to motivation, creativity, and productivity is to tap into the individual's drive to move toward his or her ego ideal. In general, this simply means giving people an appropriate challenge, and then getting out of their way except to ask what support they need and if possible provide it.*
6. *Celebrate your successes! Recognize and revel in the real satisfaction of accomplishing.*

Leading—More Than Managing

Organizations don't just happen. They are created by people who have a dream—something they want to see in the world that was not there before—and who can inspire others with that dream and rally their efforts to a common purpose. Leadership is what keeps organizations from stagnating into bureaucracies and then collapsing from their own weight. What are the qualities of leaders and leadership? How do leaders lead, and how do they go astray? Can leadership be developed, or is it just *there* in certain people? Being a leader is "stressful." How can one survive—and succeed?

What Is A Leader?

A leader shows people what they want themselves to be, and makes the achievement of their dreams and ideals seem more possible. People want to be like the leader, and want to do what the leader thinks should be done—this is called identification. This does not mean all people want to be leaders themselves, only that they want to share some of the qualities the leader exemplifies and participate in accomplishing the larger purpose which the leader envisions.

A Legend In Your Own Time

A myth, according to historian William McNeill, U. Chicago, is a general statement about the nature of the world, especially about a particular group of people (nation, tribe, religion, profession), which is widely believed by that group and serves as a basis for action.[1] One nearly universal myth is that of the superior leader. Almost every group has a way of deeming certain members special: by their crown or collar; by the votes they receive or the money they make; by their beauty or bravery. It seems that when people believe in someone greater than themselves, they can summon up the best in themselves.

This is crucial to the man or woman who wants to be a leader in an organization. You will not only be expected to be superior in certain objective ways, such as experience or success, but also will be expected to fulfill certain psychological needs for your subordinates—to act in their myth. (Probably you believe in the myth yourself, or you wouldn't be there.) Though successful leaders come in every flavor, certain traits are necessary:

1. You must have a sense of self-worth, a feeling that you are reasonably close to your ego ideal. History is full of highly regarded people racked with self-doubt; Ulysses S. Grant and Marilyn Monroe are examples. They accomplished marvels, but often came to grief, or were just plain unhappy. If you feel too far from your ego ideal, the role of leadership will only widen the gap.

2. In order not to be swallowed whole by your role, you need to be able to attend to your own dependency needs. The leader who willingly, or even insistently, takes everything on his or her shoulders, will suffer. No one has *all* the information and insight they need, and a leader must be willing to be helped.

3. Of course, the ultimate mythical leaders are parents. And all leaders will have people's relationships with parents projected onto them to some degree. That is why psychological sophistication is so important.

Does it seem like no one short of Bogart could take the job? Actually, a good many people can. Every day, men and women fulfill their roles as parents, teachers, managers, and officials, helping others and approaching their own ego ideals.

The Safe Haven

It takes a leader to hold an organization together during times of change. The leader creates identification with himself or herself, regardless of the level at which he or she operates. A leader inculcates and supports values with which people can identify, and then evolves organizational supports in the form of structure and processes that support that value system. Processes include compensation, modes of appraisal and recognition, and modes of communication. Finally, the leader establishes some mechanisms through which people can have an effect on what's happening to them, along with a follow-up monitoring device. In other words, the leader gives people a center around which they can organize themselves. When the leader remains stable, even rapidly changing organizations can weather the resulting storms.

Christmas List

When Robert McNamara became president of the World Bank in 1968, he was immediately struck by how few needy countries were being helped. His advisors gave him reasons: most of the money came from Wall Street and from the U.S. Congress, neither of which was feeling very generous. McNamara shocked them all by closing his first meeting with these words: "I am going to ask you all to give me very shortly a list of all the projects or programs that you would wish to see the Bank carry out if there were no financial constraints."[2]

Of course there were financial constraints. But McNamara raised more money and got more done than anyone thought possible at the time. His success demonstrates vividly the power of a deeply felt organizational purpose (see p. 35). He knew what he wanted the Bank to do, and he started right out by having the members of his council state their ideal goals for the organization. Making a Christmas list began the work of getting them out of a certain rut. In this way the question "What can we do with the resources we have?" was focused, and became "How can we achieve our special goal with the resources we have?" or at least, "How much of our special goal can we achieve?"

You could ask a group of managers to list what they would really like to do with their units, if nothing stood in their way. You might find some surprises: people with ideas for inventions, or grand schemes to increase the efficiency of an operation. Present your own ideal goals, too, and try to arrange for one or two others to do so, so that people see they're not going to make fools of themselves. An exercise like this lifts people's vision above the routine of daily survival and responsibility. It reminds them *why* the organization should survive, and why they should take their responsibilities seriously.

Take Us To Our Leader

European leaders tore their hair out trying to get Jimmy Carter to provide strong leadership. Ronald Reagan was more than willing to do so, yet found his hands more than full trying to get Europe to go along.[3]

The difficult fact is that people crying out for leadership are not necessarily easy to lead. Mental health workers often diagnose difficult and disobedient children as actually craving parental guidance and authority, yet the children fight it tooth and nail when it comes. The same can happen in business. Subordinates may show clearly that they crave strong leadership, with such symptoms as: 1) internal bickering; 2) inaction and paralysis; and 3) fantasies of a heroic leader who will rescue the company. Yet if a strong leader tries to take control, he or she may face frustrating passively aggressive behavior. That's because, after the "honeymoon," subordinates discover that the new leader is not perfect and cannot make all problems disappear. Also, they find they are dependent on the new leader, and don't feel as autonomous as they may have under weaker leadership.

Head And Shoulders Above The Rest

People rarely acknowledge heroes of any kind these days, asserts Reynolds Price. We scrutinize our leaders so closely that their human failings become too obvious. Heroes, he explains, must be grand and distant "because grandeur is best perceived from a distance—an eye pressed to the floor of the Grand Canyon is seeing only grit."[4]

Sad to say, too many organizations are encouraging this trend. They create too many levels of authority too close to each other, blurring the distinctions between them. It's that much harder for leaders to inspire others when potential followers see themselves as peers.

But often managers themselves reject the "grandeur and distance" that Price rightly suggests heroes need. They feel uncomfortable setting themselves up as models because they fear being autocratic or dictatorial. These managers—many of whom are overly chummy with their subordinates—are like parents who want to be pals with their kids. They deny the differences in their roles and abdicate their role as leaders.

Most people want leaders who demonstrate a more profound understanding of significant issues, a greater maturity, and a higher level of creativity. They want role models who can inspire and guide them. But at the same time many people feel burned by past hero worship that has proven to be misguided. That doesn't mean that frustrated, disillusioned, or cynical people don't need heroes—they certainly do. But heroes for our time must appeal to people's intellectual as well as emotional needs. Heroes today must work harder to embody the principles and capacities they want others to emulate. They must stand above and apart from others, but they justify their position by reaching out to help others along.

Leading The Flock

During his 1979 visit to the U.S., Pope John Paul II personified the leadership characteristics we often talk about in the abstract. He stood out, he stood up, he stood for. He stated his positions clearly, and explained why he held them. He reassured people that the structure of the Church would remain, and that change would come slowly, carefully, and thoughtfully. He didn't flinch about stating hard truths and controversial positions, but his obvious feeling for others and personal magnetism were so great that even people who disagreed with him warmed to him.

Leaders inspire more people and accomplish more of real worth when they're not overly concerned with pleasing as many people as possible. Good leaders state their views with forthrightness and integrity. But they temper their tough-minded analyses of the facts with a tender-minded concern for others. Such leaders, like Pope John Paul II, earn both the respect and the affection of others.

The Crisis Preventer

One mark of a good manager is that you find her handling more potential disasters than real ones. For example, in July 1980, officials of Ohio U. realized that the recession in Ohio was going to be worse than expected, affecting their state funding. They immediately cut spending by 1% and raised tuition and fees 10%. State funds were indeed cut back the following spring, but Ohio U., although "pinching pennies," could do so "in carefully planned rather than panicky ways."[5]

Planning like this takes more than brains. It takes guts. It isn't easy to sacrifice, and to make other people sacrifice, when it doesn't seem necessary yet. People admire the successful crisis manager, and often for good reason. But the crisis preventer shows an informed courage that is just as admirable, though less spectacular. Managers ought to prepare optional plans and budgets. There's always a chance that things will go haywire.

Having your group purpose clear in your mind will make this easier, because you'll have a way of deciding what can be sacrificed and what must be preserved. Ohio U.'s planning council, which included faculty members, voted to increase stipends for graduate students, rather than increase their own salaries. They felt that getting good grad students was more important to the future of the university. Obviously that council had a strong sense of its group purpose.

At the unit level, this can be a good way to prove your worth. Most superiors appreciate having a problem spotted and solved before it becomes a disaster—and gets dumped in *their* laps.

Eyes On The Horizon

One of the traits that differentiates unsuccessful executives from successful ones is that they "can't see over the hill." They're preoccupied with today's activities and today's profits. They can't anticipate, let alone plan for, upcoming events and situations. Managers in growing organizations or units are most likely to get in trouble through shortsightedness. They can no longer have their fingers on everything that happens, yet they are afraid to let go and turn some of the work over to somebody who has a broader purview and can pick up the ball and run with it. Seniors of such people must assess in advance the amount of foresight that will actually be needed in a particular position, and lay that assessment out for the subordinate. The big problem in most organizations is that seniors don't act fast enough. Both individual and organization then suffer.

Good Teachers Demand The Best

Some managers, including many who pride themselves on developing their people, want so much to be liked that they don't demand the best of their people. They're like parents who can't bring themselves to discipline their kids and wind up communicating that they don't know enough or care enough to help them become fully mature and competent. The niceness of such managers is selfish, and their subordinates know it. People aren't easily fooled when their professional growth is sacrificed to their manager's need to be liked.

Many people want the opportunity to work for a manager who is talented and tough. They know there's no better way to learn a craft. Comedy writer Abe Burrows, who worked with playwright George S. Kaufman, explains the process this way: "I respected his knowledge and talent so much, that when he agreed to direct *Guys and Dolls*, I told my wife, 'I'm going to do *everything* this man tells me to do.' That was a tough decision because I thought of myself as a pretty good comedy writer; but I had to trust the teacher if I was going to learn anything."[6]

I'm not saying that managers or parents have to be rigidly authoritarian—or that people can learn only by signing themselves over to an expert. I am saying that managers and parents who can say, "Hold it—that's not good enough," show they care enough to help people do better. When people want to do well, a friendly "anything goes" attitude can effectively quash their best efforts.

The Winning Combination

Kissinger's genius is to have united three roles—the politician, the bureaucrat, and the scholar—whose integrity was thought to depend upon each being separated from the others, according to Prof. Sheldon Wolin, Princeton. For some time now, he says, the boundaries have been dissolving as politics became more bureaucratized, bureaucracies became more politicized, and scholars began to feel more at home in government bureaus than in the stacks of libraries.[7] A significant shift in leadership style is under way. Management and management development programs should take it into account. Executive candidates today have to know more than their predecessors—they have to be more scholarly—and they have to be more capable of managing the complexities of organizations. This requires them to be skilled bureaucrats, and to be more political in order to cope with the multiple internal and external forces that influence their organizations. No person can make it in contemporary large business organizations unless he is skilled in all three dimensions.

Dare To Dream The Impossible Dream

Management is an art when it begins in fantasy, an imagination of what can be. It then translates that fantasy into a clear plan, brings the plan to life, capturing the attention of others and involving them in the work.

How To Lead

Leading consists more in the way things are done than in what is done, so it's not easy to pin down how to lead. But there are certain qualities that you can bring into play more than you might otherwise, because you understand their inspirational value. Some thoughts, feelings, and experiences are more worth sharing than others. Some qualities and inclinations are best constrained at work and only used, if necessary, in other arenas.

How Does A Leader Lead?

The managerial alliance is my name for a healthy relationship between a superior and his or her subordinates. The alliance exists when they can stand together to attack the organizational task at hand. That doesn't mean they are coequal. The leader has to be in charge. It simply means that they have to be actively trusting each other. A managerial alliance cannot exist either when the leader is manipulating the follower to make himself or herself look good, or when the follower is trying to undermine the leader's authority. It exists when they give mutual sanction to their separate roles by focusing on the task.

Leaders function primarily as models. They help people define the realities they face, then support people in the process of licking them. They must constantly redefine priorities and help people balance alternative costs of choices they have to make. They will exercise sufficient control to keep the group working toward a common purpose—at standards they hold up—so that people are not played off against each other.

The leader acts as an umbrella also. He or she shields people from unnecessary psychological static arising from conflicts existing at higher levels, yet transmits to them all the information they need in order to make appropriate decisions in their own self-interest. He or she protects them from the failures which are bound to come as they take risks on behalf of the organization, but also represents them adequately to those above him or her. Good leaders will support their subordinates by taking time to listen and talk with those several levels below them as well, so that they will know the leader stands behind their own supervisor.

Your Town, Our Town

Organizations are essentially communities. They are groups of people gathered together for a common purpose. The more people are closely interrelated and develop a sense of community about what they do, the more likely it is that they will achieve their goals and purposes. A major function of the leader, of any part of the organization or of the organization as a whole, is to instill and sustain a sense of mutual support of the participants toward their common purposes and goals. One of the interesting aspects of a community, just as in a family, is that not everybody has to like each other. People may quarrel, fight, and have significant differences. The fact that people do have such differences is less relevant than the fact that being in a community provides mutual support. People in a community should know that no matter what their differences are, they are better regarded and find more protection and support within the community than they do outside of it.

All leaders at every level in the organization therefore should maintain that network of relationships that transcends individual differences, points of view, quarrels, even dislike, for the broader purpose of giving people a sense of where they belong, who cares, and why they are there.

Management Styles

Management styles have been classified in various ways, often by describing a certain way of carrying out the managerial function, as Michael Maccoby did in *The Gamesman*.[8] However, it may be easier to see styles and their effects by looking at behavior. Here are a few examples:

1. *Management by impulse.* People who are uptight about the bottom line and about being fully in control are quick to criticize and often

jump on subordinates impulsively. These managers exert constant pressures, hound subordinates, and demand results yesterday. They are easily upset by the least threat to their competence or results. Turnover among their subordinates is high; they don't build organizations, although frequently they are quite bright.

2. *Management by procrastination.* These managers can't seem to make decisions. They postpone action, avoid coming to grips with the competition—in short, they can't get off the dime. They may be afraid, they may not have clear signals from higher management, they may be too dependent, or they may lack adequate information. The results are the same: their subordinates can't function and frequently vent their frustration by fighting among themselves.

3. *Management by humor.* Some managers have an excellent sense of the ridiculous. They can lighten the heavy burden for subordinates by pointing to the lighter side, by making fun of some of the unrealistic demands from above. Many times they can also kid their bosses out of being irrationally upset or overreacting to a problem. These are not clownish jokesters, but responsible people who intuitively lighten the oppressive load of conscience borne by so many conscientious people.

4. *Management by touch.* The touch need not be physical, but these managers keep in touch. They make the rounds, visit, make phone calls to those who are at a distance, and generally convey their awareness of and concern for their subordinates. Such managers are especially important to people who are widely scattered and would otherwise feel isolated. Ideally, meetings and individual contacts increase managers' interdependence with their subordinates, strengthening the mutual support that all managers need.

5. *Management by steps.* This behavior usually occurs when good managers are dealing with ambiguity. They have the choice of either procrastinating or taking some form of action. Since circumstances make comprehensive action difficult, wise managers will take short steps in a direction they believe to be useful. Such managers create structure for themselves and their people, and by doing so they support their leaders. Frequently an ambiguous situation exists because the leaders are not prepared to give sufficient direction. They appreciate the initiative subordinates take to keep things moving.

Although I've been speaking of managers who operate in one characteristic way, flexible managers will find themselves operating in almost all of these ways. They will even use the first two, which are the least desirable. There are times when a decision or action must be delayed until conflicts are resolved, or more information is available, or the direction becomes clear. Sometimes impulse, based on good intuition, brings valuable results. The flexible manager manages by opportunity, choosing a course of action based on his or her diagnosis of the situation.

"But I Want My People To Be Strong And Independent"

Managers habitually neglect the importance of being available to their people. They think it's silly to have to "hold people's hands." They want their subordinates to take initiative and to act independently, so they try to model a self-reliant stance. All this is very rational. It just isn't valid psychologically. People need to be able to touch the manager, to read her face, to see her recognition of their existence reflected in her eyes. Managing by objectives does not alter this fundamental human condition. People still need contact and support. Managers at all levels should recognize this as one of their primary tasks.

Sign Of The Times: Power Outage

Too many managers these days pretend they don't have power over others. But in trying to be one of the gang, they create a "web of dependence and resentment" that enmeshes their subordinates, says Richard Sennett of SUNY at Stony Brook. People don't know where they stand with a manager "who has power . . . but doesn't want to be dictatorial."[9]

Managers who pose as peers are like wolves in sheep's clothing. Even when they mean well—and when the last thing they want is to be wolves at all—the disguise frightens people and throws them off balance. Subordinates know that when managers want or need to use power, they will. So they're never comfortable pretending the power doesn't exist. Even when the manager seems to want familiarity and group decision making, subordinates fear he or she will snatch off the lambskin at any moment and reclaim the manager's power and prerogatives.

Power operates in all human relationships—between spouses, parents and children, friends. It can be manipulative or supportive, punitive or liberating. The point is to use it well. Managers who fear or dislike using power aren't in fact giving up power. If anything, they increase their power over others—but it's the disguised power of uncertainty and ambiguity. These managers don't lead their people, but keep them hopping and ducking. It's a waste of everyone's energy.

What Do You Manage?

I once asked a teacher what she taught. "Children," she answered with a bright, affirmative smile. There aren't many managers who would answer a similar question, "People." Yet that is what we must learn to do.

Let Your People Know

When something goes awry in an organization which may be judged immoral or inappropriate, it is highly important for the head of the unit or the head of the company to go out and talk to all the people in the organization, explaining the situation honestly and straightforwardly, answering questions, and allowing people to satisfy themselves. Corporate leaders are sometimes reluctant to explain, feeling that it is better to dampen the issue and let it die out, but that does not take care of the powerful psychological forces within people.

Matters of conscience are disturbing to people. They need to have some way of justifying themselves and the organization—they need to explain to their friends and colleagues, and they need some way to restore good feelings about themselves and the organization. If they do not have enough information to do so, they are left with secret uneasy feelings and a distaste for what has happened. They will feel that the leadership has said one thing and done another.

These issues should never be washed away, nor should it be assumed that ignoring them will have no effect. It will create employee anxiety and hostility, which will take a greater toll upon productivity than the original controversy itself.

Moral Reefs

In the Middle Ages, the lives of saints and heroes were told as sequences of good omens, noble deeds, and righteous victories. These days, we recognize openly that even those who have done the most good also have caused others to suffer and have violated their own moral codes. It's impossible to do very much good without doing some wrong. As William Fox, Columbia U., puts it, "At the leading edge of choice, moral imperatives seem to get in the way of each other."[10]

Every manager faces this on some scale. A manager always has multiple constituencies, whose just claims will sometimes be mutually exclusive. A manager has to take risks; he or she can never be sure that actions meant to be right and just will prove so in hindsight. From time to time, he or she must say: "I know I haven't taken every single variable into account; I know some people are going to feel wronged. But it's time to make a decision and act on it. It won't be a perfect decision, but it's the best one I can make." Not everyone can do this. That's why one thing to look for in promoting managers is the way they cope with being wrong and with the possibility that what they're working on may not work.

Developing Leaders

Some people are not cut out to be leaders, and nothing will ever make them into leaders. But many people have qualities that will enable them to lead if properly developed. What are the best ways to bring these people along? What kinds of experiences will help them, what will hinder? How much independence do they need, how much close supervision and guidance— and when? Mentoring is a big topic these days—who can benefit from receiving it? What are the pitfalls of devoting your energy to another person's success—and what are the gratifications?

Exxon: Developing Succession

Developing succession is the most crucial part of a leader's role. It's interesting to see that a company as manifestly successful as Exxon invests a great deal of time in finding and nurturing future leaders. The eight top executives of that giant multinational meet several times a month to "review the progress of the company's top 500 managers and the pay of the top 3,000." A similar procedure takes place at every level of supervision. Exxon's elaborate rating system includes recommendations for developing employees in addition to comments on their shortcomings. Every employee is evaluated, and the results are discussed with him or her by the immediate supervisor. The system is popular—people know where they stand, and they like that.

People know that "the system intentionally breeds more top managers than the organization can use, to assure an adequate supply." In fact, Clifton Garvin, chairman of Exxon, seemed amused at the question of whether the company could get along as well without him. The system is set up so that there are a number of people who have all the ability and experience necessary to head the organization.[11] Managements of less effective, less developed companies often fail to realize that the top executives of the most successful organizations really do spend a lot of time on the succession issue. If perpetuation of the organization is the real goal, developing future leaders is clearly fundamental.

Personalize Your Development Activities

Developing subordinates is not a single activity. Success in giving appropriate support to different people often hinges on an assessment of their psychological needs. I distinguish four types:
1. Some young people come to managerial roles through solid identification with managerial or professional parents. They have learned certain values and skills and developed certain competences already that are readily transferable. They progress naturally and confidently. People like this chiefly need room to grow. They should be

turned loose, so to speak, with only general direction and guidance.

2. Those from working classes often have strong identifications, but their models won't be managerial ones. If they are adequately motivated, they will need modeling for the managerial role. Their managers should take more time to spell out the "how to's"—how to deal with higher level officers, how to present yourself, how to dress, how to handle expenses, what to do if . . .

3. Some have motivation and good models, but lack confidence. They need permission to develop themselves through constant encouragement and reassurance. Sometimes a nod of the head will be enough; occasionally an outright assertion that "I know you can do it" may be in order.

4. Some have models and permission but still have problems. They may have unconscious conflicts that lead them to stumble. If you have discussed the same work issues with a person several times and are satisfied that you have given straightforward feedback, and you still see no change, you can assume that the person needs a different role or therapeutic help. You should point out that his or her career development will be affected by whether he or she tackles the problem. This may be painful to hear, but it gives the person a realistic motivation to change as well as permission to get help.

Let Them Try Their Wings First

The Soviets' greatest military weakness in Afghanistan is their operations against guerrillas. The junior officers who lead these small units must make instant decisions without speaking to their higher command. But most of these officers have little experience or training in making such decisions, because of the Soviet emphasis on centralized command. The resulting lack of flexibility increases the small units' likelihood of failure.[12]

Organizations that have been highly centralized and then move toward participation and decentralization would do well to watch out for similar failures in their small unit operations. As decision-making power is pushed down in the organization, top management may inadvertently be setting people up to fail. They may be asking managers to make decisions they have no training or experience in making. It's important to accompany decentralization with training. People who will head decentralized operations should be provided with opportunities to "try their wings" first on smaller, less consequential decisions and in situations where there is backup review of decisions. And when a decision is overruled, the manager should be told why another choice is better. This makes the incorrect decision an opportunity to learn instead of an example of failure.

"No"

Most organizations realize they need young talent, as well as experienced hands. But having recruited this young talent, do they know what to do with it, so that both the organization and the young people are best served by the relationship? Given free rein on the basis of early and spectacular success, young people sometimes produce equally spectacular failures.

The solution is to have managers and mentors who know how to say "No" to success. The manager can't suspend his or her judgment just because the subordinate has had a spectacular success. It's not easy—affection, admiration, and ambition all stand in the way. But sometimes it's part of a mentor's job to be discouraging. It can be done, without damaging the relationship. Sherry Lansing, head of Twentieth Century-Fox film studios, is known for her tireless encouragement of the projects she presides over. Says a colleague, "She has to say 'No' to us on some projects. But she states her reasons so clearly, and somehow, just the way she does it, it doesn't really hurt that much."[13]

Ten Nights In Twelve Cities

The common practice of giving people a range of experience by rotating them through positions at two-year intervals may not be as sound as it seems. It takes most of that period to move, get established in the new organization or division, and get things running smoothly. That can only mean that the people who are rotated never really adapt and get integrated. They can only float on top of the organization, as it were. As a result, the depth of their investment in the organization and their satisfaction with what they can do may be seriously called into question. Picking up and putting down again is not an easy task; it takes its toll on the individual as well as the organization, not to mention the people who have to keep "breaking in the new manager." Organizations that rotate people with such rapidity in an effort to develop their skills, competence, and breadth may not be doing them as much of a favor as they think they are. It may be a good thing that organizations have reduced the amount of moving around. The whole issue needs much more careful thought than most organizations are giving it.

Only Losers Expect To Win

How do managers make it to the top? What kinds of experience teach them what they need to know, and what characteristics do they cultivate? In interviewing 105 senior executives of three Fortune 100 companies, Drs. Michael Lombardo and Morgan McCall, Jr., Center for Creative Leadership, found:[14]

1. Successful managers don't necessarily make fewer mistakes. But when they make one, they admit it, anticipate the effects and warn others, work hard to correct it, and then forget about it. As one executive put it, "Only losers expect to win all the time."
2. The characteristics of leaders come in balanced pairs, not single extremes. Confidence without humility becomes arrogance; toughness must be tempered with sensitivity to human needs; the ability to take charge must be complemented with the ability to depend on others.
3. Poor role models are as important as good ones—they teach people what *not* to do. It's the variety, and the willingness to take what each has to offer, that counts. Attachment to a single mentor is actually dangerous. If that person's star falls, so does yours.
4. Job rotation doesn't season managers unless the type of situation varies, not just the content. Starting up a project is different from turning a failing unit around is different from expanding an existing unit. Starting up a project three times is three times one experience.

This research bears out several points I've been making from my experience working with managers and organizations. No one succeeds all the time, no one does everything right the first try. The important thing is to learn from one's experience, to recognize what one has done and go on from there.

Stuck In The Middle

What do you do with middle-aged people who are stuck in middle management ranks because there's no room to move up? Many companies are using horizontal moves and special project assignments to stimulate people without promoting them.[15] With a little thought, this kind of moving around can also provide managers with useful experience, and increase their value to the company by increasing their skills. Instead of just moving people mechanically or randomly, think about the way those individuals operate. What contexts have allowed them to blossom, and what ones have not made use of their best abilities? Using that information as a guide, many can be placed in situations which further broaden them, not just provide a change of pace.

Keeping Ahead Of The Times

You can keep people from being disappointed in themselves and in their managerial roles by helping them keep up to date on trends both inside the company and on the outside. This can be done with periodic one-day refresher sessions with outside speakers, conducting workshops, reading groups, or by having specialists in your own organization summarize the latest developments in their fields. People can use themselves best when they are abreast of changing expectations and when they are helped to become more proficient in meeting those expectations. These are fundamental twin needs in all organizations. When we find obsolescent executives, we usually discover that they simply don't know what's going on in the world outside. Frequently they don't even know what's happening in their own companies. They have been allowed to die on the vine.

Champing At The Bit

Bosses who supervise women managers often have a real prize on their hands, but many act as though they don't. Because there are so many male managers, they cover the normal curve of distribution—some are exceptional, most are average, and some are below average. But the women who move into managerial roles tend to be the cream of the academic crop. They have had to push their way through business schools and compete effectively. They represent the high end of the ability range. Unfortunately, this can create a major problem. It is all too likely that they will show up the inadequacies of some male bosses, and then one of three things will happen: 1) those bosses will try to constrain them; 2) there will be continuing friction; or 3) the women will move elsewhere.

People in mentoring roles or more senior management positions must look carefully at male managers who are supervising women, to be sure that they are capable of handling the quality of women managers coming to the organization. If they are not, the organization is already suffering, and it will suffer more from the restraint, friction, or loss of talent as the women move on. In addition, those young women will be disillusioned when they discover that they can't count on skill and competence to enable them to rise, since their capabilities can be suppressed by managers of longer experience but lesser competence. Of course, the same thing can happen with female bosses as well, but it occurs more often with men since there are more of them. I am surprised to run up against this problem so frequently, because I would assume that higher level managers would pay more careful attention to their own subordinates. All too often, they do not; contemporary performance appraisal systems don't compel them to.

Pass The Word

A good manager looks out for the interests of subordinates. Sometimes that means telling them about advancement opportunities. But a study of one large organization indicates that many managers ignore or forget this aspect of their jobs. In that company, most newly promoted people learned of job openings through informal channels. And many of those who were informed through the formal manager-subordinate relationship said their managers first got the information through the company grapevine.

This pattern is common elsewhere. Managers do well to remind themselves periodically that as much as they'd like to, they can't hold onto their best people forever. They therefore do well to keep abreast of the good opportunities within their organizations. When holding on becomes holding back, no one's best interests are served.

Know It All

"I knew merchandise, I knew cost, I knew selling, I knew customers, I knew everything. . . that's the advantage we had." It was a great one, and Sam Steinberg saw Steinberg, Inc. grow from a family-run grocery store in Montreal to a billion-dollar corporation.[16]

Steinberg's advantage was immersion—sixty years in the food business. Over and over his decisions and innovations proved successful. If they seemed like intuition, it's because they were based on knowledge so fully absorbed and integrated that it became second nature. Immersion like this is not just a matter of time, of course. It takes a constant effort to learn, understand, and keep up with change.

What are the psychological requirements for immersion? If you want power in order to compensate for some other lack, you probably won't have the patience. You must desire fluency in translating ideas into reality. Immersion will give you that. To encourage this, the organization must make people feel secure and keep them challenged, assuring them that decades spent there will not prove wasted. Companies that value immersion naturally tend to promote from within.

Every organization and every field has knowledge that must be gained by osmosis. If you are thinking of a new career, make an effort to find out what about it has to be learned over time: culture, personalities, traditions. The same goes if you want to advance in your present field. How many "I know's" can you say?

A Worthy Guide

Can you teach management? No, because management is an art. As with any art, techniques can be taught—but the creative and sensitive application of those techniques is what counts. Bernard Malamud, speaking both as a writer and as a teacher of writing at Bennington College, describes his teaching role this way: "You can't teach writing, but you can teach talented people; you can hasten their way through certain travails by pointing out roads that have already been taken. You can help young writers, who often have no idea what they're doing, to understand the insufficiencies of their work, and, possibly, the direction they have to go—in some cases, they ought to get out of writing entirely."[17]

A mentor can serve a similar function for younger managers. First you can offer yourself as a model—not that you are perfect, but you have developed competences beyond theirs and you have experiences to share. From the perspective of longer experience, you can try to show them what they lack and where they shine, and what they might have to do in order to make it. You can help them avoid certain problems and hassles. And in the case of people who clearly aren't going to make it, it's important to tell them that they don't belong in management at all. It may seem cruel, but in fact it is far more curel to allow people to waste years of their lives trying to be something they simply aren't cut out to be.

It's All In The Family

A mentor may be a person's closest business associate, but he or she shouldn't be too close. Mentors who follow a parental model risk cutting off communication, because children cannot talk as freely with parents as they'd like. A mentor modeled after an uncle or aunt creates a psychological distance allowing for more growth in the relationship. The younger manager can let down some defenses without worrying about reprisals, and the mentor can give personal advice that will not cloud the working relationship.

Drawing The Line

Managers who take and use the guidance an older manager offers are usually favored by the older manager. After all, the student is a credit to the teacher. A warm relationship develops, but then something goes wrong. The older manager may become critical, or distant, or start restricting the younger manager's area of responsibility, perhaps telling him what to do or countermanding his directions to others—in general making life difficult for the younger manager, or even causing harm to his career. This happens when the younger manager begins to succeed on his own, thus becoming a threat to the older manager—a rival. It doesn't matter whether the younger manager intends to compete. What matters is the older manager's perception.

Apparently Edward Finkelstein experienced this when he was Macy's New York president, and his former mentor, Herbert Siegel, was corporate president. Macy's had been in trouble, and had begun to turn around under Finkelstein's direction. Finkelstein received an offer to take over at Abraham & Straus, which was also having some problems, and he could write his own ticket. His resentment of Siegel's interference was considerable, so with this ammunition he went to Macy's corporate chairman, Donald Smiley, and insisted that the dividing line between the corporate office and his division be strictly observed. "If Mr. Siegel crosses that line once more," he said, "I will be out of here the same day." Apparently it worked—Siegel kept to his side of the line, and Finkelstein stayed.[18]

Terror Tactics

Women who so fear success that they unconsciously sabotage it are plagued by irrational guilt, says psychiatrist Doreen Schecter, Albert Einstein College of Medicine. Such women, she says, unconsciously perceive their success as an attack on their mothers. And they fear retaliation from mothers whom they perceive as omnipotent.[19]

Women in our culture traditionally were reared to be dependent. It's therefore not surprising that many who were socialized that way feel guilty when they attain a measure of independence. They're often afraid that professional success means they've become unacceptably aggressive. Unconsciously they view their professionally successful behaviors as rebellious and hostile acts against their dependent, family-centered mothers. This guilt is such an intense emotional burden that some women trip themselves up rather than carry that weight.

If you have a woman subordinate who suddenly botches her otherwise excellent chances for promotion, don't assume she will never make the grade. Meet with her to explore the reasons for her failure and her feelings about success. Since the underlying reasons are unconscious, you won't learn them, but your discussion will call her attention to the irrationality of the failure. You may want to suggest some form of career counseling or therapy. Managers who help women weather such crises are doing what their organizations need most—developing the people on whom the organizations depend.

Surviving—And Succeeding

Clearly, being a leader is not an easy role. The potential for burnout is great, when many people depend on one, and when achievement results from the efforts of followers as much as from one's own efforts. Leaders must learn where to get the support and revitalization they need—who to ask for help, and how. And leaders need to learn how to accept themselves—their failures and limitations as well as their considerable strengths.

In Demand? Conserve Your Resources

The more skilled you are at developing others, the greater the demand you create for yourself. You'll be sought out for in-depth discussions; you'll be collared for informal advice. People will expect you to live up to the highest ideals you and your organization espouse. You'll be a model for others, as well as a source of insight and inspiration.

If you're in demand, you'll feel increased pressure for your time and attention. What can you do? First, conserve your time. Schedule people; don't let them take your time impulsively. When you're not constantly reacting to spur-of-the-moment demands, you can respond more thoughtfully—and you'll be conserving your physical energy and emotional reserves, too. Second, think about the implications of your words and behavior. These take on more importance as you become more respected. A hasty act or judgment can have worse consequences the more people look on you as a leader. Finally, find someone who can support and lead you as you support and lead others. All leaders worry from time to time that they can't measure up to the expectations or fill the needs others want them to. They all have doubts, worries, and insecurities that others blissfully fail to see. A trusted friend, mentor, spouse, or professional therapist can help you express and examine such natural but troublesome feelings. And if you get help when you need it, you'll be better able to help those who demand it of you.

Anything You Can Do

One hallmark of great achievers is that they are also great students, and remain so all their lives. When they see a remarkable achievement, they want to know how it was done, and perhaps to try it themselves. Once Leonardo da Vinci went to see a piece of sculpture discovered near Florence. When he arrived, "he walked round and round the masterpiece, saying nothing. Finally, he took a string from his pocket and began measuring each of its dimensions."[20]

One of the traits of a leader is the ability to learn from the competence of others. This means not just noticing who's doing well, but also closely observing how he or she does it. Leonardo measured the sculpture he admired. Perhaps you should take notes during meetings: How does that fellow phrase the proposals that always seem to be accepted? Where does that manager find the facts she is always citing? Write things down when you think of them at odd times of the day; don't let your perceptions slip away as unobtrusively as they appeared.

Besides observing, you can ask people directly how they accomplish things. Of course, there may be some politics to consider here. You don't want to appear prying or opportunistic, or you may not want to create an image of yourself as a novice. But people are often flattered to be asked about their techniques for success. They feel good about passing along what they have learned.

Hiding Fire With Flames

Success is stressful for some people because they aren't sure they've earned it or that they can meet the demands of their new positions. And some people handle their fear of failure by putting obstacles in their own paths, according to Dr. Steven Berglas, McLean Hospital Stress Management Clinic. If they have a "legitimate" problem, such as alcoholism or a neurosis, or even stress itself, there will be a reason if they don't succeed. They won't have to feel that they failed, so much as that their problems got in their way. They can still tell themselves that they would have succeeded if it hadn't been for . . . . "Given the current popularity of psychological thinking, mental illness itself has become a great cover story for breaking rules," says Berglas.[21] In this case, you might say that mental illness is a symptom. It's a way to deny another problem: fear of success or fear of failure. It's possible that people may use our discussions of characteristic behavior as an excuse, too. "I can't help it," they may think, "that's the way I am, because of things that happened to me when I was too young to do anything about it. I'm not responsible for being the way I am." But that isn't the whole story. First, we are who we are because of the way we respond to our life experience, not because of our experience. Second, we can modify the expression of our behavior, within certain limits, choosing the most productive and least self-destructive modes. Third, it is possible, with hard work and competent professional help, to change in deeper ways. People who hold on to symptoms, using them as excuses for their lack of success, are displaying once again their own characteristic behavior of placing the responsibility for their lives outside themselves—and therefore outside their control.

Misfortune: Opportunity In Disguise

Difficulties are inevitable. One's attitude toward them is not, however, and can have a profound effect on the results of a situation. In *The Oak and the Calf: Sketches of Literary Life in the Soviet Union,*[22] Aleksandr Solzhenitsyn quotes a Russian proverb: "If trouble comes, make use of *it,* too." So often, when faced with difficulties, we avoid them. We run away, get angry, and do all kinds of things out of frustration. But sometimes we are wise enough to take the circumstances, whatever they are, and turn them to advantage. It may not be a material advantage, it may be personal growth. The proverb is a powerful reminder of that opportunity.

Superstars Sweat It Out

Want to make it to the top? If so, don't rely on raw talent alone to get you there. That's the observation of coach John Nicks, who grooms Olympic skaters. Champions, he says, mostly need dedication, self-discipline, support, courage, and the ability to perform best under pressure. And, he adds, they need complete self-confidence *before* they've mastered the technique.[23]

This news should hearten many managers—too many assume they're not really cut out for tasks they can't master effortlessly. Many people wrongly assume that the fast learners will always dominate a given field, so they don't work as hard as they might when a skill doesn't come naturally. That's a mistake. Much learning and mastery involves sheer hard work and determination. Those who persevere at a task that can make them feel awkward, incompetent, or even stupid, often find one day that they've nurtured an ability that's become second nature. They can now apply the laboriously learned skill creatively.

They've also learned the value of perseverance along the way. It's an old-fashioned virtue that gets short shrift too often. No significant effort, no sustained change is possible without it. And organizations certainly need "tortoises" who stick it out to the end.

In Summary

1. *A leader has a vision of how things could be, and moves confidently toward that goal, thus inspiring others to work with her toward that goal.*
2. *A leader models the kinds of behavior that people can both respect and strive to emulate.*
3. *A leader maintains direct contact with subordinates, supports them through difficulties, represents them to higher management, and deals honestly with them.*
4. *Leadership can be developed by giving people opportunities to solve new problems, by supporting and guiding their efforts to solve those problems, and by letting them know in what way they are meeting or surpassing expectations and where they need to improve.*
5. *Leaders can tolerate the dependence of others on them, because they know how to depend on others. They can accept their own failures and shortcomings, because they recognize and value their own achievements.*

Relationships That Work

Wherever you are in an organization, there are people around you. Getting work done depends on your relationships to those people. The apparently trivial and tedious activities of management look different when seen as the vehicle for creating and maintaining the relationships by means of which you move toward making a shared vision into reality.

Communication

In order to lead, one must *communicate. How can you be in more control of your communications with subordinates, and superiors as well? How can you make sure the message you want to send is the one that's received? And how can you make sure you're receiving the messages your coworkers send?*

The Medium Is The Message

What do managers do all day? Prof. Henry Mintzberg, McGill U., recorded the specific activities of a number of managers to find out. They sort through mail, talk on the phone, attend meetings and ceremonial functions—and deal with constant interruptions. Half their activities lasted less than nine minutes, he noted. And though most managers claim their job is to plan, organize, coordinate, and control, in fact most of their activities are routine and ritualized—or, conversely, spontaneous and disorganized.[1]

Is your job what you think it is—or what you think it ought to be? To find out, try using Mintzberg's method. Observe yourself closely for a day or two, and record your specific activities. How much time do you spend going through your mail? Dictating form letters? Being collared in the hallway? Leaving meetings to make phone calls? Chewing the fat with colleagues or clients? Then write down your purposes and goals in your job, and compare the ideal with the reality. You may be wasting a lot of time on meaningless details. But you may also find, on a closer look, that some of those details, interruptions, rituals, and snatches of conversation are the heart of your job. Some managers are hard at work when they're pricking up their ears at business rumors, renewing contacts with old associates, or pausing to congratulate newly promoted managers. Such tasks aren't a waste of time when they're used to channel information, maintain rapport, and establish an overview of an organization. You may not be organizing and controlling as much as you'd like to. But you may be oiling the gears of a cumbersome machine more than you know.

The Unspoken Message

Subordinates read the signals of their managers' gestures, intonations, and subtle behaviors. They know what their managers want even when the message isn't communicated directly. New managers in particular are inspected and "read" by their subordinates in this way, says Prof. John Gabarro, Harvard. Subordinates in one company, for instance, knew very well that a new manager who arrived first and left last expected a special measure of commitment from them. And they responded in kind.[2]

Wise managers are sensitive to the nuances they give off and the impressions they create. They catch themselves when they're interrupting people, rushing off, and acting impatient—in effect, telling people they don't want to be bothered. Instead, they make a point of dropping into offices. They seek out suggestions in informal conversation, and communicate through all their actions that they are part of a cooperative effort.

Cat Got Your Tongue?

What makes it so hard for managers to communicate with their subordinates? Here are four common obstacles:

1. They aren't sure how to go about it, and are afraid to try. This is more common among people trained in objective, factual disciplines, especially those who sought such roles because they are uncomfortable with personal relationships.
2. They may be too caught up in work demands. Either they don't have the time to communicate, or they don't realize the importance of making time.
3. They may have too much guilt (see p. 38) to talk comfortably with others.
4. They may be too tied to management objectives. This allows them to focus on the concrete, and at the same time to avoid interaction and those aspects of behavior which affect the achievement of the objectives. In short, they are trying to manage mechanically.

If you're the manager of someone who doesn't communicate, try to find out whether one of these four factors or some other is at play. You can go at it by asking the questions we ask about our cases: how does the person handle affection, aggression, and dependency, and what seems to be the person's ego ideal? Then you are in a position to talk with your subordinate about the nature of the communication barrier and what steps might be taken to correct it. Perhaps the person needs to learn how to interview (see p. 83). Perhaps the person is not aware of the cost of being overly preoccupied with the details of the job, and once aware of that could set aside formal times for communication. Perhaps the person is so uncomfortable with interpersonal relationships that he or she avoids personal contact. Or perhaps the person thinks too concretely to allow for the interpersonal communication required of managers. In either of the last two instances, the person simply should not be in a managerial role—and the sooner you come to that conclusion and do something about it, the better.

If you yourself are having a communication problem, you may be able to size it up by these criteria. Then you can decide for yourself whether some kind of training would help. You might want to seek professional help in dealing with your guilt or other discomfort about talking to people. Or perhaps you would be better off investing yourself in your technical role and not in trying to manage people.

Missing Your Cue

As managers grapple with that facile dictum, "We must improve communication," many encounter a frustrating situation. Their doors are open, they see anyone who wants to see them, they can chat comfortably with whoever comes in—but still they are criticized for not listening. What's going on?

Sometimes the emotional climate in the listener's head prevents him or her from taking in what's being said, especially if it's not being said directly. There are several climates that are particularly unfavorable for picking up subtle cues:

1. People who tend to repress their own feelings too heavily are often so preoccupied with holding them in that they can't be alert to others' feelings. These people are likely to choose occupations where there are lots of rules and prescribed ways of dealing with things, which minimize uncertainty and support their overcontrol.

2. People who are overly preoccupied with how they're doing—how they're measuring up to their own and others' expectations—have little energy left over to attend to what others are thinking and feeling.

3. People who are characteristically self-centered invest all their energy in themselves, and other people don't count for much. They may feel it isn't worth the effort to pick up subtle cues from others.

Some people apparently pick up the cues, but don't do anything with them. In one study, subjects were asked to interview a person on three topics, and if a topic seemed to make the person uncomfortable they were to drop it and move on to the next topic. In talking with the subjects afterward, it appeared that they had all picked up the cues of discomfort. However, some felt the person had no business being so uncomfortable about such an innocuous topic, and barged on with the questions. They made judgments about how the person should behave, and acted on the basis of that opinion rather than the evidence from the other person.[3] People might also disregard cues because they don't know what to do with them; they aren't sure of their perception or interpretation of them; or they're afraid of dealing with the feelings these signals imply.

If you find yourself trying hard to be open and communicative but still being criticized for not listening, try sitting down after a conversation and writing down the interchanges. Then look over the record with some-one who has some skill in communication, who perhaps can point out what you are missing. You might also try tape recording an interview, if the other person agrees. Or perhaps your organization has a training program using videotaped role playing. The point is to step back from your own behavior and take a more objective look at what you're doing during conversations.

Breaking Bad News

Many executives conscientiously take time to explain to their subor-dinates why decisions have been made or will have to be made which are counter to the recommendations or wishes of the subordinates. When you do this you are not only giving information, but also conveying respect for the subordinate. This consideration for the other is frequently helpful, but it sometimes goes awry.

If a person's recommendations are not followed or if someone is pro-hibited from doing something she thinks she ought to do or wishes to do, she is usually disappointed if not angry. When a manager goes to great lengths to soothe ruffled feelings, he runs the risk of unwittingly trying to keep those ruffled feelings from being expressed. The manager may need to be liked too much, or may find it unpleasant to incur the disappointment, hostility, frustration, or dismay of the subordinate. Try-ing to get the subordinate to agree to a decision, or at least sit still for it, can be perceived as seduction and coercion. This can only increase the subordinate's anger.

It is far better to give a simple explanation of the facts and then let your subordinate react with all her disappointment and hostility. This indicates that the expression is acceptable in itself, and that you aren't going to be angry just because the subordinate feels wronged. It's an important means of developing trust.

Surveys: Questioning The Answers

Many organizations use morale studies, opinion polls, and attitude sur-veys. Some people swear by them; others, like myself, have considerable doubt about their value for a number of reasons:
1. You get answers only to the questions you ask. The way the ques-tions are expressed often determines the answers. In addition, the questions may not mean much to those being polled, yet the polls fail to ask about the importance of the issues to those being sur-veyed. And people sometimes do not talk about their real feelings, particularly if they think it is inappropriate, not nice, or immature.
2. The very fact of a survey implies, "Tell me what's wrong and I'll fix it." But many situations cannot be fixed, and even when they

can, polls rarely ask those affected what responsibility *they* will assume to correct problems. And situations worsen when managers don't respond to problems after asking about them.

3. Surveys tend to bypass levels of supervision, and those supervisors often take survey feedback as an indictment and criticism of their methods. In fact, higher level management sometimes uses surveys for just that purpose. But to magnify the helplessness of supervisors is to do yourself, as well as them, a great disservice.

4. The usefulness of survey feedback hinges on the professional competence of the person interpreting the data. Responses frequently contain internal contradictions. In some reports, for instance, 80% of those polled have said they are satisfied with their jobs, but 60% would change if they could. Without a theory to explain such data, they don't mean much. The interpreter must understand unconscious motivations and the meaning of the answers in deeper terms. Then survey feedback can be a helpful part of a comprehensive study of an organization.

Survey feedback is most likely to be valuable when it is used as a basis for discussion and to engage with people around the problems to be solved.

Conflict Resolution

The competitive nature of work organizations and the problem-solving orientation of most work means there will be conflict. It's up to the manager to make conflict constructive—to channel the energy that could be wasted on fighting each other into fighting obstacles and producing useful goods and services.

The Hatfields And The McCoys

When trying to resolve an organizational conflict, diagnosis is as vital as ever. Techniques for resolving conflicts are worthless until you know what type of conflict it is, when and why it started, and who has a stake in resolving—or prolonging—it. Looking at an organization's history, we frequently discover a history of conflict. Often the conflict appears early in the organization's development, perhaps over which of two departments will perform a certain function. People may come and go in each of the departments, but the departments themselves remain, as does the conflict. None of the transient people may know why there is a conflict, where it came from, or why it continues. The effort to resolve it then runs afoul of a standing partisanship with no logic behind it.

If you are in a department or unit which has had a running battle with another, stop before you carry that battle any further. Take a look at how long the conflict has been going on (in one form or another), where and why it arose, whether it is an institutionalized form of a power struggle between two long-departed people, or whether it reflects a historic battle over power or turf that no longer has any meaning. Such a perspective may enable you to arrive at a reasonable solution, instead of carrying on a Hatfield and McCoy feud, which produces only casualties.

Like Bickering Children

Is intense competition necessarily a problem in peer relationships at high levels? How can it be handled?

People are competitive in a competitive society and in competitive organizations. There's no way out of it. But that competitiveness is sometimes exacerbated into conflict by the manager. Here are four common ways:

1. The manager may play people off deliberately, in order to retain power. This is generally done to take the heat off the manager. If people are busy fighting each other, they can't compete with the manager.
2. Ambiguity, whether intentionally fostered or the result of neglect or incompetence, unnecessarily intensifies competition among peers. When the manager doesn't provide clear direction and clear boundaries, people are likely to try to cover all bets. So they try to enlarge their own turf as a means of protection, which of course puts them into conflict with others.
3. The manager may independently agree with both sides in a conflict, for any number of reasons. Each party then thinks the manager is on his or her own side exclusively, and is more willing to do battle with the other.
4. If there is no cohesive thrust in the organization, rivalry will be more intense as people try to pull each other in the direction they think best. The direction of the organization therefore must be made clear. People need to meet with their leaders and talk it through as a group. They need to analyze and examine the future and then divide up roles. Otherwise each can only do what he or she deems relevant—which may be in competition with somebody else.

When peers are put into this kind of conflict, for whatever reasons, there's a great tendency for the manager to want to sit on them, to say, "Stop it!" That may stop the behavior, but the feelings just go underground. Then you don't have an arena in which the rivalry can be transformed into successful problem-solving efforts on behalf of the organization. That's the problem Lyndon Johnson got into, as described by David Halberstam in *The Best and the Brightest.*[4] No one wanted to be unacceptable to the group so everyone agreed too much, at considerable cost both to the president and ultimately to the country. Every organization needs a loyal opposition—a set of people who can examine the other side of any problem or decision. You can get that out of appropriately channeled rivalry.

When rivalry is neither squelched nor channeled into problem solving, people's energies go into battling each other. When you start to analyze a problem and somebody differs, the difference tends to become a personal difference. We saw this between Reagan's budget chief David Stockman and energy secretary James Edwards,[5] and between Alexander Haig and Caspar Weinberger. The first person has to protect what he or she said, or take the offensive against the other person, instead of looking critically at the problems that all share. Intense competition is costly and not particularly helpful. Some managers think it's important to see who will win the battle. That may get you the defeat of some and the victory of others, but it won't get you clear thinking about what you need to do or a commitment to do it. You get that from turning rivalry into cohesive teamwork.

Untying The Knot

Internal conflict can tie a group in knots, bringing its work to a halt. How do you disentangle the knots so the group can get on with its task? There are several possibilities, and the best one to use depends on the type of conflict.

1. *Setting boundaries.* When the group is confused about its purpose, describe what the group is to do and what is beyond its scope, suggests my colleague Dr. William Hausman. Restate its charge and remind people of those boundaries when they stray from the subject or task.

2. *Relieving the pressures of conscience.* Members of a group often vary in their degree of concern about accomplishing the task or the time it takes to do so. Focus on the person who is most concerned with completing the task, and support that person's position by calling attention to the fact that there is a task to be done.

3. *Taking charge.* This has to be done with rebellious groups—groups that are testing the leader's authority or challenging the validity of the group's purpose or existence. The leader might state that there is a real task to accomplish, perhaps give the reason for it, and spell out the consequences of failure. Allowing rebellious turbulence to continue simply paralyzes the group.

4. *Refocusing.* As the work proceeds, the group's original purpose may be obscured, or even changed. It is necessary, particularly when this surfaces as confusion and conflict, to raise the question of the

group's objective, so that people can return to the task at hand.

5. *Confronting*. At times one must take a stand and point out the nature of the conflict, which may be going on underground or in very subtle ways. Bringing it out into the open may enable people to drop the side issue and resume working toward the group's goal. For example, in a group meeting it became necessary to point out that two members were vying for dominance and power over each other, thus preventing the group from functioning at all. The person who was supposed to be leading the group took a passive role, and the meetings were frustrating and fruitless. Once the conflict was in the open, the leader could take charge and the two who were fighting for power backed off.

Each method deals with a particular type of group conflict. The leader must diagnose the conflict before attempting a resolution. Taking charge of a nonrebellious group could arouse serious resentment. Refocusing a rebellious group would escalate the conflict. Setting boundaries is beside the point when there is an underground struggle for power. Throwing a random technique at the problem is likely to make matters worse, not better.

Raising The Issue

When two factions are blaming each other for a problem and both are two levels below you, how can you reestablish communication between the groups? Say, for example, that you have complaints from customers about product quality. The sales group complains that the manufacturing group turned out a shoddy product; the manufacturing group says they were pressured by the sales group to put the product on the market before they were ready. Try raising the problem another level. Generalize the point of contention into an issue with broader application that needs to be discussed—how to maintain quality control. Then follow these steps in setting up the discussion:

1. Prepare the person to whom both groups report to deal with the generalized issue. She may have considered the original problem too hot to handle, fearing that an open discussion would erupt into an emotional free-for-all, and that she would lose control of the meeting. With the discussion one step removed from the original argument, that is less likely to happen.

2. Prepare the heads of the two groups—or the members—to discuss the generalized issue. This can be done by means of a memo or, preferably, face-to-face discussions.

3. Prepare the person who originally raised the point (the sales manager who received the complaints) to deal with it as a generalized issue (maintaining quality control) and present the issue to the meeting.
4. Attend the meeting yourself. Guide and support the manager who chairs the meeting; help her keep the discussion focused on the issue, and avoid letting it slip into unproductive blaming.

This technique can be useful in any situation where meetings are avoided. A prime reason for that avoidance is the fear of things getting out of hand. This fear is particularly common in accounting and law firms, but is also encountered in business organizations.

You Did! I Didn't! Did! Didn't!

Are you a successful arguer? Can you bring a disagreement to an amicable conclusion? It's a skill that can be learned. John Gottman, U. Illinois, studied the differences between the conflicts of happily married couples and those of unhappy couples. He says there are three stages to a conflict: agenda-building, arguing, and negotiating. In the first stage, successful arguers acknowledge each other's complaints, rather than trying to counter one complaint with a "worse" one. This doesn't mean you have to agree with the other person's point, only that you listen to it sympathetically.

In the second stage, the whys and wherefores of the agenda items (complaints) are explored. Most people do some "mind reading" here, saying what they think the other person feels. If you're correct and don't sound accusing, this can give the other person a feeling of being understood. But it's dangerous to phrase these thoughts as anything but questions, and if you feel accusing, you'll probably sound that way no matter how you phrase things. Another part of the second stage is making a comment about the way the discussion is going, such as "You aren't listening to me," or "You're shouting," or "We're going around in circles." (This is called metacommunication.) Successful arguers use these comments to correct the direction of the discussion. Less successful arguers make the comment the subject of further argument: "I am so listening!" or "I'm not shouting, you are!" or "That's because you . . ." Obviously, this doesn't resolve anything.

In the negotiating stage, successful arguers reach an agreement fairly quickly, either through compromise or by one person deciding to give in (with no hard feelings). Less successful arguers are likely to respond to a proposed solution with a counterproposal—which, as you may have guessed, becomes the subject of renewed argument.[6]

People at work run into some of the same problems in trying to settle conflicts. If they don't listen to each other, all they get is cross-complaining. If they think the other person is wrong, they'll never understand what's really bugging him or her. And if they need to be right more than they want to reach a solution, the negotiations are likely to deteriorate into a renewed argument.

When arguments go around and around, never reaching a reasonable conclusion, there's a good chance that the real subject of the argument hasn't been discovered. How can the real subject be uncovered? First, it's helpful to have an outsider listen—a person who has no interest in which person or which side of the argument "wins." Then, try to identify the level of disagreement. That is:

1. Is it a conceptual difference? Do the parties disagree as to what is the problem or what is the goal?
2. Is it a methodological difference? Do the parties disagree about how the goal or solution should be reached?
3. Is it a personal (power-seeking) difference? Regardless of the stated problem or goal, is it power that people are really after?

Having identified the real problem, it can be discussed. But the skills described above must still be used: *listening* to the other's point of view, letting him or her know you empathize, and being willing to compromise, to give as well as take.

Healing The Breach

Sometimes we feel injured by another but that person doesn't see any-thing wrong with what he did. The person is, in effect, denying the way we feel and invalidating our experience. Invalidating a person's experience is a serious threat; it's almost like acting as if she doesn't exist.

The urge to reaffirm one's existence and the validity of one's experience can be overwhelming. Hence, revenge: causing the person who harmed us equal harm. But revenge doesn't undo the original harm, and it doesn't make the person acknowledge that we hurt. And we know, deep down, that revenge doesn't make things better.

On the other hand, if the person acknowledges the hurt, we do feel bet-ter. If the person regrets that we hurt, better still. And if the person acknowledges having caused the hurt, we're pretty much ready to go on as if it had never happened (unless the effects of the hurt are very long lasting). Intention doesn't seem to come into it much, as long as the per-son regrets the harm.

Next time someone accuses you of injuring him, think twice before defending yourself. You can deny the injury, put up a wall between the two of you, and shoot back and forth at each other. Or you can hold your temper, acknowledge the person's pain, express empathy for his situa-tion, and acknowledge any part you played in creating the situation—saving explanations of what you *didn't* do for later. That way you heal the breach instead of widening it.

Being The Boss

You're in a position to lead, to inspire, to take charge and get things done. But you're also in a position where you're responsible for what others do and for what happens to them. You need enough psychological understanding to manage subordinates with a whole variety of personalities, and you need to know yourself well enough to be a help to your people, not a hindrance.

Oh No, It's Me Again

Being a good boss may come naturally to some people, but most managers have to change some of their habitual ways of reacting to people and situations. Even after managers have developed new habits of interaction, their old ways come back from time to time, particularly when they are under stress. The first sign of stress is to be more intensely and more conspicuously your typical self. In other words, a quiet, unassuming person will tend to withdraw more under stress; a highly conscientious person will try harder to be in control of more things. The second indication of stress is physiological symptoms without physiological causes. The third is a radical change in behavior.

If you have changed your behavior significantly in your efforts to be a good boss, your subordinates may be thrown off balance when, during some particularly stressful period, you suddenly revert to your old self. If your supportive concern is suddenly transformed into detachment or into pressure and harsh criticism, people will be confused, angry, resentful, and frustrated. They also will have difficulty sustaining the trust you had built up.

How can you prevent this from happening? Chances are you can't, entirely. But you can nip it in the bud, if you understand your own characteristic response to stress and are alert to it. Many times we don't realize we are under stress—or at least, that it's severe—until we hear ourselves snap at a subordinate, child, or spouse for very little reason. Withdrawal and flightiness are even less obvious signs of stress. Also, it's hard to see our own characteristic behaviors, precisely because they are characteristic. We are accustomed to them, so we don't notice them.

This is where a "trusted other" comes in. We each need one person whom we know well and can trust, and who will show us the things we need to see when we are blind to them ourselves. It might be a friend, colleague, secretary, child, or spouse. Whoever it is, ask that person—give him or her permission—to point out to you when your own behavior is getting in your way or making life difficult for others.

Erratic behavior really tears people apart. As long as you're consistent, whether good, bad, or indifferent, people can adapt. They can learn when not to approach you, or how to approach you on sensitive topics. But they can't very well cope with inconsistency, wherein every tack that works once fails the next time. We all need protection from ourselves, particularly when in positions of power over others, whether as parents or as bosses. A trusted other provides that protection by lending us some objectivity.

What's Sauce For The Goose . . .

Do you subscribe to Theory Y but prescribe Theory X? If so, you're not alone. Or so say researchers James Driscoll, Daniel Carroll, and Timothy Sprecher of MIT. In a study of randomly selected managers and first-level supervisors, they found that while both groups said they believed in humanistic theories of motivation, they agreed that the managers over-controlled the supervisors. Even when the managers saw the supervisors' painful dilemma, they just couldn't let go.[7]

When people try to maintain rigid controls, they indicate that they feel inadequate. They want to meet their own expectations of perfection but cannot, and they overcompensate for their failure by directing their energies into power struggles. But if overcontrolling managers also tell their subordinates to have more autonomy and self-respect in their jobs, then they're creating a double bind—a no-win situation. The subordinates will fail no matter what they do, because they can't meet the managers' contradictory requirements for success. They can't offer the line people the carrot or the stick, because the managers in theory don't want that; but neither can they use more flexible approaches when they're controlled by a firm system of reward and punishment from above. The result: frustration, anger, and cynicism. Managers need to ask how their behavior affects their subordinates' performance. What are their problems? How would they like to operate? What gets in their way? Managers may not be able to—or want to—give subordinates as much flexibility as they want. But there's no need for the tensions that dissonance creates. If you want or need control, say so. Then at least your people can work under clear directives.

Kangaroo Management

When things go wrong, the first impulse is to express your anger or frustration at those you assume to be responsible, and get the facts later—ready, fire, aim. Often you find that there are reasonable reasons why things happened as they did, quite beyond the knowledge or control of those you blamed. At that point, it's a good idea to apologize for your short fuse. Your subordinates probably are aware that they had no control over the situation, or that they had no way of knowing the necessary information to prevent it, so they feel unfairly used. They can't tell you they resent the blame, however, because you're the boss and the boss is always right (or so the incident might make them think). So communications close down. An apology is a good way to reopen them— especially one accompanied by renewed efforts not to jump to conclusions.

Some managers have trouble apologizing. Some dislike admitting a mistake to others. Some can't bear to recognize a shortcoming in themselves. And some can't accept the reality that some things *are* beyond their control and that of their subordinates. They make themselves ridiculous by requiring ever more stringent controls, instead of accepting the fact that there are unforeseeable circumstances and that precautions can be carried to the point of absurdity. They would stand far higher in their subordinates' regard, and possibly in their own as well, if they ate a piece of humble pie.

Hostility: How To Take It

Managers often have difficulty differentiating the times to stand up and take the anger of their subordinates from the times they are being run over and should put a stop to it. Whenever a leader encourages interaction, differences and anger arise. If feelings have been bottled up a long time, the degree of hostility that breaks through when discussion opens up may seem overwhelming and inappropriate to the leader. But she need not dump participative management at this point. She can counter her own fears of being put down and attacked with the knowledge that she can turn all that energy toward problem solving.

When criticism starts coming hot and heavy, you should not answer it, but should ask people to specify the details of whatever they are concerned about. This focuses their attention on the problems—on examining them—rather than on personal attack. If people persist in personal attack, you can simply ask them to stop and to look at the problems instead.

When people are discussing a problem related to a decision made at higher levels, ask them why they think the decision was made that way. By holding back the explanation you have, you give them the chance to express their expectations of management's thinking and you compel them to look for potential logic behind the decision. Then if you need to offer a different explanation, they will be in a better position to listen.

From time to time, try to summarize what people have said to you, clarifying both factual and emotional issues. This gives them the chance to correct you if you have misunderstood anything, and it proves to them that they have been heard.

Once they have agreed that the issues have been clarified, you can address the question of what to do about the problems. Even if deciding on a solution is not in their power, ask them what they think ought to be done. As differences of opinion arise, point them out and ask how they might be resolved. When people come to realize in this way that authority figures can't please everybody, they can either begin to resolve the differences among themselves or give the authorities permission to make compromises for them. They can trust management more because they have been heard.

To sustain the momentum of this increased trust, you should come back to the group frequently to report progress and check out how things are going. Much progress has been lost by failure to follow through.

Smooth Sailing Or Becalmed?

What kind of subordinates are likely to give you the greatest headaches? It's not the obnoxious ones, but those who idealize their manager, who have a marked, but subtle, dependency on him, and who have specific fears of making demands on the manager or coming into conflict with him. The subordinate's high opinion of the manager protects the manager from the fear the subordinate will leave him for a better manager, and the subordinate's fear of conflict protects her from encountering hostility from the manager. There just aren't any problems. Things go along very well, but that is the rub.

If there aren't any problems to be dealt with or differences to be examined, it is difficult to take a critical look at the work. It is also difficult for the manager to push for greater initiative on the part of such an admiring subordinate. If the manager tries to get his subordinate to behave differently, he feels guilty because he thinks the subordinate will feel attacked—which isn't surprising, because that is exactly what the subordinate is trying to avoid.

When a manager is too comfortable with a subordinate, perhaps he should take a second look. He may well be undermining his own capacity for action.

First Lieutenant

Many managers have a lieutenant of some sort—a managerial assistant who can act in place of the manager, whatever the title of that position may be. Since an assistant is a stand-in for the manager, he or she holds a sensitive position. It's important that the assistant's actions and interactions with people be consistent with the manager's. Nothing can undermine communications more painfully between manager and subordinates than an assistant who throws his or her weight around, trying to be a big shot and arousing the wrath of subordinates. People are not likely to tell the manager how the assistant is acting, because the assistant has the manager's ear more frequently and on a higher level of confidence. People fear that speaking against the assistant may antagonize the manager, or lead to vengeful behavior from the assistant. So the manager must pay attention to the assistant's manner. If there are hints of inconsistency between your subordinates' expectations and their direct experience of you, it would make sense to check out whether the expectations were created by one who acts in your name.

Black Hat, White Hat

Managers and their assistants sometimes get into a relationship where one plays the "black hat" and the other is the "white hat." This phenomenon, technically called *splitting,* was described well by Charles Peters of *The Washington Monthly:* "Jody Powell often speaks for Jimmy Carter's mean, petty, and defensive side. Many bosses have this kind of assistant. He permits the boss to be a wonderful fellow, serenely above the battle, while still making sure his real thoughts are injected in the meeting so that he can hear others' reactions to them."[8] This can happen unconsciously as well as consciously—for example, a secretary's attitude is often a dead giveaway of his or her boss's attitude toward you, whether or not the secretary intends to let you know.

The subordinates in such relationships put themselves in a difficult situation. They are likely to draw the lightning of people's anger to themselves, which may prevent them from having positive relationships of their own with those people. In addition, if the assistant moves into a managerial position, he or she is likely to take the negative image along. The new assistant then is viewed as a white hat, while the new manager is stuck in the same old black hat role. So if you are in a relationship with your manager in which you split out and portray the negative side, be careful of your impact on others and its ultimate effect on your reputation.

Spell Out What You Want

Managers who want to establish a standard of behavior for others to follow need first to state a principle and then to outline some steps. Both aspects are important, especially when the issue is sensitive—as with sexual harassment in the workplace. What HEW Secretary Patricia Roberts Harris did was issue a memo both warning that her department would not tolerate sexual harassment, and outlining formal complaint mechanisms.[9]

It doesn't do much good to state a principle if you don't let people know just how you expect them to carry it out. That's true whether you're creating complaint procedures, asking for increased productivity, or demanding a greater degree of professional job commitment. People need to know how they can represent your principles and fulfill your goals. (They also need to know how you expect them to act when they make a mistake or fail to measure up—or when something in the system breaks down.)

An added point on the Harris memo: it's not surprising, of course, that a woman executive would be the first to take this action. But in any organization, managers do well to find and assign a woman—preferably of middle age—to hear out any complaints and charges of sexual harassment. Distressed women will find it easier to talk with such a person—and their managers most likely will, too. You might find such a woman in human resources; or she may be a respected and experienced person who has been in the organization for some time, and knows many of the people in it. In that case, she might give valuable insights about what seems to be going on in the charges and countercharges. It's worth remembering that although sexuality is an issue when men and women work together, sexual harassment is a matter of power and control, not sexuality.

Playing Leapfrog

The tendency of senior managers to go several levels down into the organization to get information they want is a major problem in many companies. This practice is usually justified on the grounds of time constraints and expediency. No doubt such claims are valid. But think of it this way: you wouldn't walk into another person's library and take a book without telling her; how can you do the same thing with a person's subordinate? Asking someone else's subordinate for information causes problems for the subordinate, who is torn between the obligations to his immediate manager and to the more senior manager. And the immediate manager usually fumes with anger at the intrusion and consequent undermining of her role.

It's often important to get information quickly, and to avoid loading an intermediate manager down with the demand for such information. However, if you're going to skip over an intermediate, you ought to talk it over with her, particularly if it's going to happen often. There should be a distinct plan of action, so that the intermediate manager does not lose status or control, and is always informed. It's hard, feeling ignorant about something your subordinate knows. And it's easy for subordinates to want to be one up on their managers and thereby undermine their power and control, when they have the chance.

Being Subordinate

If you work in an organization, you have a boss. That manager or executive has power over you, so you're in a better position if you form an alliance with him or her—if you have the boss on your side, using his or her power on your behalf. It's worth the effort to "psych out" your manager, using the model of affection, aggression, dependency, and ego ideal—not in order to manipulate the relationship, but to understand your manager and coordinate your efforts so everyone gains.

When Your Manager Doesn't Take Charge

Subordinates often complain that they take a problem or demonstrate a need to their managers, but nothing happens. The managers sit on the issue and don't take charge, leaving the subordinates feeling frustrated and angry.

Before deciding how to approach a manager who doesn't take charge, it's important to assess what's holding him or her back. Some people are by nature unable to take charge; they never have and never will. If your manager fits this pattern—you can determine that by looking over past behaviors—stop beating your head against the wall. Other managers, however, are constrained from above. When subordinates are sensitive to this constraint, and ease the pressure from below, they can help their managers take small steps toward desired goals. Finally, some managers feel inadequate to implement their subordinates' requests or demands; they can often take charge when their subordinates give them detailed information, considered advice, and continued support. In short, when managers don't take charge, subordinates often have room to maneuver. But they must choose their goals and tactics carefully.

How To Help Your Manager

Subordinates should not be fooled by an overly assertive, individualistic manager. They should recognize that underneath such behavior, the manager needs to be able to lean on them. He won't admit it to himself, nor can he admit it to them because he is unaware of the need. When they recognize they have such a manager, subordinates should make a special point to stay in touch with him, to keep the manager informed, to reassure him by giving facts and figures which allow the manager to feel the situation is well in hand and that he can depend on the subordinate. When subordinates do this they are supporting their manager, recognizing the manager's needs, anticipating and preventing anxiety and concern, and providing the manager with the opportunity to have an effect on what's going on in the operation.

Once a manager develops this relationship with a trustworthy subordinate, he may have significant difficulty in separating from that subordinate, just as parents have difficulty when their children grow up and leave home. When the trustworthy subordinate begins to move up organizationally, she may be encouraged by the manager to do so, but may also receive complaints, anger, and, in extreme circumstances, rejection from the manager for leaving.

Sometimes the subordinate is puzzled by the negative side of the manager's ambivalence. She feels rejected by a manager who had previously trusted her so much. This may become a particularly pressing issue if the subordinate advances beyond that particular superior.

The separation process, then, needs to be managed carefully. The subordinate should continue to stay in touch with the former superior just to say "hello," to recognize the importance of the relationship, and return occasionally to talk over mature problems with the old manager. This keeps the manager from feeling totally deserted and this kind of care will also help the manager until he develops other relationships to pick up the emotional slack.

Looking Down Can Trip You Up

Many people underestimate their managers, and then wonder why their managers don't think better of them. For example, many Levinson Institute seminar participants claim that, while they're interested in what we teach, their managers are too narrow, too stupid, too critical, or too insensitive to pay any attention to our ideas. These people, prejudging what their managers are willing or able to understand, block the flow of information to them.

Of course it's true that many managers don't share their subordinates' interests, and many aren't as smart as their subordinates. But it's also true that subordinates often err in underestimating their managers. Too many times they're wrong. I can think of one person who didn't want to discuss the significant incident method of performance appraisal with a manager whom I knew to be disenchanted with traditional methods. And I frequently see people in human resources functions who are fearful of discussing various kinds of counseling with their managers, fearful of having "shrink talk" rejected—unaware that these same managers are in psychotherapy. If you're running scared and therefore withholding information from your manager, ask yourself whether you're cutting your own throat by cutting off information. Chances are your manager knows when he or she is being condescended to—and doesn't think highly of you for it.

Mixed Messages

What do you do when your manager is giving you mixed messages? She says she wants you to do a project, but acts as though the material you need to do it is her private property. Or he says he wants you to take on more responsibility, but bites your head off every time you make a false move. Mixed messages put you in a bind. If you respond to the overt message, you get the covert message that you're doing the wrong thing. If you respond to the covert message, you're in trouble for not following the overt directions. You feel helpless, and that makes you angry. But expressing your anger probably won't help. You can go around and around for hours about whether his anger has anything to do with your ability to take more responsibility, or whether her proprietary attitude has any effect on your progress with the project. You can dig yourself into quite a morass that way—largely because the person who's giving the mixed message has no intention of doing it. And he or she is probably furious with you for paying attention to a message he or she didn't intend to send. Add to that a little feeling of helplessness, if the person was trying *not* to send the covert message and failed.

What you have to do is follow the overt directions (start gathering the materials you need to do the project) until you get the covert message ("I don't want that taken out of my office," or "You don't need that," or "Where is such and such? I need it."). Then point out that you're having difficulty with the project, because you don't have the resources you need. Would she prefer that you left the book with her, or that you work on the project? This allows your manager to go with the overt message, and possibly to think about how the other one got there.

People can't avoid giving mixed messages when an unconscious need or strong wish conflicts with a conscious desire to act a certain way. A manager who needs to be in control may consciously want to develop her subordinates, but unconsciously want to keep a tight hold on the reins. The subordinate who makes the conflict clear allows the manager to make a conscious choice. In order to do this, the subordinate needs to recognize the manager's behavior as a conflict within the manager, not a reflection on the subordinate.

How Much Is Too Much?

I've been hearing more complaints lately about overcontrolling managers. It's a tricky situation to work with, because overcontrol can be a matter of perspective. Sometimes the person who is complaining about the controls is sloppy or lazy. Perhaps he or she previously worked for a manager who was too concerned about being liked to make people toe the mark. Perhaps the previous manager didn't know that it wasn't necessary to tolerate the person's slapdash style, or simply had lower standards. At any rate, the new manager strikes the person as making outrageous demands when, in fact, the demands are legitimate—as in requiring detailed analysis of situations, possible solutions, and anticipated consequences of implementing each solution, before listening to recommendations. As organizations have tightened up their operations, controls have become more stringent and standards have been raised. The increasing use of computers makes more detail and stricter controls possible, too. It's just part of the way the business world is changing.

Business attracts people who want to be in control, who need to know that the work is being done with some rigor. But some managers really are overcontrolling. They need to be involved in the details. They must have all the figures in order to recheck all the calculations. They go over the report with a fine-tooth comb and nitpick over every insignificant detail. Their behavior in general is compulsive.

What do you do if your manager really is overdoing the controls?

1. Consider how long you've been in your present position with this manager. The manager is responsible for what you do; it's reasonable for him to check your work, perhaps quite thoroughly, until it's clear that you can be trusted to work up to his standards. That takes time, plus meeting or exceeding those standards consistently and taking any criticism or suggestions seriously.

2. If demonstrating your competence for a reasonable amount of time—and it may take longer than you would like—doesn't help, tell your manager how you see the situation. Point out—courteously!— that working with this degree of closeness is not efficient. The manager is taking on an unnecessary burden, and in effect the same work is being done twice. Point out also how you feel, being over-controlled, how it undermines your sense of competence, independence, and value to the organization. Point out that it interferes with your ability to act, to get things done; that it blocks communication and slows things down.

3. If the manager can see your point and let go, then you know the overcontrol was situational. The old behavior may return when the manager is under severe stress, but should ease up again in response to a reminder.

4. If the manager can't respond to your need for more independence, or if he tries to let go but tightens the reins again almost immediately, then you're up against the manager's characteristic behavior. It isn't likely to change, unless it's getting him in considerable trouble from above. If you can't work effectively, start looking for a position where you can.

"Not That They Die, But That They Die Like Sheep"

Some people repeatedly allow themselves to be bullied by their managers or other superiors. Just as in the school yard, they must stand up to the bullies, making it clear that they won't give in without a fight. In her personal retrospective, *Civil Wars,* June Jordan, a widely recognized black poet, recalls a beloved uncle's advice when she was being bullied by her father: "Probably you can't win. . . . But if you go in there, saying to yourself, 'I may not win this one, but it's going to cost you; if you hit me you better hope to take me out because I'll be going for your life.' If you go in there like that they'll leave you alone. And remember: it's a bully. It's not about fair. From the start, it's not about fair." She herself goes on to say, "The outcome matters less than the jumping into it. Once you're on, there's adrenalin pumping of self-respect that compensates for terror . . . fighting is a whole lot less disagreeable than turning tail or knuckling under."[10]

The consequences of standing up to a bullying manager may be costly in financial terms. But enduring the bullying is far more costly in loss of self-respect and in chronic anger with yourself and your manager. And sometimes people do endure such situations for far too many years.

In Summary

1. *The willingness to hear what people are trying to tell you is the key to communication—actually receiving the messages that you would rather not hear.*
2. *The key to resolving a conflict is finding out what people are really fighting about. The source of the conflict may be historical, rivalrous, rebellious, a matter of perspective, a result of ambiguity, or any number of other things. Only when the true conflict has been identified can you choose the appropriate technique for resolving it.*
3. *As a boss, you need to be dependable in your actions and in your expectations of subordinates, and make sure those who act in your name provide the same consistency. You need to be close enough to your subordinates for them to feel you are engaged in a common enterprise, yet distant enough to be an authoritative guide to their endeavors. When you give your subordinates what they need, they are more able to give you what you need.*
4. *As a subordinate, you can help to lighten your manager's load, just by looking at things from his or her perspective. When you give your manager what he or she needs, he or she is more able to give you what you need.*

Managing Change

Change is becoming a way of life in organizations. That doesn't make it any less stressful, it just means more of the organization's energy goes into adapting to change. It makes sense, then, for managers to think carefully about why they want to reorganize, whether a particular change they have in mind is really necessary, and how to introduce a change so it will be least disruptive and most easily accepted. It makes sense to study and understand your organization first, then anticipate the effects of the changes, and finally, evaluate the effect of a particular change after it's made, before rediagnosing and planning further change.

The Process Of Change

All change entails loss—the loss of what has been. All loss is psychologically costly. If the leader fails to manage the feelings of loss that inevitably accompany change, if he or she tries to ignore or deny them, people will resist their new tasks. The leader's job is to redirect energy from resistance into solving organizational problems.

By defining organizational purpose and the goals and objectives derived from that purpose, and by confronting people with the realities of the organization and the problems they face together, the leader gives people the information they need to understand the need for change. By enabling them to discuss the past, present, and future together, the leader enables people voluntarily to break their ties with the past and to get to work on the tasks of the present and the problems of the future. Such discussion, particularly of the past, constitutes a mourning process. The new cannot be seized until the old is successfully mourned.

Change For Its Own Sake

It's always time for a change, according to some managers. Even when things are going smoothly, they say, it's a good idea to shake things up a bit and jolt people out of their ruts. What they don't realize is that the jolt may send them in an entirely different direction than they expected. Arbitrary change makes people feel powerless and out of control. It leaves them fluttering around feeling helpless because no one has explained the changes and given them a chance to master them.

If you're looking seriously at what you're doing, you keep changing what you do as needs, events, problems, and issues change around you. That way changes are made systematically, based on continuing diagnosis of the situation, and you understand why you're doing what you're doing. You can help your subordinates confront these changes, understand the reasons, go through the mourning process that change requires, tackle the problems, and adapt to the new situation. Without these steps, change can only be threatening. Instead of gaining a new perspective on problems, people get bogged down in their feelings about the change. Change for the sake of change is worse than useless. It's downright dangerous.

I Didn't Bargain On That

People enter organizations with psychological expectations, including some basic assumptions about social norms, relationships with fellow workers, work load, areas of responsibility, what constitutes a legitimate crisis and how it will be met, and so forth. The company makes similar assumptions. Altogether these form what I call the *psychological contract,* which covers three major areas: 1) dependency, or the balance between reliance on the work environment for support and the need to build independence; 2) distance, or the limits of intimacy or isolation one expects in various relationships with people at work; and 3) change, or the kind of help one expects in coping with alterations in the market-place and the economy or in one's own life. Companies and people vary as to what seems fair and appropriate. Although most people can't specify all the reasons, this is why they gravitate toward some companies and not others.

Whenever there's unilateral change in personal or organizational relationships, the psychological contract is broken, and we see signs of stress. For example, any change in top management upsets the working balance of these factors. A violation of the unspoken expectations produces anger, and sometimes strikes. If the violated expectation isn't the sort of thing people are accustomed to thinking about, they will grab the nearest handy irritant in its place. There usually is one. Whenever an employee or a union is insisting on something and management is dead set against it, you can be fairly sure it's a psychological issue that's at stake. A strike represents a breach of trust that goes well beyond the points explicitly spelled out in a union contract.

Before making significant changes, managements should weigh the dimensions of the operating psychological contract and take steps to re-adjust it openly. Employees can be sounded out by interviewing if necessary. (See p. 82 on how to interview.) When ample and adequate discussion precedes change, people feel they have renegotiated the psychological contract. If they then choose to accept the new contract, they know what they're in for.

Built Upon Sand

Say the structure of your organization changes around you, or under you. You may never be told the reasons for the changes, but you still have an important part to play. As a manager, you must spend a great deal of time helping your people deal with the change. If you don't, it will take years for things to settle down, and both the personal and organizational prices will be very high. Suppose, for example, higher management calls in a consultant who redesigns the organization and lays things out differently. Supposedly this is going to solve problems, but no one necessarily knows how or why, and even if someone does, your efforts to find out may be fruitless. The changes may or may not solve the original problems, but unless you handle the changes in your unit with some psychological sensitivity, you can expect some new problems in the wake of the change.

When change occurs without explanation, there appear to be no plans, no priorities, and no concern for the needs of the people involved. As a result, people are in a continuous state of disquiet, uncertainty, fear, and anger. They may have trouble identifying and expressing such feelings; they may consider such feelings unreasonable and therefore unacceptable, having no clear idea where they come from. You can help by encouraging people to express their feelings, however unreasonable they seem. You can help by talking with your colleagues or friends about your own feelings, thereby keeping yourself clear to help your subordinates with their feelings. You can help by clarifying for yourself what your unit is doing and needs to do, and passing that understanding on to your subordinates. And you can help by being straightforward with them about what you *don't* know. It will still be an unstable time in many ways, but by maintaining contact and open communication within your unit, you can ease the stress for everyone.

Worry Is Useful Preparation

People operate better when they know precisely what they are up against, even when the realities are anxiety-provoking. Why feed people's worries? Because normal worrying is useful preparation for meeting a difficult situation.

This principle is beautifully illustrated in a study by Prof. David T. A. Vernon, U. Mo., of three groups of children entering a hospital for minor operations. One group was given no advance preparation. The second group saw a film of a child wincing and saying "ouch" as he got a shot. The third group saw a film of a child reacting calmly and without pain to a shot. When those children entered the hospital and received injections themselves, those who had seen the realistic movie showed the least distress, followed by those who had seen no movie. The children who saw the "painless" film experienced considerable distress. As Prof. Vernon points out, they not only had to endure unexpected pain "but also feelings of betrayal and distrust in authority figures who let them down."[1]

For companies, this means not only trying to help their people to anticipate the future, but also holding back on facile promises meant to comfort people momentarily. How often, when a merger has taken place, is the newly acquired company reassured that nothing will change? And then things do change. That is betrayal.

Risk Is Where You See It

Why do people fear one thing and not another, when the dangers may be equal? Dr. Robert L. DuPont, director of the Phobia Program in Washington, says it is because of the way our assessment of risk is affected by three unconscious perceptions:

1. We tend to deny that a risk exists if we think we control it—as in skiing or driving a car. We might see a risk as being greater than it is, however, if we feel it is controlled by big, impersonal, mistrusted institutions such as a bureaucratic government or a huge corporation.
2. One big event is seen as a greater hazard than a series of small events spread over time and space. Although the same number of people may die in one plane crash as in 100 car accidents, the fact that the car accidents are not all in one place attenuate the effect—even if they all occur on the same day.
3. Familiar risks arouse less fear than unfamiliar ones. Cars and cigarettes are so familiar, we lose our fear of them. Jets and nuclear power plants are unfamiliar, therefore more frightening.[2]

Organizational change, innovation, learning new information, and many other aspects of managerial life present risks. But managers and executives can present these risks to their subordinates in ways that seem less threatening. Introducing changes gradually and providing as much information as possible makes the changes more manageable and less uncertain. When people have the opportunity to ask questions and express feelings, and when they feel they are being heard, they feel more in control and see the situation as less of a risk. And when the necessity of change is made clear by taking a firm look at the facts, people are better able to manage their fears and get on with the work.

The Importance Of Diagnosis And Planning

You cannot introduce a technique into an organizational system without creating a ripple effect and altering the balance of forces. Therefore the *way* a technique is chosen and introduced is more important than the inherent value claimed for it.

Before you introduce a new technique, method, or practice into an organization, it is necessary to make a comprehensive diagnosis of the organization. Try to understand what your organization is all about. Against this background you will see more clearly what the problems are, and what specific techniques or interventions will address them. Otherwise, you're just assuming that your favorite technique is the one the organization needs.[3]

This diagnosis should also include an assessment of the problems you are likely to encounter in introducing the technique you determine to be appropriate. The new technique must be integrated with the established policies and practices of the organization. If not, the new technique will be extruded from the system—not maliciously, but simply because it doesn't fit into the existing system.

When something new is introduced, certain behavior patterns and norms must change, and the power distribution is altered. Unless you plan these changes carefully, there will be an equal reaction to every action, as Newton showed us, and your planned improvement will backfire. Many things which have value in themselves fall by the wayside as a result of inadequate planning. That's one of the reasons useful techniques deteriorate into fads. They die because they're not firmly rooted.

So the next time somebody comes down the pike with a new technique or method to sell, or when you yourself have a great new idea for your organization, stop. Don't do anything without making a comprehensive diagnosis.

These Things Take Time

The type of organizational diagnosis I advocate is a major undertaking, but often I have only a limited time when I go into an organization to develop some understanding of the situation. There are a couple of shortcuts that can give you a feel for an organization's mental health, just as a person's appearance and demeanor can give you an impression of his or her general state of mind.

One way of sensing an organization's problem is to ask people to think of the company as a person, and then describe that person. They may describe it as a decrepit old man or as a vigorous youth, providing a picture of the organization as seen by the people in it.

Another way is to try to sense the degree of lightheartedness. Do people laugh and smile? Do they seem friendly with each other, as you walk around? Or is this a cold and distant kind of organization, with considerable guardedness? One sign that children and adults are in good mental health is when they can laugh and their sense of humor comes through; when they can't laugh or kid around, something is probably troubling them. So it is within organizations. When people can be free and comfortable with each other, which is easy enough to see by walking around and talking to them, then the organization's mental health is likely to be reasonably good. When they cannot, I begin to ask myself why, and raise some questions to be further investigated.

And how can an organization be changed in a couple of days? The answer is simple: it can't be. People can be brought together for team-building meetings so they can learn to communicate more effectively with each other; members of the organization can be helped to more clearly define their common purpose; executives can be helped to look at ways they might work more effectively together, and they can be shown a better way of understanding what's going on in the organization. These things can open up some doors and help people begin the process of change. But it is unreasonable to expect a large organization to change significantly in less than ten years. Beginning to understand the problems does not magically solve them. There are many new roles and new arrangements to be created. No matter how well you handle the changes, it takes years for things to settle down into a reasonable new routine.

A senior executive in a new role pointed out that it took him two years to move into a new organization, get established, and do what had to be done to get his function in order. When you reorganize an entire organization, or even a division, you multiply that unsettledness by the number of people moving into new roles. Then add to it the adjustments to the changes around them that must be made by all the people who don't actually move. Rather than being impatient at the time it takes for organizations to change, we might well be amazed at the human adaptability that allows eventual change without disintegration into chaos.

FOCUS ON . . . . Support During Change

Significant change in any organization arouses many uncomfortable feelings; expressing and sharing these feelings is an important means of coping with them. Yet people who know perfectly well what they are feeling, and that it is legitimate and necessary to express those feelings, don't. Why?

In consultation I see groups of managers who can easily say that changes in their organization stir up feelings. They know they should speak out their frustration, disappointment, anger, and fear. But outside the context of consultation, they fear their superiors and peers will think less of them if they express anxieties, and that these negative judgments will affect their careers. They know that peer counseling and group discussion of common problems aid in adapting to change. But they can't participate in those activities, they say, for fear of losing their colleagues' respect.

On further examination, the fear of others' opinions usually turns out to mask a greater fear of their own. They don't feel good about expressing their feelings; they feel they should keep a stiff upper lip. So they are always fighting themselves, but projecting the fight outside themselves by attributing hostility to peers and superiors. Of course, this only makes their work environment more uncomfortable.

Some of these managers have established ties to people in various parts of the organization over the years. They recognize the value of the moral support, information, broader and more balanced perspective, and occasional leads for new roles that these networks provide. They also see the need for family support and family integrity. Yet they don't speak of their deepest feelings to members of their network in the organization or their family. They *do* note that when they take the initiative in coping with their problems, their self-esteem improves.

Others have not developed supportive networks. When told that they can stay with the company through the reorganization if they find their own new roles, they are at a significant loss. They are desperately in need of organizational supports.

Psychological Scaffolding
What supports can organizations provide? First, top management officers should state publicly what feelings people are likely to have. Institutionalized recognition of their pain makes people's feelings more acceptable to them. Top executives should also describe the company's resources for helping people talk together, bring their feelings to the surface, and help each other formulate ways to take the initiative in coping with their situations. Second, there must be institutionalized ways of helping those who want to stay in the organization find suitable roles, if any exist.

You could think of these activities as a psychological scaffolding for organizational change. A scaffolding is erected to serve as a temporary support for a building while it is being remodeled, and to facilitate the work. In preparing for organizational change, a psychological scaffolding must be erected to support the people involved and to facilitate their psychological work in adapting. It is predictable that people will become depressed and fearful, and that this will be costly to the organization in its effect on their work. One can only wonder why, with sophisticated leadership in so many organizations, such predictable feelings usually are not anticipated or dealt with.

When Institutional Supports Are Lacking
If the organization as a whole is not dealing with these predictable feelings in a formal way, what can responsible managers do for their own units?

First, they can increase the frequency of staff meetings as a means of enhancing communication and maintaining group spirit. When departments are broken down into temporary functional groups, each of these subgroups may be held together by its own leadership. The groups are likely to be interdependent working units, such as matrix teams, project teams, or task forces. Maintaining the boundaries of these groups enables each group to be a source of mutual support for its members. Boundaries are reinforced by frequent meetings and problem-solving activities.

Second, managers must provide direction for their units. They must define their own accountabilities so that subordinates can define their accountability to their manager. People adapt more easily when they have more say in defining their new roles. But in order to do that, they must have: 1) information on which to base decisions, 2) power to implement their decisions, and 3) the capacity to understand their roles in the context of the larger organization. These conditions are less likely to be met during times of change. When they are not met, it is necessary for the manager to conceptualize for the unit.

Third, managers must build trust in themselves by fostering their relationships with people. Under conditions of change, and with multi-project or matrix orientation, it is more difficult to solicit opinions and have decisions made at lower levels. People are more likely to follow their manager's direction when they trust him or her, even if the frequency of contact must be reduced.

Finally, with wider spans of control and more mobile subordinates, managers often have less opportunity to observe what people are doing and ask them how they feel about what they're up against. That means managers must encourage more peer interaction. However, they must also provide specific coordinating times and mechanisms. Otherwise people simply will be milling around together.

Slow And Steady Wins

In times of change, managers need more than ever to have their own strategy as clearly articulated as possible, both for their own peace of mind and for that of their subordinates. But at these very times it is more difficult to get clear direction from superiors. Managers must therefore take greater initiative, using a method called *successive approximation*. You take a step in a direction you think is appropriate, check it out with a superior, refocus, take the next step, check again, until you get where you need to go. You have your manager on board both along the way and when you get there. Of course, a certain amount of caution is required, along with the risk taking. As my associate Dr. Ralph Hirschowitz points out, managers must take time for deliberation before acting.

Since you can't always be available to your subordinates, you also want *them* to take initiative. That means you can't be in a hurry to punish failure, either your subordinates' or your own. If you do, both you and they will become wary of taking appropriate risks. This is not the time to be hypercritical.

Change requires managers to maintain the mentoring and guidance role more intensively than ever. People at lower levels are also experiencing stress, and must be heard and reassured. If there are new roles to which people must gain access without the aid of institutionalized networks, then the manager may need to take advantage of his or her own position, contacts, and ability to persuade, in order to protect the career interests of subordinates. The manager may have to help them lay out and follow their career paths, if institutional mechanisms are inadequate.

All in all, managers shoulder greater responsibility for attaching subordinates to themselves. People will want that attachment anyway, when all around them is ambiguous and uncertain. Your initial tendency may not be to encourage such attachment; but if there is to be cohesion in the organization, it must arise largely out of the relationships of subordinates to their managers.

When The Novelty Wears Off

After winning a major award for his innovative research in physics, Richard Muller decided to describe the obstacles created for research scientists by the very funding programs meant to help them. While many regulations are well intended and do serve a valuable function, they also are counterproductive in unforeseen ways. Take funds awarded for research in a particular field. "This specialization was undoubtedly designed to avoid waste and duplication, and to make certain that the monitors in charge of an area of research are those most expert in that area," Muller concedes. But it sometimes results in scientists being unable to follow a valuable lead because it falls outside the jurisdiction of their current funding, or doesn't fit any of the established categories of research.[4]

It is manifestly impossible to anticipate every ramification of a new policy. That doesn't mean you shouldn't institute it—but you should check up afterwards to see how it's really going. And you should wait until the novelty wears off to see how the new system will work, once people get over their initial enthusiasm or resentment.

Don't just ask how things are going. Ask specifically: what's better and what's worse? Ask how the change affects other tasks people must perform. Prohibiting researchers from teaching and from being their own machinists might ensure that they devote all their time to research, but it also prevents them from constructing the most efficient experiments and equipment and from clarifying their own thoughts by conveying them to others.

Finally, be sure to watch for any unanticipated benefits. This knowledge is both useful for designing future programs and personally gratifying to the originator of the program.

The View From The Top

People in lower and middle management have considerable power to change their organizations, as people at the top sometimes admit. Sir Adrian Cadbury, chairman of Cadbury-Schweppes, says he's not in the best position to sell his ideas to the company. The best someone at the top can do, he says, "is to try to create a climate in which people can at least see your pet idea as an alternative, which might be favorably received if somebody would get behind it. The fact remains that, at the end of the day, it is the chap in the operating division who can get the new lines on. You are not in a strong position at the top of the pyramid to get into that act, and if you get into it too much, you tend to foul it up."[5]

It's true that people at the top are constrained because they're far removed from the guts of the operation. But the people below can feel so constrained by directives from above and pressures from below that they constantly react; such people soon forget that they have the power to act as well. When people assume that they can't change anything from where they sit, they become indifferent, cynical, or hyperactive. Even when they're working hard to keep things running, they're not serving their organizations as well as they could.

Middle managers can become proactive by first imagining how the organization looks to top management. What are their pressures and frustrations? What problems do they want to be rid of? What changes might they be grateful to see? Putting yourself in top management's shoes accomplishes two things: 1) it helps you see that no one has a premium on power; 2) it helps you conceptualize some of your organization's needs. At that point you'll be in a better position to assess how you can best help out.

Anyone in an organization can initiate successful change by doing the following: 1) define a manageable problem, and approach it in small, discrete steps; 2) build support for your idea or project as you go along; 3) define goals in terms of your own turf and expertise; 4) raise your sights only as you successfully complete one aspect of the project. If you try to do too much at once, you're likely to fail—or become too discouraged to continue. But if you build a pattern of proactive behavior, you can become a catalyst for significant change. Whatever your place in your organization, if your ideas and approach are on target, chances are your leaders will want to follow you.

Don't Bother Me With Facts

When it comes to a choice between new facts and old assumptions, most of us choose the assumptions. Sociologist I. I. Mitroff, speaking of lunar scientists and theorists in particular, noted the lack of willingness to "give up their ideas in the face of facts" and to "think logically" about the data gathered by the Apollo moon missions.[6] This tendency to stick with our assumptions, untroubled by the facts, is particularly important these days. All computer technology will be based on assumptions, and people will tend to operate with the data rather than look at the assumptions. So the data may turn out to be useless because of the assumptions on which they are based.

We are all in the position of having to give up some of our personal theories about the way things are and how they happen to be that way. The necessity is particularly pressing for managers. If you're not able to change what you're thinking about and the factors you're looking at, then of course you stay stuck in the same mold, undissuaded by facts. A lot of companies have gone down the drain because their executives had such limited perceptions.

Petrified Perfection

Plato's philosopher-kings are often thought of as open-minded thinkers applying the best ideas of their time to the daily tasks of government. Not so. Plato described them as possessing absolute knowledge of what is good and right, and having absolute power to kill or banish any who disagreed and did not keep silent. "Plato was not interested in progress ... but in stability. He wanted to create a perfect society and therefore a changeless one, since any change from the perfect would by definition be imperfect," says I. F. Stone. "For Plato, change was the enemy."[7] But change is a fact of life. Indeed, change is one of the qualities that defines life. We can dream of perfection, but we can't expect to attain it. Perfectionistic managers striving to achieve the perfect state of philosopher-kings become too rigid to manage change. They are destined for the stagnation that would have overcome Plato's Republic, had it ever become a reality.

A Changing Environment

The environment changes, and the organization must adapt. What are the likely effects of specific structural changes, such as decentralization? How can you be prepared for recession, how do you handle contraction? What is the effect of relocation? The more circumstances you anticipate, the less likely you are to be caught off guard.

Logistics For Change

All organizations should evolve three kinds of strategies for the organization as a whole or for its components: one for growth, another for a stationary position in the marketplace, and a third for possible decline. A growth position may require the infusion of larger numbers of people who are capable of highly abstract thinking. A stationary position may require merely maintenance people, but it is certainly not for those who would be impatient with an extended status quo. A declining position may require contraction with rearguard action using, primarily, older people for whom retrenchment will not be a severe blow. A delineation of the strategies will make it possible to define the necessary structure and, in turn, the kinds of people required to accomplish the chosen course.

How To Cope With Decentralization

Decentralizing an organization means that much authority is taken away from staff units and given to operating units. This places staff units in a consulting role, and along with their loss of authority, they experience a sense of severe psychological loss. It is important to provide solid training and consultation immediately after such changes take place so the staff units can begin to practice their new role, to identify with it, and to recognize that they are acquiring new skills to enable them to operate in new ways, rather than being left with the feeling that they have been castrated by the changes.

The Trouble With Hierarchies . . .

When an organization is power-oriented, people tend to judge their success in terms of how close they get to the manager and the manager's power. Any shuffling of organizational boxes becomes a defeat for them if the reorganization places their department or activity at a greater distance from the manager. It communicates to them that they have become less important. This is one of the problems of the hierarchical model and is yet another argument for bringing about organizational change with the involvement and permission of the people who are going to be subject to the change.

Moves To Make When Moving

When people are moved from building to building, they not only change offices, but they also change social arrangements, social networks, communication patterns, support systems, and access to resources. Only rarely is the impact of these changes taken into account. It is simply assumed that people will manage somehow and that everything will be all right soon.

Building changes should be carefully anticipated. People should be walked through a mock-up or blueprint of the new facilities. They should be encouraged to ask questions about the kinds of problems that the new setup will pose for them, and about any issues that may have to be resolved because of the move. They need to have sources of support information—where do they now get supplies, personnel services, security protection? They particularly need to remain in touch with people they have been associated with for a long time. They should have the opportunity to learn in advance where their friends are to be located by being given maps which have their own new locations marked.

Coping With Recession

When there are economic downturns, managers will want to be alert to people who won't cope well. In every organization, even those not hurt economically, some people will be thrown off balance, and will respond to uncertainty with undue anxiety. Left to their own devices, such people will compound organizational problems. Wise managers will therefore watch for people with the following vulnerabilities, and will take the steps outlined below to help them:

1. *Rigidity.* Compulsive people who have always operated in highly structured organizations are likely to overcontrol themselves. If so, they don't have the flexibility to adapt old ways to new conditions; they can't respond rapidly to change, especially under stress. But they can benefit when their managers teach them new ways and rehearse them in new roles.

2. *Dependency.* People who, under ordinary circumstances, are dependent on systems and higher authorities to take care of them and tell them how to function, become even more dependent in hard times. When they must deal with adversity on their own, these people are likely to panic or withdraw. They need increased communication and contact with their managers in stressful times. Dependent people function best when managers make incremental changes which allow the subordinates to master a new step before giving up an old procedure entirely.

3. *Perfectionism.* People who place impossible demands on themselves are likely to blame themselves for any adversity. In their own eyes, any problem that occurs is proof they haven't been good enough. When they confuse real-world problems with their own internal difficulties, perfectionistic people can't judge adequately how best to tackle a difficult and fast-changing situation. They're likely to become depressed and lose effectiveness. These people need managers who help them accept their limited control over situations, and who reassure them that no one is perfect.

Wise managers won't fight downturns by focusing all their attention on the bottom line. They'll watch their subordinates' ups and downs as the economy vacillates, and therefore know how to invest in their human resources for the most solid long-term gain.

I Thought You Knew

Many managers feel betrayed as the economy or the threat of takeover forces organizations to cut back and revise their plans and goals. They expected their CEOs to run the organization well, their superiors to know more than they and to adapt more readily, more effectively than they. Unfortunately many are discovering that their superiors aren't that good and never were. And they are resentful because they feel that they themselves are paying the price.

Handle With Care

When 53 managers were about to be laid off from a corporate office, I told one of the officers that I hoped the corporation would develop a program to help them. He said, "Give me three practical reasons why we should go to that much trouble when we lay off our employees." My answer:

1. You don't fire 53 employees in a vacuum. This will create a lot of insecurity among other employees; and the less information and reassurance they have, the more insecurity they will feel. You can expect anger, stress from "survivor guilt," and decaying commitment to an organization they're no longer sure they can trust. Some employees will look for new jobs instead of waiting for the ax to fall on them. All of these effects decrease productivity. It will pay to make sure everyone understands why the layoff is necessary, and to show people that the company cares about them.
2. Your company doesn't exist in a vacuum. It exists in a community of its town, its clientele, and related or competing businesses. There's no use creating any more bad feeling than necessary when something unpleasant has to be done. You just earn a reputation for being heartless. Then people will turn on you if they get the chance, and those chances are more and more common these days.
3. The managers who have to preside over this layoff are human. If company policy forces them to behave cruelly to their coworkers, they're going to feel badly about themselves and about the company. Firing a subordinate is a frightening experience for any manager. These managers need support, too. If your company allows them to fill up with guilt and resentment, their performance will suffer, and so will the company's.

Out—But Not In The Cold

When a plant closes, people lose a community, a way of life, and their trust in the world's order and fairness. So says Prof. Walter Strange, Virginia Polytechnic, who studied the effects of a plant closing in a company town in Appalachia. The experience was so traumatic, Strange found, that people bore the psychological scars long after they found new jobs.

If you're hiring such people, expect them to worry about more than lost jobs and money. They'll grieve over lost friends, rankle with guilt and resentment, and struggle to regain their equilibrium. They're likely to worry about market or production fluctuations, fearing that any change means disaster. And often they feel alien and inferior working in a new place with people who haven't shared their recent misfortune.

Managers can help these people first by letting them air their feelings, then by reassuring them about unfounded anxieties. These people need information about seasonal fluctuations, past layoff patterns, and present market conditions. Where the "gun shy" employees' fears are realistic, managers can help them see the range of choices and make decisions. When managers can meet distressed employees' needs for affection and dependency, these people can become integrated into the new work community.

Cutting The Fat

Just as some parents are always ready to criticize their kids and to point out that society is going to hell, so some top managements are perennially ready to scapegoat their middle managements. This is seen in many of the contemporary efforts to reduce costs by "cutting the fat" or "pruning the deadwood"—which usually means middle management. But with rare exceptions, to talk about deadwood is to talk about bad management from above. There are a number of reasons why deadwood occurs:

1. Organizations create deadwood with their extended hierarchical model, when that model is not based on capacity for dealing with abstraction. For every person promoted many others are left behind feeling defeated and depressed.
2. Due to inadequate feedback, many people do not know they have been passed by until it is too late for them to correct their performance. Merit plans and appraisal systems are honored more in the breach than in reality.
3. People are not adequately supervised in the form of coaching, consultation, direction, appropriate criticism for development, and making clear what is the person's responsibility and what is not.
4. People are not given enough support in coping with new jobs and new roles, with political forces in the organization, with situations that are not clear, with interpreting policy and carrying it out. As a result, most people run scared and many, after a while, get tired.
5. People must use new technology, often without enough preparation and without being taught how to cope. It is difficult for them to learn the steps (however simple they may seem) when the new technology requires a radical change in the way people see themselves.
6. A one-track system requires people with technical competences to go into management if they want to move up. But they are not necessarily of a managerial bent. When they become managers, a lot of good technical and expert knowledge is lost—and often they become poor managers.

In good times, organizations retain people they can't afford to retain when the times are hard. Some people plateau or are no longer carrying on their functions. These situations should be handled in a straightforward fashion as they arise, but usually they're not. And that creates the opportunity for some people to be heroic by suddenly launching an attack on middle management. It's as if middle management were at fault for all the things that have gone wrong. This can only demoralize middle management and undermine its identification with top management.

One cause of drastic internal cuts is that there are also top managers who can't handle the increasing complexity they face. One way of coping with that is to turn inward: to cut and chop and attack the organization, rather than try to figure out how to deal with external complexity. To attack the outside is to fight with vigor; to attack the inside often is to self-destruct. Too heavy an internal concentration may weaken the organization's capacity to attack the environment. The goal is to get ready for the next big leap, not to further demoralize the troops.

I don't mean to say that organizations do not need to become more efficient. But there is no excuse for the manner in which all this is discussed publicly, or for the way some people become heroes by launching such attacks. It contradicts the underlying effort to survive.

Creative Destruction

The recent recession was a symptom of what Austrian economist Joseph Schumpeter has called the "gales of creative destruction" that periodically sweep through economic life, according to a *Forbes* article by James Cook. They destroy parts of the economy that have become inefficient: labor-intensive agricultural methods in the early 1900s; the railroads in mid-century; and now labor-intensive manufacturing industries such as steel and rubber. This destruction makes way for the new: mass production of consumer goods in the early 1900s; autos, suburban housing, and education in the 1950s; and now electronics, computers, and service industries. If earlier industries "were an extension of the human hand and back, the new ones are an extension of the human brain and nervous system," writes Cook. "After all, decision making—the conversion of information into action—is probably the only really productive activity there is." Many workers will be displaced by this process, and those who cannot or will not learn to do the jobs that are becoming available in new industries will suffer. But the economy, he says, will survive—and probably prosper.[8]

It's important to help people whose jobs become obsolete understand that that is what's happening. Calling cutbacks "layoffs" when there is little chance that the people will be rehired only makes it harder for people to accept the reality that times are changing, and that they must move on to something else. Offers of retraining are more likely to be accepted by people who see that they must change and learn new ways. And retraining is likely to be easier and more effective when people feel it is their route to survival.

Role Changes

Every role change requires adaptation on the part of the person in the new role and the people around that role. It requires saying good-bye to old associates and old ways of doing, and getting to know new associates and new ways of doing. It also requires you to think of yourself in new ways—to say good-bye to the old you in order to be the new.

Hey, That's No Way To Say Good-bye

Saying good-bye is more difficult than most of us are willing to acknowledge. Many of us attempt to avoid the pain of parting by letting those who leave slip quietly out the door. But failing to say good-bye can have serious consequences for those who remain in an organization, as well as for those who leave it.

When a manager who has been well-liked and highly regarded leaves an organization without saying good-bye, the person who succeeds him or her will be in a difficult position. People will have trouble letting go of their allegiance to the old manager and committing themselves to the new one. They will tend to feel that no one can take that manager's place. They will be in a state of mourning, and as long as that mourning is incomplete, the successor will have a very hard time filling those psychological shoes. The problem will be most severe if the previous manager was the one who started the unit or department, or was a charismatic individual, or had some other unique quality.

What can you do if you're going to be the new manager? Try to explain to your predecessor the importance of saying good-bye to each person, thereby detaching himself or herself from the organization and the people who stay behind. If that doesn't work, you must do what you can to help your people mourn. You will need to include these five phases in the process:

1. Get everyone together and indicate that your predecessor is, in fact, gone. In group discussion they could recount the previous manager's contributions and note the degree of esteem people feel for him or her. You can then summarize what they have said. If for some reason you can't have a meeting, then you yourself might speak. This will help people recognize their loss. In effect, you must deliver a eulogy, and reassure people that letting go is not the same as forgetting. There can always be a place for that person in their hearts.
2. At the end of that review, announce that it is time to look ahead and to move forward again. Life is for the living, so to speak, and those who are gone are best served by our renewed involvement in achieving the organization's goals.

3. After that meeting, make the rounds and ask people what, ideally, they would like to do in their roles. Put those wishes together with your own into a statement of organizational purpose.
4. Look at the organizational constraints, then make a decision about how resources are to be allocated and what demands are to be made of people.
5. Let people know, both individually and collectively, what they are accountable for, and which of their goals can be pursued and how. Then, get on with it!

Take Them Just The Way They Are

Everybody gets a new manager from time to time. One of the problems subordinates face with a new manager, particularly if they had very close and admiring relationships with an old one, is that they keep trying to remake the new manager in the image of the old. There's no way that's going to work. For one thing, these subordinates will be beating their heads against a wall. It's a very rare character who will want to be like her predecessor. For another thing, the new manager will justifiably view them as nagging, unhappy, and unable to accept the new manager for what she is.

A new manager may be disappointing compared to the old. If the previous manager was charismatic and the new manager is not, no amount of effort is going to create charisma. If the previous manager was proactive and the new manager is more mediative, pressure won't make the new manager change. Managers develop their own leadership styles. A new manager may not meet the needs of people who have had different kinds of relationships with previous managers, but trying to force the new manager into a mold won't help. It will only induce anger and discontent.

Subordinates who find themselves acting this way ought to ask themselves why they are doing so. They're likely to discover that their attempts to help the new manager "adjust" to the job and the company are really attempts to get her to satisfy their own needs for a manager like the one they admired so much. Essentially that makes them manipulators and exploiters. It can't work.

First Get Your Bearings; Then Forge Ahead

When you move into a new position, assess your role and relationships before taking any significant action. That way you'll know what people expect and what managerial strategy is most appropriate. To assess your new role, first ask yourself the following questions:
1. Who are the key figures remaining in the organization after your predecessor's departure?

2. What have these key figures devoted their work lives to? What have they achieved and built? What are they proud of? In other words, what represents their ego-ideal striving?
3. Who are their allies? A network of associates within the organization? A group within the board? Significant people outside the organization?
4. What stake do these people have in various aspects of the organization's operation? What are the organization's vested interests?
5. What is the political terrain? How do people traditionally advance? What are the common pitfalls?

These questions will help you assess where the organization has been, how it has functioned, and where it is going. They'll also help you avoid stepping on toes. Then you can assess your own role. Will you be intensely pursuing your own ego ideal in your new role, or will you be subordinating your own aims to those of the organization? If you're expected to carry out what others have set in motion, you'll need first to test the political waters and adapt to the organization's set ways. But if you're expected to initiate your own program, you'll have to build your own base of political support, and make sure you have sufficient charge to carry through. Either approach can work, but only when you get your bearings and evolve your plans before taking the plunge into action.

How Possible Is Possible?

When coming into a new job, managers usually want to cover all bets and get on top of things as quickly as possible. Those are justifiable wishes, but the key lies in the word *possible*. You can't always move as fast as you would like. Conscientious people are likely to put themselves under great pressure—too much pressure. So it's important to specify a prognosis. That is, determine what you can *reasonably* expect to accomplish, in what amount of time, with what problems, given the resources available and your own skills. If you don't do that, and if you don't organize your work into steps, then you'll have a sense of being overwhelmed. You won't be able to see your own progress, so you'll tend to run scared all the time. In defining what you can expect of yourself, you'll gain a perspective that is critical in budgeting time, in avoiding burnout, and in coping effectively with the tasks at hand.

I'm assuming that you already will have evolved a diagnosis of the organization. You can't make a prognosis for yourself out of context. You should bring to your new job some understanding of the organization's history, values, historic conflicts, past and present leadership, and major mistakes. (Gathering such information is part of considering a prospective position.) Then you can get a sense of the internal momentum and the role of your particular job in that context. If you go at it without a prognosis, of course you'll learn by trial and error. But you may never have an adequate picture of what you're up against and why, and you may well wind up behind the frustrating eight ball.

Missing The Boat

Most management development programs don't address the anxieties and concerns of knowledge workers moving into managerial roles. The skills specialist or technician—engineer, accountant, lawyer, scientist—soon discovers that he is expected to assume managerial responsibilities. In some cases he is sent to a management development program; just as often he is merely put in charge of others. He immediately runs into two problems: 1) he must shift his self-image and ego ideal from performing in his specialty area to helping others get the specialized work done, which up to that point meant little to him; 2) he must deal with and sometimes control other people (as well as accept their hostility), which many specialists avoid by choosing their fields.

To become a manager, the knowledge worker often must turn against his own psychological grain. He must shift from being a doer to being a manager. That means losing control of his previous function and the opportunity to demonstrate his personal competence. It also requires that he deal with greater ambiguity. The specialist is rarely comfortable with these experiences.

Therefore, whatever formal skills are taught in management development programs, they often are imposed on a person who is a mass of internal insecurity. All people moving into these roles should have the opportunity to understand what it means psychologically to be in that position. They need to express their concerns and anxieties, and to have the benefit of discussing with more experienced managers the problems they have had in supervising others, in negotiating the political terrain, and in exercising authority.

When In Rome ...

Managers who move from one part of the country to another are, in a sense, moving from one culture to another. One manager described the differences he saw between managers in the North and in the South. Southern managers, he said, are much more gentlemanly. They control their emotions more. They are reluctant to get into hassles with each other, and place great store in being "good ol' boys." A former faculty colleague told me something similar about business school students. In the North he found them much more inclined to take part in T-groups, get into conflict with each other, and hassle for position than in the South. He theorized that this was one reason Southerners so often "made it." They let others fight themselves out, and then move into position. They themselves have not antagonized either side, being "good ol' boys."

No doubt this generalization, like most, is a bit exaggerated. However, it does point out that regional differences, though subtle, can be significant. It follows that such concepts as openness and engagement must be applied with subtle differences in regionally different cultures. When managers move around the country, they must think quite carefully about each new culture they enter, and learn to work with it.

Surprise!

Why is being a newcomer so hard? The fact that there are many new things to learn doesn't fully explain the disorientation we feel when taking on a new job. Many of the changes are known in advance, and we expect many things to be different, yet we continually are surprised. One reason is that there are more kinds of surprises than most people realize. Meryl Reis Louis, U. Ill. Urbana-Champaign, has identified five forms of surprise:[9]

1. Newcomers' conscious expectations about the job are not met in early job experiences. For example, they are told they will analyze data but at first are only involved in data collection.
2. Newcomers have assumptions about the job which are incorrect. It may not have occurred to them, for example, that there would be no windows in the building.
3. Newcomers' expectations about themselves are unmet. The expectations may be unconscious, or conscious but incorrect. For example, a person may expect to enjoy working independently and then find he or she needs more direction in order to work confidently.
4. Newcomers sometimes anticipate correctly what will happen, but are surprised by how it feels. A person may know that many hours of overtime will be necessary and agree to that condition, but may not realize how tired he or she will feel after doing it for a month.
5. Newcomers make cultural assumptions that are often incorrect. For example, they may be committed to producing results and assume others feel the same, only to find that others are committed to putting in their 40 hours and staying out of trouble.

Clearly many of these surprises are inevitable, since they result from unconscious expectations and assumptions. And the effort of making sense of surprises is what makes being a newcomer so hard. That effort can be reduced somewhat by spending time with peers and other non-supervisors who have been in the company for a while, and checking interpretations of events with them. They may be able to tell you the reason your manager didn't say much about your first presentation is that his wife is in the hospital. Newcomers also need time and the support of subordinates, superiors, and peers in adjusting to the unexpected changes. If you're an old-timer, take the newcomer to lunch on the first day and introduce him or her around. And newcomers can help themselves by taking life a little easier and seeking support from family and friends during the transition to a new job.

In Summary

1. *All change is loss; all loss must be mourned. People must identify what they are leaving behind, and let go of it psychologically before they can invest themselves in what is new. Letting go is made easier by recognizing what people will be able to keep or take with them, either as memories, or as part of their situation.*
2. *The consistency of behavior makes it possible to predict the effects of change, if you diagnose your organization.*
3. *Change takes a lot of psychological energy. People need to know why the change is needed—why they should go to the trouble of adapting. And they need lots of contact with superiors to reassure themselves that their efforts are appreciated.*
4. *The need for change often can be anticipated, so orderly plans for change can be made. Anticipation itself is an important part of adapting to change.*
5. *Most role changes require a change in self-image, as different tasks allow you to work toward different aspects of your ego ideal.*
6. *The psychological effort required to adapt to change cannot be sidestepped. It may involve some pain, but the payback is growth. Seek extra support (contact with people whom you know love and value you) in times of change.*

Troubled Waters

Life requires growth and change. Sometimes it comes easily, sometimes not. Understanding the process of change and how to help yourself before situations become overwhelming is one way to make change easier. Understanding what kinds of support are helpful and appropriate for others can make change easier for family, friends, and coworkers. Knowing when to ask for help or suggest it to others, and knowing where to get the help that's needed, can prevent a change from becoming overwhelming, or prevent an overwhelming change from causing destruction instead of growth.

Personal Change

You want to be a better manager, if you're taking the time to read this book. That means you're interested in changing. How much change is possible? How much can you change without losing your sense of being yourself? I have said a lot about unconscious feelings—what are the clues in your behavior to your own unconscious feelings? And what are some of the things you can do to increase your own sense of stability, well-being, and satisfaction with your life?

The New You Has To Be The Real You

Integrity is one of the qualities needed to cope with change, according to Shirley Letwin in *The Gentleman in Trollope: Individuality and Moral Conduct.* It is necessary to change with the changing world, but not simply to give in to change, because some changes are for the worse. It is necessary to be able to relate to others and speak their language, but not to make oneself into what others want simply to please them.[1]

Integrity is an important trait for managers, with the business world changing so rapidly. With management fads coming and going all the time, it's important for managers not to shift with every new wind that blows. When they do, subordinates become confused and don't know what to expect next. In addition, it's very hard to maintain self-respect when one is always doing what someone else says is right. When a new idea comes along, it's important to look at it, study it, understand its theoretical base and implications, evaluate it, and decide whether the whole or some parts are worth adopting. Whatever is worth adopting needs to be integrated into one's past behavior and ideas about the world. Otherwise one begins to feel like a montage instead of a whole person.

Working It Out

An adult's life doesn't change much when a parent dies—at least on the surface. But a parent's death often precipitates a period of soul-searching, crisis, and personal change. So say Drs. Dennis Malinak and Michael Hoyt and Ms. Virginia Patterson of U. Calif.-San Francisco, who interviewed adults who had recently lost a parent. Some felt irrational guilt for not preventing their parents' deaths; others felt guilty when the death didn't seem real because they'd had so little daily contact with the parent. Still others felt themselves becoming more like the dead parent. And some came through the experience with a renewed appreciation of life and intensified relationships with their children.[2]

Most people think of grief as bereavement; psychologists speak of grief as *work.* That's because people come to terms with death or other loss only when they express, confront, and examine their feelings openly and fully. That process is work—difficult work. But it allows you to understand the emotional and symbolic meaning a death carries for you. Some people will feel a parent's death as abandonment, and their insecurities and resentments will be aroused. Others will feel they're only now true adults. These people may feel renewed strength and purpose, but they may be more aware of their own mortality as well. If your parent dies, or the parent of someone close to you, it's a good idea to watch your reactions and feelings and think about what they're telling you. A therapist, counselor, or clergyman may be helpful in this process. But until you complete your grief work, your unconscious feelings will be turning to the past, even while your conscious mind is working toward future goals.

Discomfort May Contain Opportunity

T. S. Eliot produced his poem *The Waste Land* in a period of severe emotional stress, explains Harry Trosman, M.D., U. Chicago. A series of personal crises had left Eliot depressed, exhausted, and unable to concentrate. Fearing derangement, he sought treatment through an early method of psychotherapy. Yet he was able to transform his suffering into a work that is considered representative of a struggle that faces all of us.[3]

Eliot's gift, in addition to his well-developed poetic talent, was the capacity to tolerate his own suffering long enough to work out a creative solution. Many who come to normal crisis points in life are tempted to drown the attendant anxiety or depression with alcohol or drugs. This allays the discomfort, but also the motivation for solving the problem. The symptom-palliative-symptom-palliative cycle can go on indefinitely. An alcoholic is one who has never dealt with the problem that started the cycle. Those who can share and examine their discomfort in some way have a far better chance of working out a lasting solution. This is why it is so important to have someone to talk with during any sort of crisis.

Too Old To Cry

The idea that emotions are valid and need to be expressed is gradually gaining acceptance, although feelings about expressing feelings remain mixed. A good illustration of this mixed feeling is David Brinkley's comment about leaving NBC: "It was a wrench for me. I'm too old to cry, but I did manage a tear or two."

I hope the notion of being "too old to cry" will not be with us much longer. Certainly, as one gains experience and perspective, small hurts don't have the impact they had when one was young and every loss felt irreparable. But leaving an organization where one has spent most of one's adult life is no small matter. Thank goodness for those who can shed "a tear or two" and say so in public. They provide encouragement and

permission for those who might otherwise stop themselves from expressing their sense of loss, because they feel "too old" to do so.

Sign Language

We've long known that stress takes many forms, and now a study indicates that males and females are likely to manifest different symptoms.
Dr. Marianne Frankenhauser, U. Stockholm, and her colleagues studied
49 Finnish high school students, during both routine classes and a special matriculation exam. The girls reported feeling more tension during
the exam than did the boys, but the boys showed more physiological signs
of stress. Neither group out-performed the other.[4] We see here the effect
of social conditioning. Boys more than girls are expected to control their
emotions. And when people can't express their feelings openly, they
express them in less obvious ways. Here the boys expressed their tensions internally, and the physiological effects are ultimately costlier than
the girls' conscious anxiety.

Everyone needs some acceptable way of expressing and releasing tension. And each way is a metaphor for feeling. Using marijuana is a way
of decompressing tensions; drinking is a way of drowning them. People
who develop psychosomatic symptoms are trying to hold onto and contain their tensions; people who engage in perpetually frenzied activity
are whipping themselves. If you want to learn more about how you really
feel, look at your everyday activities and little quirks of behavior to see
how they express your affection and aggression.

Name That Tune

Another clue to how you're feeling is the songs you hum unconsciously
during the day. A middle-aged man with children leaving home sings
"Sunrise, Sunset" from *Fiddler on the Roof.* Happy moments bring other
songs. What have you been singing?

Break On Through

People sometimes shy away from professional psychological help because
they believe it's their neuroses that make them achieve. Actually, they
are achieving despite their neuroses. This is apparent in some people who
reach a certain age or level of competence, or who come through certain
intense physical or emotional experiences. They suddenly discover that
they don't have to press as hard, as if they had shifted into overdrive.
They look with greater equanimity at what goes on around them and
what they do. And they can devote their energies to more creative efforts
in doing the job than they could in their previous, more frenzied period,
when they needed so badly to prove themselves.

When we observe this change in people, it raises the question of whether all of us shouldn't go into overdrive earlier. Most of us continue the same hard-driving pattern of behavior long after we have thoroughly demonstrated to ourselves and others that we are indeed able and competent. Some may be able to make the shift on their own by simply altering their perspective. Others may need professional help—but from where I sit, it seems worth it.

I've Raised My Prices

In response to my critique of the notion that neuroses make people achieve, one of our readers shared the following anecdote. A sculptor of his acquaintance accepted an offer of free analysis as part of an examination of creativity by the New York Psychoanalytic Society. The sculptor claimed that several other artists declined to participate in the experiment for fear that their creativity might be irreparably altered. When, a few years later, our reader asked what analysis had done to or for the sculptor, he replied, "Well, I'm more creative than ever; but I've raised my prices drastically since I now value my works and myself more highly."

Busily Seeking With A Continual Change

With self-improvement so much in vogue, the question arises as to whether and to what extent the personality of an adult can change. The answer seems to be a matter of definition and emphasis. No one denies that people adapt to changing circumstances. But some psychologists and sociologists emphasize the stability of the basic personality as the person adapts, while others underscore the change that occurs in order to adapt. As Orville Brim, Jr. and Jerome Kagan, editors of *Constancy and Change in Human Development,* put it, "There is, on the one hand, a powerful drive to maintain the sense of one's identity, a sense of continuity that allays fears of changing too fast or of being changed against one's will by outside forces. . . . On the other hand, each person is, by nature, a purposeful, striving organism with a desire to be more than he or she is now."[5]

The debate centers on whether you consider "being more" to be a matter of personality change, or new expressions of the same personality. What most people call change tends to be the modification of one or another trait. The person continues to be recognizably the same as he or she always was. Yet a change that is barely noticeable to other people may make the difference between misery and contentment for the individual, and therefore alter some aspects of behavior. Others are likely to notice and react to the contentment differently than they reacted to the behavior which was a product of misery.

One change may be a matter of recognizing and accepting that one is a certain way, and finding a personally and socially acceptable way of expressing that part of oneself. Another change may be a product of realizing that a characteristic way of dealing with the world doesn't accomplish what it was meant to accomplish. Are those personality changes? A matter of definition. The needs to give and receive affection and support, and the need to act on the world—they don't disappear, but they can take different forms. And often those forms are modifiable, sometimes by oneself (that's what "maturity" means) and sometimes with professional help. Those modifications won't destroy that basic something that each of us recognizes as "myself." Fear of losing "myself" keeps many people from undertaking psychotherapy, and that's too bad. Consistency of self is not so much a limit to change as a foundation for change: the root and stem which enable us to grow and flower.

The Need For Solitude

Solitude is an important element of our lives. We need time to allow our unconscious processes to work: time free from interruptions. We need time to turn things over in our minds, away from people, noises, and all the things that demand our immediate attention. When people talk about the importance of enjoying nature, or going out to the countryside, the mountains, the ocean, or taking time to smell the flowers, they aren't just talking about aesthetics. For many people the beauty is secondary to the freedom to think, or to just let the mind wander where it will. In directed pondering of problems or random thought, we make connections that need to be made, and ideas, experiences, and feelings settle into place. All of us need that kind of break from the hustle and bustle of our daily routines, so we can return to the world refreshed.

Most studies on solitude have dealt with special conditions having little to do with a normal person's daily life. However, Reed Larson and Mihaly Csikszentmihalyi, U. Chicago, studied the role of solitude in the lives of 75 volunteers from Chicago high schools. Although teenagers have a reputation for being inseparable from their friends, these students spent an average of more than a quarter of their waking hours alone. The proportion of time spent alone was fairly stable over the course of the week, and the amount was generally not affected by outside forces such as playing a team sport, having a boyfriend or girlfriend, or having one's own room.[6] The unconscious self-regulation apparent in these findings supports the notion that solitude is necessary. Although the teenagers reported being in better spirits when with others, they also found that the time they spent alone allowed them to return to the company of others feeling more alert, stronger, more involved, and more cheerful. So if you find your son or daughter seeking solitude, don't worry about it unless it's really excessive. Most teenagers need it. And if you find yourself wishing you had more time for yourself, it would probably be worthwhile to arrange things so you get it.

Playing

I have a friend I admire because she still knows how to play. She can sit down and build a castle out of twigs on the ground.

By playing together, children learn the arts of living together. They learn to express and control affection and aggression. They learn the social skills of their society. And they experience morality: they *feel* what fairness and injustice, honesty and treachery, are. They also learn to explore and enjoy their own imaginations.[7]

Because adults are presumed to have learned these lessons, they may feel they have no need to play. But play is a way for adults to remind themselves that there is a lot more around them than they usually notice, and a lot more inside than they usually show. Play, in this sense, can mean taking a long walk with no destination, or making up stories and silly songs for your children or your beloved. Ann Landers often advises couples with stale sex lives to spend a weekend in a hotel and act out their fantasies—in other words, to play.

To play is to admit that your sensible head and heart are full of candies and rare jewels. If you're willing to do that, they're yours for the taking. What? You've never flown a kite in bed, never walked with ten cats on your head? Take Dr. Seuss's advice: "If you never have, you should. These things are fun, and fun is good!"

Helping At Work

Help comes in many sizes and shapes. When people are in distress, their memory and concentration are poor—just a reminder of a meeting or deadline can be an important help. Sometimes people don't know what the problem is, or even that there is a problem until someone asks and they put their situation into words. Some people will never tell you what the problem is—all they needed was for you to ask, so they know someone cares. On the other hand, some people have serious problems that are too big for them or for you to handle. They need to be referred to someone with the appropriate training and experience. The worst thing you can do is just hope it will go away. It won't. It will only get worse.

Solving The Wrong Problem?

When a subordinate comes to you for help with a problem, a quick solution may be a solution to the wrong problem. Therapists know that the problem a person presents first is usually not the real source of difficulty, which later becomes evident. Managers will encounter the same phenomenon. Often a subordinate walks through the door with one problem, when he or she is really struggling with another. For this reason it's important to hear the subordinate out, not simply respond to the problem as presented. If the person is given sufficient time to elaborate and to examine the difficulty, something more important might develop. Managers must resist the tendency to deal with problems expeditiously. That may seem to be the sign of a good manager, but it usually results in premature closure . . . followed by the recurrent appearance of the person, to the irritation and dismay of the manager.

Sorely Needed: A New Attitude Toward Feelings

More than 100 supervisors surveyed by the Hahnemann Medical College in Philadelphia reported a more negative attitude toward subordinates under treatment for mental illness than toward those who smoke marijuana on weekends, are obese, have some heart ailment, are age 60 or over, are being treated for skin cancer, are atheistic, or are part of a racially mixed marriage.[8]

Uneasiness about emotional matters makes it difficult for most people to endure looking at their own feelings in any depth. Many are reluctant to consult a professional or suffer repercussions when they do, because of prevailing social attitudes. Organizations can display a different attitude in several ways. One is to disseminate up-to-date, solid information about mental health and the normal crises of everyday living through pamphlets, seminars, training programs, or other available channels. They can set up internal counseling systems. They can stimulate discussion by inviting local clinical professionals to speak on special aspects of adult development. In addition, executives can model for their subordinates appropriate concern for people's feelings. One need not become embroiled in people's personal lives to do this. On the job, the question should always be how people feel about what is happening at work.

To Help You Ease Your Pain

Peer counseling is an important self-help device. It has been used widely in colleges and self-help groups. Managers, too, can use peer counseling as a way to think about difficult work situations and as a source of support for the trying tasks of improving those situations.

How well does peer counseling work? For a group of widows studied by researchers at the Clarke Institute of Psychiatry, Toronto, peer counseling helped them reach landmark stages in adapting to their bereavement sooner than widows who were not provided with any assistance. And the difference in rates increased over the two-year period of the study.[9]

It's important to note that peer counseling—or any counseling—doesn't change the stages of adaptation or magically take the problem away. That's not the point. Each of us has to do his or her own emotional or psychological work; each of us has to solve his or her own problems. The point of peer counseling is to have a source of another perspective, and the reassurance that you are not alone. You are not the only one who has to solve difficult problems, and such problems have been and can be solved.

So Many Good Years

An elderly woman who had just been widowed was being comforted by a friend. "You had so many long good years together," the friend said. "Yes," replied the woman, "but because you ate yesterday doesn't mean that you will not be hungry today."

The terrible losses that people experience are not assuaged by telling them how good they had it for how long. Yesterday is yesterday. They must live today and tomorrow and the tomorrows thereafter. The better the relationship and the longer it lasted, the more severe the loss and pain. When comforting another, it's more important to touch him or her in sympathy than to offer lectures. Your presence and acceptance of their pain can make them feel less alone, and safer to do the grieving they must do.

How To Get Someone Talking

"Talk things over." Any manager who sees value in this small piece of advice has undoubtedly run into countless problems applying it. Many people don't want to talk—especially about how they feel.

There are several ways to support a person who finds it difficult to open up, all of which revolve around demonstrating to him that how he feels is important to you. First, be specific about your interest. Ask directly about a situation you think the person might be reluctant to bring up. Second, be personal. Talk about some of your own experiences that you think might have relevance for him. Third, generalize. If you know of certain experiences he's bound to be running into, you can observe, for instance, that "Most people around here sooner or later run into so-and-so, who seems to act as if the department were her private possession." Then you can ask if he has, and if so, get him to describe what happened and how he handled it. Here, however, you must be careful not to prejudice the person or lead him to support internal factions. Fourth, direct the conversation away from the person. Those who find it very difficult to talk about themselves usually deal with emotional issues better by looking at what someone else is up against or how someone else might feel in a certain situation. Ask such a person to tell you what he thinks his various subordinates have to deal with.

In addition, everyone finds certain kinds of talks anxiety-provoking. The uneasiness is generally rooted in the unconscious feeling, left over from childhood, that words can kill. You can't make unconscious anxiety disappear, but you can make yourself more comfortable if you take it into account. In such situations, rehearse with a trusted peer beforehand and anticipate the other person's probable reactions. Try to put yourself in the other person's shoes. Sometimes what seems to you uncomfortably like an attack on another person is only a reflection of your differing values. What is important to you might not be equally so to him.

A Cure As Bad As The Disease

One of the most effective ways to get an alcoholic manager to seek treatment is to put his job on the line. Under those conditions, the recovery rate is 60% to 80%. The first step is to make sure that the manager gets the message in no uncertain terms, and that he knows you mean business. But it's possible to go overboard, and that's how I would describe the type of "confrontation" used by Dr. Joseph Pursch.[10] How is a person likely to feel after being confronted by a roomful of people—spouse, children, superiors—knowing they all know about a problem he can hardly admit to himself? That's the test of any procedure. Even if he recovers, the memory will remain.

The best thing to say to a manager whose drinking interferes with his work is:

1. You can't drink and work here.
2. If you get professional help and fall off the wagon, we will put you on sick leave, according to our regular provisions. When your doctor says you can come back to work, we'll take you back.
3. If you don't get professional help and you fall off the wagon, that's it. Period.

Another Cover-Up

"The second most likely person to cover up for a drinking executive was his immediate boss," according to a summary of a study of 25 top-level executives who are recovering alcoholics. (Personal secretaries took first place.) Charles Shirley, N.Y. Council on Alcoholism, attributes the bosses' behavior to "embarrassment or reluctance to admit that hiring the executive might have been a mistake."[11]

Alcoholics get by with the help of what Alcoholics Anonymous calls "enablers"—people who enable them to drink and not face the consequences. Some enablers pick the fight that lets the alcoholic rationalize the drinking; some pay the bills and cover up with friends and neighbors. Apparently, some managers cover up the fact that an alcoholic isn't really doing his or her job. In fact, 16 of the executives in the study "advanced steadily up the corporate ladder during their years of active alcoholism." Obviously, that ultimately didn't do their organizations much good. Presumably it made life difficult for their bosses, who had to have *someone* do the work. And certainly it didn't do the alcoholic executives any good. Hiring the person may have been a mistake, if he or she can't shape up when it's called for, but keeping the person on only compounds the error. And if the person does shape up, hiring the person may not have been a mistake at all.

Battered Women At Work

As the pervasiveness of wife beating becomes apparent, it becomes clear that many women in the work force must be battered wives. What does this mean for managers?

1. A woman who is beaten will have to show up at work with bruises and injuries, or miss a lot of work while recovering from them.
2. A battered woman is characteristically passive, or she would not remain in her situation. There will be a helpless quality to such a person, and once she gets over her reluctance to admit she is being beaten, she can be expected to lean heavily on the organization and her manager.
3. When a manager discovers such a situation, the impulse is to try to help, but he or she must avoid giving in to rescue fantasies. (For a discussion of rescue behavior, see p. 28.) If a battered wife leaves her husband at someone else's suggestion, she generally ends up going back. She must be ready to leave of her own accord, or it won't work. And that means rescue can't work.
4. If the woman misses too much work, the manager has a problem. Since the manager can't improve the woman's situation (because rescue efforts don't work), the manager tends to become enraged at the woman.
5. When the manager finally decides to deal realistically with the work situation by insisting that the woman come to work regularly, the woman is likely to be angry. And she will probably displace her unexpressed anger at her husband onto the manager and the organization.

What can you do to prevent this sequence? When a wife-beating situation is discovered, refer the woman for professional help *immediately*. Make it clear that the woman has a job as long as she comes to work and does her work, but no longer. If she stays in her situation, things are unlikely to change, except if both partners are getting help. It's sad, but true. The manager can make a referral, but the woman must go for help. If she won't, there's nothing else to be done. Getting more involved won't help anyone.

I Need The Eggs

People often stay in painful situations, even when an outsider would say there was no reason to do so. There may be an obvious way to correct the situation, but the person doesn't see it or won't act on it. And the person can come up with a hundred flimsy excuses for not just walking out. It's difficult to watch anyone do that, but especially distressing if you care about the person and want him or her to be happy. The fact is, the person is getting something out of the situation that he or she needs to maintain his or her psychological balance. In *Annie Hall*, Woody Allen tells a joke about a man who is seeking help from a doctor because his brother thinks he's a chicken. When the doctor asks why he doesn't have his brother put away, he replies, "I can't do that, I need the eggs." If you point out options and people refuse to take or even consider them, there isn't much else you can do except try to understand: they need the eggs.

Life's Business . . . Choice

What happens when one of your subordinates develops a disability, through accident or illness? When physical limitations make it difficult or impossible for the person to continue performing his or her duties, the impulse is to take action on your subordinate's behalf. You want to protect him or her from the consequences of the disability. But in doing so, you may find yourself making a unilateral decision about the person's life—and you can't do that.

In one case, a sales manager developed arthritis, a common complaint among people over 40. However, his pain was severe enough to limit his driving ability and keep him out of work for weeks at a time, interfering with his ability to maintain contact with customers. It was also a blow to his image of himself as an active, athletic person. His manager is worried because the man denies the problem and drives anyway, and may hurt himself. At this point the manager *can* make a decision: no, you may not drive, and you may not stay in your present role. This is necessary, to contend with the denial. But beyond that, the manager's role must be to develop and present options, and to invite the subordinate to do likewise. The manager may veto any unreasonable options the subordinate presents, on the same grounds that he vetoed staying in the original role. But the subordinate must choose among the remaining possibilities. If the manager decides what is best for the subordinate, he will be wrong by definition. The subordinate must retain responsibility for his own life.

ADDENDUM: Emotional First Aid

Managers faced with deeply troubled associates or friends often feel helpless, inadequate, and confused. They don't feel professionally equipped to help, but they know they must do or say something. They feel simultaneously worried and guilty about the troubled subordinates' increasingly poor performance at work. These managers don't want to be dragged into messy personal problems, but they don't want to be unfeeling taskmasters either. They often ask for guidance steering through these troubled waters: "What can I do? What *should* I do? Where can I turn for help?"

Managers aren't professional psychotherapists or social workers, but they *can* help troubled colleagues and subordinates. Faced with an emotionally disturbed subordinate, a manager usually takes one or more of three roles: a firm parent figure, a friend in need, or a lifeline to professional help. But before he or she can decide on a role and course of action, the manager must understand the nature of emotional disturbances.

Emotional disturbances are the most common illness, and everyone suffers from them. They're often very mild—like a temporary fit of anger or a day-long feeling of the "blues." Other common emotional disturbances are more severe—depression, alcohol dependency, unusual excitability or agitation, migraine headaches. Such disorders affect people's judgment, physical health, and self-control. Emotional disturbances also upset relationships. A troubled person who goes to bed with a nervous headache is out of touch with others for at least a short time. Highly excited people are difficult for others to understand or keep up with. Some distressed people retreat into a shell; others engage in inappropriate behaviors that create problems for the people around them.

It's important to remember that all these symptoms are cries for help. A troubled person needs constructive relationships to gain the psychological strength to cope better. That's why an understanding manager who offers support and lends an ear can be so helpful. The manager's personality and ways of relating to others are the most important instruments he or she has for helping an emotionally disturbed subordinate.

How Can You Recognize Emotional Disturbance?
We all work to keep our personalities in balance. When we succeed we talk of "being on an even keel;" when we fail we say we're "having ups and downs." When emotions are temporarily upset, automatic mechanisms try to bring them back into balance. Just as the body responds to disease or infection with a fever, so a person responds to anger with shouting, striking, greater efforts at self-control, or physical symptoms like

hypertension. When the troublesome feelings are successfully met, equilibrium returns.

Anxiety is the most common response to emotional distress, and it triggers our psychological balancing actions. When we face an external threat like termination, anxiety in the form of fear motivates us to marshal our forces. If we violate a rule of conscience, anxiety in the form of guilt motivates atonement. And anxiety prevents us from acting on primitive, unconscious emotions that our rational selves cannot accept. Although prolonged or excessive anxiety is a sign of emotional disturbance, anxiety initially is an important mechanism for self-protection, adaptation, and motivation.

Anxiety sends clear warning signals that someone is worried or upset. People may become tense, restless, or listless. They may perspire or tremble; they may eat less and drink more. Anxious people often can concentrate only on the problem disturbing them. The more severe the anxiety, the more it disrupts the ordinary, ongoing activities of the personality. It's at that point that we usually speak of an emotional disturbance.

Because anxiety has this disruptive potential, the personality cannot tolerate too much for too long. We have all learned characteristic ways of coping with situations that make us anxious. In the process of growing up, these ways of coping have become predominant characteristics of our personalities. The shy person is most comfortable alone; the "life of the party" thrives in groups. But sometimes our ordinary mechanisms for warding off excessive or prolonged anxiety don't work. Then three major signs of emotional disturbance appear:
1. The anxious person intensifies his or her characteristic ways of coping. The shy person withdraws even more from others; the gregarious person socializes at a fevered pitch.
2. The distressed person develops strong symptoms of anxiety—panic, jitteriness, excessive perspiring, flushing, inability to concentrate.
3. The person breaks down and can no longer adequately control thoughts, feelings, or actions. Thinking becomes irrational. This person may become obsessive about small matters and ignore work, family, friends—and the real source of distress. This person can no longer adequately assess the problem alone.

How Can You Help A Troubled Person Find Relief?
People with mild, temporary emotional disturbances don't pose special problems for managers. Most of us have learned to interact with people who are feeling down or grouchy or otherwise out of sorts for the day. Where more severe disturbances are concerned, managers either find they must confront the subordinate, or the subordinate approaches them.

If a manager sees that a subordinate is performing less adequately, causing more friction with others, or having increasingly frequent interruptions from work, he or she may be reluctant to add to the distressed subordinate's burdens by criticizing his or her work. But that's a mistake. These subordinates need a manager who, like a firm parent, can set reasonable limits. Of course no one likes to be told of unsatisfactory job performance, especially on top of other problems. But it's neither helpful nor fair when a manager sits by while a subordinate's work deteriorates. The manager will have to act eventually, and it's best to let the subordinate know early on just what the organization's tolerance limits are. A frank performance appraisal often helps a subordinate pull himself or herself together.

A 19-year-old black secretary, for instance, hired by a large company under the federal EEO guidelines, was troubled by marital conflicts and child care difficulties, and was often preoccupied, late, or absent from work. Her manager made exceptions for her, and held his tongue longer than he normally would. But the problem didn't go away, and he finally spoke up. "Look," he said, "I know you have real and pressing personal problems. But everyone has to show up for work here, and on time. I can't make exceptions for you. And I don't want you to fail here, because you're a model for all the young black kids who know you're working with us." After this meeting, the young woman resolved her immediate problems. She made carpooling arrangements with other secretaries and came to work on time. By confronting the problem, her manager helped this young woman make an initial move she felt unable to make alone.

Those who are more troubled also need someone to open an avenue of help. Sometimes a frank discussion of poor job performance or erratic behavior motivates an emotionally disturbed subordinate to seek professional help. And when problems are more severe—like those of a paranoid manager who became convinced that everyone was out to get him—a superior may have to put the person on sick leave or disability and insist that he or she get professional help before returning to work.

In other cases, the manager as a responsible and respected person in the organization is approached by someone spontaneously seeking help. The troubled person may state the problem directly, allude to it indirectly, or talk of a vague feeling of distress. In this situation (as well as when the manager initiates the discussion) the manager can become a "friend in need." Being such a friend helps in three ways:

1. It relieves anxiety by putting another person's resources at the troubled person's disposal.
2. It gets the problem outside the troubled person and helps him or her gain a new perspective on it, easing the decision of what to do next.
3. It prepares the troubled person to seek additional help if necessary.

But at this point the manager's own anxiety is often aroused. The behavior of the troubled person may be frightening; the problem may touch the helper's own conflicts; the helper may be asked or required to take burdensome or unpleasant action. At this point managers must first *listen* to discover just what the problem is; and second, they must *limit* their role in terms of their particular business situation.

How Does Listening Help?
Listening is the key to emergency relief for emotional distress. Listening to someone express painful feelings demonstrates a willingness to help. It shows respect for the troubled person as a fellow human being, and it acknowledges that we all need to feel as we do. Good listeners are sounding boards who allow others to talk, explore their feelings, and come to their own conclusions. They don't impose their own logic or reason on the other person's revelations. They give a sympathetic hearing and ask open-ended questions that help the troubled person gain fresh perspectives.

Most people know intellectually that listening helps. But listening is perhaps the most-discussed, least-understood, and least-practiced principle of human relations. Listening is much harder in practice than it seems in the abstract. But failing to listen tells the troubled person that he or she has come to the wrong place for help.

Listening fails when listeners can't control their anxiety and impatience. Often when another person's distress arouses our own anxiety, we want to pontificate, blame, criticize, or reason. We have all said to someone else, "You shouldn't feel that way." And though we mean well, we're really saying that we don't understand how the other person feels.

Troubled people often don't know themselves why they feel anxious. And it's dangerous for listeners without professional training to presume to tell other people why they feel the way they do. Everyone has unconscious feelings and thoughts that motivate much of his or her behavior. Those unconscious feelings are like microbes—they can't be seen without special techniques or skills. And just as microbes cannot be washed away with water, unconscious feelings cannot be washed away with reason or sweet words. Psychotherapists have learned from long experience that people can't use knowledge about their anxiety unless they discover it for themselves. Telling them disrupts their thoughts and arouses their defenses. It shuts off the expression of feelings—and thus delays the time when the troubled person comes to terms with them.

In most cases, the troubled person must decide alone on a course of action or means of coping. Even so, the listener can play an important role. People can feel a tremendous relief after unburdening themselves. A manager who can let out his regret and guilt and worry over a son who has flunked out of college may find he now has new psychological strength for coping. A subordinate with a desperately ill or retarded child may be too upset to know where to turn for help; someone whose spouse wants to take a job 1,000 miles away may be too distraught to assess the alternatives. Listeners can help such people clarify the problems and examine options.

But managers offering emotional first aid should remember that the more ill and less in control a person is, the more active the helper's role will be. A manager can't tell a 40-year-old woman what to do if she's accidentally pregnant. But if a hysterical subordinate sees visions in the office, the manager must get that person to a hospital immediately.

Listening fails when the listener loses patience. Listening to a troubled person *is* difficult—people in distress often go around in verbal circles and lapse into long silences. Troubled people use repetitions, vagueness, and silences to try to pull their thoughts together under the press of strong emotions. The process of understanding and analysis will break off if the listener can't wait it out. Listeners also become impatient when troubled people can't resolve their problems or make decisions quickly. But people don't *want* to be upset. If they could just "snap out of it" they would. Listeners often think (and sometimes say), "You think *you* have problems!" Their impatience and resentment tell the distressed person that his or her problems are insignificant. But problems that cause people pain are significant for *them.* And patient listeners are more likely to discover *why* such problems are significant.

I saw a dramatic instance of this principle after a major flood many years ago. Among several thousand people waiting for emergency medical help was a man who complained of athlete's foot. "How long have you had athlete's foot?" asked the physician, scarcely able to control his anger. "Four years," the man replied. With great difficulty the physician continued to hold his anger in check. After asking a few more questions, he learned that this man was homeless, alone, and frightened. He desperately needed someone to talk to, some way of reaching out for support and affection. The few minutes the physician spent listening to this man helped him as much as surgery would have helped someone with a physical ailment.

Impatient listeners often want to escape. They may suddenly find pressing business elsewhere; they may suddenly become coldly businesslike and aloof. They may quickly close the conversation with a piece of advice and then act as if nothing special has been said. No manager who feels uncomfortable with the listening role *must* offer emotional first aid. But those who do should listen long enough to get the troubled person's basic message. That way, they'll understand the problem well enough to make sound managerial decisions—including whatever referrals may be necessary.

What Limits Must Be Set?

Setting limits of emotional first aid is as important as taking action. A manager is not a professional psychotherapist. He or she can therefore perform only a relief function. The manager must remain within his or her professional role. Occasionally managers criticize themselves for failing to help people with whom even the most skilled clinicians would have great difficulty. Their expectations are unrealistic, and such self-recriminations are unwarranted. Relief counseling is to psychological treatment as first aid is to medical treatment. First aid efforts are critically important in their place. But they don't replace psychotherapy any more than they can replace major surgery.

Emotional first aid helps most when problems arise from sudden external stresses, such as immediate family or job difficulties. It doesn't much help inflexible people with little awareness of their problems or sensitivity to their feelings. People with chronic problems, those in acute panic, and those threatening themselves or others need professional help. And the business situation imposes its own limits on what a manager can do. A manager with heavy responsibilities and time commitments simply cannot meet frequently with a disturbed subordinate. Someone who cannot be helped in one or two interviews must be referred. In addition, managers must take care not to hear too much of a personal nature. Allowing a coworker to talk on and on about marital and extramarital relations, for instance, can permanently disrupt a business relationship. In this and similarly delicate situations, the manager should refer the person to professional help once the nature of the problem is clear.

Finally, in setting limits the manager must keep the troubled person's revelations and distress confidential. When people seek help for emotional distress, they remove some of the protective layers of personality to reveal what is troubling them. Their behavior—which may include bursting into tears or an angry tirade—is an act of confidence. If the listener violates this trust, he or she debases the dignity of the troubled person and discredits his or her own reputation for integrity.

Who Should Be Referred For Professional Help?

People instinctively turn to those in responsible positions for help with emotional problems. That's why all managers should have ready access to professionals for advice and referrals. Managers feel more secure about dealing with difficult and pressing problems when they know they need only pick up the telephone to get a competent psychotherapist to turn to in an emergency. (You can always call The Levinson Institute for advice or referrals if you don't know where else to turn.) And all managers should learn what community resources are available for help and how to use them. Any sizable community has dozens of sources of help, and a professional can help you find them. In some companies, Employee Assistance

Programs have knowledge of such resources. One important potential source of help is the troubled person's family physician.

Managers often hesitate to refer someone for professional help, either because they misunderstand what it means, or because they fear they will be misunderstood. A referral does *not* mean that the troubled person is "crazy," hopeless, or unworthy of the manager's attention. It's an additional source of competent help, and it should be presented as such. The manager should emphasize that no one should be ashamed of needing professional help. Many people need guidance through stress points in their lives, whether through marriage or career counseling, an encouraging talk with a family physician or clergyman, or some form of psychotherapy. Understanding and enlightened managers can help troubled coworkers accept professional help they would otherwise shun. And conversely, managers who distrust or fear professional help will communicate just that. Therefore, no one should make a referral he or she does not trust.

Just as medical first aid helps until the physician arrives, so emotional first aid is often the first step before referral for professional help. When talking out a problem once or twice isn't enough, managers should suggest professional help. People who have suffered severe trauma—the suicide of a spouse, death of a child, or major medical crisis—should be referred for counseling and whatever specialized help might be necessary. Many problems can best be served by outside agencies, and should be referred. These include alcoholism, truant or disturbed children, marital conflicts, and medical emergencies. Managers also should refer coworkers with whom they're especially close. They can't be objective enough about a close associate's problems, and the associate may have trouble talking freely. Finally, severely disturbed people *must* be referred. This includes anyone who is paralyzed into inactivity, who is threatening suicide or violence, whose speech or behavior is irrational and uncontrolled, or who is persistently breaking the law or the rules of the organization. Managers simply aren't trained to help people with psychotic symptoms.

A troubled person may panic when referred to a professional, thinking that he or she must be in seriously bad shape. The manager making the referral needs to let the person know it's not a last-ditch effort for a deeply disturbed person. One way to do this is to summarize for the distressed person what has passed between them, where matters seem to stand, and why the referral seems appropriate. It's also useful to indicate that the manager's door has not slammed shut and that the troubled person is not being shunted aside.

After Emotional First Aid—Then What?
People are often embarrassed and ashamed after seeking help for emotional distress. Some will feel they've said too much. Others will feel that

their needing help is an unacceptable mark of weakness. They often, therefore, ignore or avoid the person to whom they turned for help. Managers should anticipate such feelings, and let troubled subordinates know that they are common. People cope better when they're prepared for troublesome feelings.

Managers needn't ignore or avoid the people who have come to them for help. Many people feel grateful and relieved when helpers ask friendly questions and make small shows of concern. They can break the ice with someone who wants to let the helper know where matters stand but is too embarrassed to speak up. But if the troubled person doesn't respond to a casual, friendly inquiry, the executive should let the matter drop. So long as the subordinate's job performance is not in question, the manager's task is now complete.

The Need For Help

Most of us would rather avoid pain than confront it, but when we think it has gone away, more likely it has gone underground. Now that we've missed the early warning signals, what are the more indirect clues in our own and others' behavior that tell us we'd better get some help? Sometimes the prospect of change is frightening enough or inspires such hopelessness of success that people run away from it—and from life. How can you recognize the signs that someone is in desperate straits, and in immediate need of professional help? The signs may be subtle, or may be entirely hidden. It's no fault to miss them—only a saving grace if you see them.

Post-Holiday Blues

If you are one of those people who finds yourself sad, lonely, and demoralized over the holiday season, then it is time to think about your underlying feelings of loneliness and depression. Many people experience more difficulties over holidays and weekends than they do when they are at work. The holidays are especially troublesome because they are supposed to be spent having a good time with families and friends. Often people are alone during this time and the fact that others are having such experiences seems to highlight their own sense of loss and nonattachment. Rather than keeping busy, such people frequently become blue, sometimes drink too much, or become more inactive, which makes them even more depressed.

To cope with such feelings you should develop new ties, new activities, new friends. These become social support systems in the form of networks of colleagues and friends. If you find you can't do this by yourself, it's important to talk to a professional.

"Sweet Is A Grief Well Ended"

People suffering from unresolved grief often don't know it. They commonly show the following traits, says Prof. Thomas Scheff, U. Calif.-Santa Barbara:

1. Bodily complaints, often including pain in the chest.
2. Anxiety or panic attacks.
3. Disoriented time sense—time seems to have stopped.
4. Inability to form new relationships.
5. Searching behavior—looking for someone (the insufficiently grieved person) when in a crowd.
6. Setting up a shrine, where the lost person's belongings are kept.
7. Speaking of the lost person in the present tense.

Such people often benefit from grief therapy, Scheff says, in which they can finally accept the person's death as real, and feel and express the emotions they have long repressed.[12]

People are often afraid to express intense grief, as if doing so could overpower them. However, therapists can help people approach their grief by degrees so that it is not overwhelming. Therapists also provide the caring support people need in facing a pain that seems too great to bear. When people don't permit themselves the opportunity to express their grief and anguish, they never give it the opportunity to diminish. It's never expressed powerfully, to be sure; but it never lessens either. As Aeschylus, the Greek tragedian, said in *Agamemnon,* "Sweet is a grief well ended."

Attempted Suicide As Communication

Many suicide attempts may actually be intended to communicate anger or to influence family members or close friends, according to a study of self-poisoning cases in Britain. Researchers concluded that this possibility "emphasizes the need to focus on those relationships when trying to help or intervene."[13] This reinforces the point Karl A. Menninger made in 1938 in *Man Against Himself,* that suicide is more often an attempt to communicate when all else has failed than actually to end one's own existence.[14]

It is particularly easy to see self-poisoning by overdose of easily obtained, everyday drugs in this light. Self-poisoning, which the article says is noticeably on the rise, is a far cry from shooting oneself or jumping off a bridge. It doesn't have the same kind of meaning. We're all so accustomed to taking pills for whatever ails us that it's hard to believe a large dose would really kill us, not just put us to sleep. And taking pills isn't expected to be painful, as a violent act would be.

People fail to communicate verbally, either because they can't put their feelings into words or because they don't feel they are being heard. Then they find other ways to express themselves that are more destructive and therefore more difficult to ignore. If people could put their feelings into words that others could hear and respond to, they wouldn't need to resort to this desperate kind of action.

Making Up Is Hard To Do

Children from chaotic homes often become overachievers, say Dr. Stephanie Brown, Stanford Medical Center Alcohol Clinic, and social worker Claudia Black, Parkwood Community Hospital in Canoga Park, Calif. They need to compensate for their parents' failings, and to control their environments as much as possible. But such people are in danger, say Brown and Black. They ask too much of themselves, and eventually they crack under the pressure.[15]

If you're approaching middle age and feeling depressed, empty, and dissatisfied with yourself, you may be experiencing something more than a middle-age crisis. You may be reacting to the chaotic experience of early childhood. If one or both of your parents was alcoholic or emotionally disturbed, or if your parents' marital difficulties disrupted the household frequently, now is the time to review that experience with a qualified therapist. This isn't something to talk over with a friend or a spouse. But a skilled professional can help you understand how this early experience shapes your present attitudes and feelings in ways you're not consciously aware of.

Your Mind Matters

People often dismiss an illness or complaint as "psychosomatic," meaning they think the person has merely talked himself or herself into being sick—it's all in the mind. But the connection between mental and physical health is real, and more and more research is uncovering the connections between disease and behavior. For example, researchers at Duke U. Medical Center studied patients with suspected coronary heart disease for their "hostility levels" and for Type A behavior. They found that most of those who had significant coronary occlusions apparently held assumptions "that people in general are going to behave toward others in ways that are mean, selfish, and exploitive; and, furthermore, that since people are this way they should be punished—either physically or verbally." These patients also agreed with such statements as: I would certainly enjoy beating a crook at his own game; I have often had to take orders from someone who did not know as much as I did; when a man is with a woman he is usually thinking about things related to her sex; I have at times had to be rough with people who were rude or annoying.[16] Another group, at U. Mich., has found a correlation between blood pressure and styles of coping with "arbitrary authority"—that is, how you handle having your manager yell at you unfairly.[17]

Of course, these are common thoughts, and it's not as if you're doomed to a heart attack if you don't like your manager. The relationship between mind and body is much more complex than that, and is only beginning to be understood. But persistently stressful or troubled thoughts should be attended to, as if they were physical aches or pains. Pain is the body's message that something is wrong—and mental pain is a message, too. If your back hurt all the time, you would want to know why, and what to do. If you find you're nervous all the time, or can't get along with people anymore, or are obsessed with something trivial, you've got to find out why, and what to do. Maybe it's something you can figure out and solve for yourself; maybe a friend can see the situation clearly; or maybe you need a professional's help.

When Success Ends In Suicide

Many managers, unfortunately, will at some point confront the suicide of a successful associate. I was reminded of this sad fact by a recent letter informing me of the suicide of an "ace" personnel man who seemed to have a good family life as well as a successful career. His obituary lists a lifetime of achievements and honors. What went wrong?

Everyone wonders why someone who seems to have it made would take his or her life. But in fact many highly successful people are especially vulnerable to suicide. They get ahead by setting impossibly high standards for themselves, and though they surpass others, they never measure up in their own eyes. However much they achieve, they berate themselves for failure and struggle against depression.

Managers can't prevent all suicides, and shouldn't expect to. But they can spot vulnerable people, and take steps to help them. Who might be vulnerable to suicide? First, someone who has suffered a significant personal loss or professional setback. Second, a highly conscientious person who expresses irrational guilt over small imperfections. Third, someone showing signs of depression, whether increased drinking, irritability, a variety of somatic symptoms, or, in the extreme, talk of suicide.

These people can often be helped when others recognize the intensity of their feelings. It doesn't help to dismiss overblown self-criticisms, saying, "I should have your troubles—you've got it made." The feelings are very real to the depressed person, and must therefore be taken seriously by others. Managers can help in the following ways:

1. Support people depressed by a failure at work, and help them see their efforts in perspective.
2. Give regular appraisals of your subordinates' performances so they'll be less likely to blow up small mistakes into major failures.

3. Give associates who show signs of depression a chance to talk. Help ease their irrational guilt by sharing with them your own past problems and insecurities.

4. Suggest that depressed associates seek professional help. But unless they require hospitalization, keep them at work, where they can feel useful and needed and derive significant support from others. The last thing these people need is lots of empty time on their hands.

Every person's greatest asset—the wish to like himself or herself—is also his or her point of greatest vulnerability. When managers can see the feelings of inadequacy and helplessness within the trappings of success, they can often support associates who might otherwise succumb to suicide.

Seeking Professional Help

What is professional help? What kind of help works in what kind of situation? What kinds of "help" can do more harm than good? Lack of information is one of the major reasons for not seeking help—what can you and your organization do to inform yourselves and pass it on?

When The Company Can Show The Way

Although millions of Americans are now covered by mental health insurance, many do not know how to find care when they need it. Some refuse to seek treatment until the illness has progressed to dangerous levels because they fear social stigma. These are among the findings of the National Institute for Mental Health. A study discovered that many workers don't know when to seek professional help. They think only gross behavioral symptoms require treatment. After being referred to a health facility a majority of workers found the services inadequate for their needs.[18]

Employers can help overcome these obstacles by working to coordinate community efforts to provide referral information about services, and to help educate employees to recognize early symptoms of mental illness, thus also granting them psychological permission to seek help.

Psychotherapy: Beyond Good Advice

How does psychotherapy work? The process is based on trust between client and therapist, and on learning. After the client shares a great many thoughts, feelings, and spontaneous changes of subject, the therapist and client try to analyze them, looking for distortions and repetitive themes. Then the client gradually assimilates their discoveries, and begins to reorient his or her life in light of the new view. This process takes energetic activity and effort of will on the part of the client. Insight alone is not enough. Internal conflict, anxiety, and depression are not eradicated, for those are the energizers which push us toward continuous growth. The goal is to master them.

Is Help Helpful?

What stops managers from applying their psychological sophistication at work? Possibly some of the same attitudes that prevent physicians from referring patients for psychiatric help. Apparently physicians often don't think it will do any good, don't think it's called for unless someone is really disturbed, don't understand the psychological aspects of being seriously ill or laid up in a hospital, or are too uneasy about such topics (and perhaps ignorant of them) to discuss them. Some say they're afraid of offending patients. But most patients are glad of the suggestion, and furthermore, psychiatric help *is* helpful in most cases.[19]

Psychological understanding is useful in all interpersonal situations, not just situations involving particular problems or disturbed people. Something as simple as saying good morning matters a great deal to certain people, but it requires a psychological perspective to understand that, and to know when it really counts.

When a coworker is having problems that may have a psychological basis, managers, like physicians, are often reluctant to say anything, for fear of offending. But, as with patients, your coworker may be glad of the suggestion. Some people simply wouldn't think of it themselves. Others need that sort of permission to ask for help, perhaps because they don't feel they deserve it, or perhaps because they feel they ought to be able to work it out themselves.

Sometimes managers find that their own anxiety about discussing feelings—or feeling feelings—gets in the way of applying what they know. One suggestion for those who think just asking people how they're doing is contrived, or kid stuff, is to consider why you feel that way. Another is to trust me, and try it! You may be pleasantly surprised at the results.

To Seek Help Is A Sign Of Strength

A poignant comment psychologists and psychiatrists hear from clients who have begun to benefit from psychological help is, "I wish I had done this many years ago." Some people fight off help for fear that it will diminish them somehow. Wise ones take advantage of it early.

In-House House Calls

Many managers want to talk with the company psychologist about a personal or professional problem, but wouldn't be caught dead walking into his or her office. They don't want anyone to think they're incompetent, weak, or crazy. They know they need help, but they're afraid they'll doom their careers if they seek it.

If you find yourself in this situation, call the psychologist and lay out your problems and fears. And suggest that he or she regularly make the rounds, getting to know people on their own turf. That way, many people will talk about many kinds of issues without being seen as sick or desperate. And lots of people who need help will get it. When I go into organizations, managers talk with me in their offices about everything from mid-career crises to family troubles to investments. I learn more about who they are when I see them on their own ground. And they're more comfortable talking in familiar surroundings.

If your organization has no in-house psychologist because top management thinks no one will use the service, you might show them this item. People in organizations can and do get significant help from company psychologists. But companies and the professionals they hire must know in advance what they want from the relationship and how they expect to develop it.

Choose From The Full Arsenal

The sciences of neurology and psychopharmacology continue to advance, and one result is many new drugs for the treatment of mental illness. Are they replacing psychotherapy, enhancing it, or distracting people from it? Toksoz Karasu, Albert Einstein College of Medicine, tries to bring psychotherapy and pharmacotherapy into collective focus. He makes a useful comparison of the differing capacities of drugs and psychotherapy:

1. They have different kinds of effectiveness. Drugs affect psychological symptoms and emotional distress. Psychotherapy affects interpersonal relations and social adjustment.
2. They act on different time scales. Drugs take effect sooner (and so can be used preventively) and wear off sooner. The results of psychotherapy don't appear right away, but last longer.
3. They are useful for different problems: drugs for temporary "state" disorders, psychotherapy for long-lasting "trait" disorders.[20]

In theory, the more varieties of help available, the better. The danger is that some people specialize in one, and are not competent in the other, especially these days when many psychiatrists are fleeing back into medicine. The best answer is still a comprehensive workup and evaluation by a reputable person or clinic, and a second opinion if things aren't moving along. In several cases I've had to suggest this where somebody was being managed on drugs for a problem which clearly required psychotherapy. No doubt the reverse is also true in many cases.

Mind Over Matter?

People from all quarters are singing the praises of biofeedback. Prof. George Fuller, U. Calif.-San Francisco, reports that new sophisticated techniques can reduce chronic pain and replace more drastic medical measures.[21] Biofeedback is also being used to control the gastric secretions of ulcer patients, to block the seizures of epileptics, and to alleviate sexual problems.[22] And many businessmen say it's a good cure for stress—they like to measure their relaxation responses.[23]

When it's used to diminish pain where other treatments have failed, biofeedback is a helpful and appropriate technique. It gives a literal reading of what's happening electrically in the muscle and helps people get at the source of their distress. But biofeedback as a panacea for stress is just a gimmick. It can work, because it's a self-hypnotic device like Transcendental Meditation and other relaxation methods. It lets people get out from under their consciences and respond to symptoms. But it doesn't get at the root of the problem, and its effects don't last. In one study, hypertensive patients controlled their blood pressure in the lab, but once they left the biofeedback machines, their blood pressure rose again.[24] Gimmicks can sometimes help us relax, but we can't fine-tune our emotions as if we were color television sets. The electronic age isn't about to revolutionize our psychological wavelengths. As long as our basic conflicts go unresolved, or our environments unchanged, or both, we'll suffer from symptoms of stress.

Should You Share It With The Group?

Weekend group therapy, even in a well-controlled group run by highly competent people, can be a dangerous experience for some participants. For others it can be devastating. It offers no long-range help. That is the finding of Drs. Irvin D. Yalom and Gary Bond, Stanford, who studied three specially selected groups of patients who were already in individual therapy. They were assigned to two weekend groups in an attempt to speed up their therapy. Two people suffered considerable psychological damage. Even those who had opened up more in the six weeks immediately following the weekend showed no lasting positive effects at 12 weeks.[25]

People who are in an acute crisis situation, who are markedly depressed or suicidal, who have a low tolerance for anxiety and frustration, or who have strong paranoid propensities should not be in group therapy. It may be helpful for people who are highly self-centered because the group will bring out in bold relief a person's egocentrism, abrasiveness, and greed. It may also be helpful for those who are extremely shy, timid, or inhibited in social settings. People often think that all problems are manageable in groups, and therefore, group therapy is more economical than individual therapy, but the key issue here is diagnosis. There is, in both individuals and organizations, too little sophisticated diagnosis.

The Seduction Of Patients

A new "psychotherapeutic" fad has arisen in recent years—sexual therapy—whose advocates claim it to be "liberalizing." Masters and Johnson, the preeminent sexual researchers and therapists, report an astonishing number of seductions of patients by their previous therapists, particularly when these patients have been under treatment for sexual dysfunction. "Therapists have every advantage over the extremely vulnerable patient. . . . There is no greater negation in a professional responsibility than taking sexual advantage of an essentially defenseless patient, yet this often happens," they said.[26]

When you see this fad coming down the pike, put it in its appropriate place. There is little to be gained and much to be lost in providing the distressed patient with a personal sexual experience. Masters and Johnson contend that at least half the marriages in this country are made unhappy because of sexual dysfunction, but the correct emphasis is treating the marriage *relationship*. Their own experience is that couples who seek professional help of this kind are best treated away from their home communities.

A Preventable Tragedy

It's always tragic when somebody falls into the wrong professional hands. I recently came across a case in which a man undertook "analysis" with a person who claimed to be a psychoanalyst. He saw that person three times a week for twelve years, with little effect. Of course, some problems are intractable. But this man eventually saw another psychiatrist who checked out the first one, and found that he not only lacked the training he said he had, but had actually been rejected by two psychoanalytic institutes.

The moral of this story is: Check! If you or anyone in your family is seeking professional help, don't go to the yellow pages. If you don't know where else to turn, pick up the telephone and call us. We have directories next to the phone; we can check people out, make recommendations, and help you reach a wise decision. It is critically important to see a professional who is properly qualified to give the type of help you seek.

To Spite Your Face

There are ways and ways of cutting costs, but sometimes what looks like a cut can actually be a reallocation, or even an increase. If GM and the UAW aren't careful, that may be the result of their attempts to cut health care costs. At the top of the list of service areas they hope to reduce is outpatient psychiatry, followed by foot surgery, elective surgery, and treatment of substance abuse.[27]

The less physical evidence there is of a problem, the more difficult it is for an outside observer to determine whether the problem in fact exists, whether treatment is having any effect, and whether the problem has been or can be cured. That makes psychological services an obvious choice for cost-reduction attempts. But cutting back on abuse is one thing; cutting back on needed services is another. Health maintenance organizations (HMOs) have found that the provision of psychological services reduces the call on medical services. Cutting back in the wrong places could be a classic case of cutting off one's nose to spite one's face.

The American Psychiatric Association has recognized the difficulty in determining the necessity and usefulness of psychiatric services, and offers a case review service. In some instances they have found that the prospect of review has led to withdrawal of claims, but in others they have found even very long-term use of therapeutic services to be valid. But there are many questions to be answered about who should be reimbursable for providing therapeutic services (social workers are in some states but not others), and what criteria should be used for determining competence, as well as where you stop psychotherapy. These are difficult questions, and they aren't going to go away.

Physical And Mental Health: Connections

Mind and body are not really separate, as current research makes increasingly clear. A simple touch can have significant physiological effects. And the notion that closely related people can physically affect each other even without touching is not just science fiction. The state of your mind affects the state of your body—and vice versa!

Turning Off The Alarm

Hypnosis is finding greater and greater acceptance as a drug substitute. Experts disagree on the percentage of the population that can be hypnotized, but agree that hypnosis can at least partially replace painkillers, tranquilizers, and anesthesia for those who are susceptible to it. Hypnosis has been used by various practitioners to successfully treat insomnia, hypertension, allergies, asthma, colitis, eczema, impotence and frigidity, bed-wetting in older children, warts, hemophilia, and severe burns. And it has been used successfully to control habits like smoking, drinking, and overeating. Dr. Bernice Sachs adds a sensible warning, however: "Never allow anyone to treat a condition with hypnosis if he or she is not qualified to treat that condition medically without hypnosis."[28]

To Dr. Sachs' warning I would add another caution. Pain and other physical symptoms are often the body's way of telling us that something is amiss, either physically or psychologically. Removing a symptom without knowing its cause can have disastrous effects. I still remember the time in my early training days when a man's back pain was removed by hypnosis, after which he suffered a psychotic break. People who favor hypnosis tend to minimize the danger that a hypnotically removed symptom will be replaced by a worse symptom. It does happen, and my recommendation to anyone planning to be treated by hypnosis is to have a careful clinical examination before beginning that treatment.

In some cases we know what is wrong but the treatment takes time, and there is no need for the painful or annoying warning signal while the treatment takes effect. In some cases we cannot treat the problem, so symptom removal is the best we can do. For example, Dr. Wallace LaBaw mentions using hypnosis to help some terminally ill patients remain at home and reasonably alert by eliminating the need for dulling drugs.[28] Under these circumstances, hypnosis can be used safely. But turning off the alarm makes sense only after you've heard and heeded the warning it sends.

Involuntary Rescue

When children have chronic health problems that don't yield to the usual treatment, they are sometimes helped by being moved away from their parents. This has been done for many years in hospitalizing emotionally disturbed children. The late Dr. Murray Peshkin was the first to try this with asthmatic children, in the 1940s and '50s. More recently, Dr. Salvador Minuchin has demonstrated that physical changes occur when a child with intractable diabetes enters a room where his or her parents are discussing a family problem. Minuchin monitored the level of free fatty acids (FFA) in the blood, which is an indicator of stress as well as a cause of diabetic symptoms. The parents' levels had increased during the discussion while the child was in another room. The child's FFA level increased markedly upon entering the room, while the parents' levels dropped.[29]

This is an extreme example, and occurs in families where children are not allowed much independence in choosing their own activities or expressing their own feelings. In addition, there is little flexibility for change in these families—no one is really free to suggest a little more autonomy for anyone. But it illustrates the fact that family members do affect each other, to some degree, in all families. And when one family member has a problem, or two family members are in conflict, the others are going to feel the effects, one way or another. This is another case in which treating the symptom, or even the person who bears the symptom, may do little to solve the problem.

Is Stress Linked To Cancer?

Various studies show relationships between stress and heart disease, particularly the significance of loss and change (as in job security or separation and divorce). Now, similar connections have been made between stress and cancer. A group of men, whose chest x-rays were abnormal but who had not been diagnosed, were interviewed and rated on a psychosocial scale that included childhood instability, recent significant loss, job and marital stability, and lack of plans for the future. From the score on that composite scale, 80% of the benign diagnoses and 61% of the malignant ones were predicted successfully. The best single predictor was recent significant loss, and the second best was job stability. The psychosocial scale was one to two times as valuable a predictor as smoking.[30]

A study of life events and cancer in children produced a similar finding about recent significant loss, but for children, the other two most closely correlated stresses were illness of or discord between family members, and a recent move. In the comparison group, 24% of the families had moved in the past two years and 12% had moved within the year; of the patient group, 72% had moved in the past two years and 60% within the year, and many of these children had shown strong feelings of anxiety or depression during and after the move.[31]

It is clear, once again, how important it is to find ways of dealing with our own stress, and of helping our children deal with theirs. When you or your child can't shake off the effects of a loss, when feelings of anger, boredom, or depression persist, it doesn't hurt to see a professional, and it may well help avoid serious health problems later. And when making a move, do what you can to prepare your child (see p. 228). Don't count on the "natural resilience of children"—in this case, it doesn't necessarily apply.

Cholesterol Connections

The evidence relating heart disease, cholesterol levels in the blood, and dietary cholesterol is confusing, to say the least. You can find evidence of a relationship between diet and serum cholesterol in one study and not in another. Certain studies show a relationship between diet and heart disease, others don't. Some people can drastically reduce their serum cholesterol levels by altering their diet, others cannot. For those who cannot lower their cholesterol levels, there is the rather cold comfort that in some studies people with lower cholesterol levels made up for their lower rate of heart disease with a higher rate of death from other causes.[32]

The wide range of physiological responses to similar conditions reminds us again of the significance of psychological forces. A recent study indicates that although high rates of heart disease accompany high serum cholesterol levels, this relationship can be changed in rabbits by providing special attention. When rabbits were fed a high cholesterol diet, the ones that were regularly petted, held, talked to, and played with had 60% less damaged tissue than the control group, even though both groups had the same serum cholesterol levels.[33]

If touching and holding have such a positive effect on animals, it's reasonable to look for the same in people. We know that children thrive on physical demonstrations of care and affection, which make them feel secure. It's a mistake to assume we outgrow that need. We don't express affection easily in our culture; we aren't so likely to put our arms around others, and this restraint is particularly strong in men. As a manager, you can ease the stress your people feel by giving them verbal support and communicating your goodwill and concern. For yourself, develop relationships with people who are willing to exchange warmth and affection. In Japan, individuals have a right to demand attention from kin. Perhaps we can take their example as permission to request a little care for ourselves.

Find The Basis For The Action

Few people are aware that there are physical illnesses that mask as mental or emotional ones. Children are often treated by psychologists and psychiatrists for extended periods of time without any effect upon their psychological problems because the real illness lies in their bodies. Hypoglycemia (abnormal low level of sugar in the blood) is one illness that is masked by emotional symptoms. Young children with hypoglycemia become irritable and fretful; older children are confused, negativistic, sometimes even violent. Restlessness, insomnia, daytime drowsiness, an inability to concentrate, weakness, and depression are all signs of hypoglycemia as well as of emotional illness. Other sicknesses which lead to diagnoses of emotional problems are hypothyroidism and iron deficiency anemia. Both illnesses manifest themselves in lack of concentration, misbehavior in school, while iron deficient children are also likely to be nail biters and enuretic.[34] Thorough psychological diagnosis always should include thorough physical diagnosis. If someone you care about needs help, comprehensive diagnosis is the all-important first step.

The Power Of Suggestion

On the third day after a highly publicized airplane fatality, there are nearly twice the expected number of similar fatal crashes, says Prof. David Phillips, U. Calif.-San Diego.[35]

These aren't just accidents. This pattern indicates a psychological contagion. Significant public events resonate for severely depressed and self-destructive people who can't openly acknowledge their feelings. Some become morbidly caught up in news of the accident. And the event gives others psychological permission to suffer the same fate. They identify with the victims, and their inner controls relax enough to cause a similar accident.

We sometimes see psychological contagion spreading through organizations. A number of people will have a rash of similar accidents or will make a series of similar mistakes. The trouble spreads, fewer things work right, and as more people fall prey to the syndrome, it becomes harder for anyone to control the situation. If you're caught in a situation like this, it's best to call in a trusted professional. He or she can take a good look at what's going on and find the root problem that people are unconsciously reacting to. It won't help to treat the symptoms until you understand the source of the contagion.

In Summary

1. *Unconscious feelings are a major obstacle to change, precisely because they are unconscious and therefore outside the reach of our conscious intentions.*

2. *Just as we can use others' behavior to infer their feelings and motivations, we can observe our own behaviors and use them as clues to our own unconscious feelings. Knowing that these feelings exist can help to bring them into consciousness and thus under our conscious control to a greater extent.*

3. *Listening well is important. Putting thoughts and feelings into words helps the person formulate the problem, so the work of solving it can begin. Very often, troubled people are helped just by knowing that someone cares enough to listen, and that they are not alone.*

4. *Professional help is useful because it provides a neutral outsider's perspective on the situation. A professional can help a troubled person look at painful feelings and work through them.*

5. *Physical conditions can be caused by psychological conditions; psychological conditions can have physical causes. Mind and body cannot necessarily be treated separately.*

A Time For Every Purpose

Development doesn't stop when we reach adulthood. Each stage of adult development brings its own challenges and gratifications, but every stage also requires a readjustment of our relationships to our work, to our coworkers, and to our families and friends. The order in which you take up the tasks of adult life is not nearly as important as paying attention to each of the various tasks in its turn, and keeping the whole scheme of your life in mind. That way you are less likely to come to old age and suddenly find that it's too late to do what you wanted to do or share what you wanted to share.

When Is The Honeymoon Over?

Organizational relationships, like all others, go through stages of development. In romantic relationships, people fall in love, marry, and go through a honeymoon. The gratifications are mixed with certain frustrations and disappointments. The style of the relationship must adapt when children are born, and when family members enter new stages and make new demands.

In organizations, the stages of relationships among peers, subordinates, and superiors resemble other relationship stages so clearly that we borrow terms to describe them: a company woos an executive, U.S. Presidents have a honeymoon with Congress, and so on. The terms imply characteristic feelings. We start with some uncertainty and exploration, and if we find things to our liking, we develop great expectations. When the headiness subsides, it's time to begin recognizing and adapting to differences in style, orientation, focus, and level of interaction around the task. Routine relationships are finally established and are satisfactory for a while, but when people and circumstances change (as people and circumstances will), the relationships must change as well.

Everyone takes for granted the early stages, but we tend to forget that further adjustments will always be necessary. So we may not realize why we feel resentful when a coworker changes, necessitating some change on our part, or when the job or organization changes. Or we ourselves may enter a new stage, and wonder why we feel differently toward the job or coworkers.

In every organization, in every unit, it's important for managers to assess the particular stages of relationships. You might start with these questions:

1. With what psychological contracts do people come to your unit? What kinds of expectations? What have they been promised, both explicitly and implicitly, by you or others? What have they been led to assume or expect?
2. What early experiences do people encounter? Are their expectations met, not met, or more than met? What kinds of problems do people run into as a result? What is the typical honeymoon period? Is there a common "the honeymoon's over" experience?
3. Can you identify further stages that are typical of your unit? What characterizes the stages? Are there cycles of highs and lows, boredom and renewed interest? Do they correspond to other patterns of work or personnel changes?
4. What makes people feel better or worse through given stages? How do you know? Can you spell it out? How might the individuals know? What things at different points in their tenure make a difference in morale?

If you can think about these aspects of a work group, and as a manager be aware of them, then you may be able to head off potential difficulties or enhance gratification by trying to meet changing needs. But if you take progress through these stages for granted, then you're at their mercy.

Act Your Age: An Age-Old Misconception

Americans tend to assess their accomplishments and behavior in terms of their age, says Prof. Bernice Neugarten, U. Chicago. But, she adds, this cultural tendency—and much of the recent literature on life ages and stages—is misleading. Our developmental courses are actually flexible and idiosyncratic: "Our society is becoming accustomed to the 28-year-old mayor, the 30-year-old college president, the 35-year-old grandmother, the 50-year-old retiree, the 65-year-old father of a preschooler, the 70-year-old student, and even the 85-year-old mother caring for a 65-year-old son."[1]

Our psychological development patterns are as varied as our patterns of physical growth and development. Some of us age sooner than others; some of us are "late bloomers." No one is on a rigid track system. There's no need these days to dismiss ourselves too readily or to assume pessimistically that a chance once ignored is gone for good. It's rarely too late to go back to school, launch a new career, return to the workplace. Conversely, for a number of managers it's not too early to retire at age 50 or so. How do you know what you can manage appropriately at any point in your life? Well, you must simply assess what feels good as you do it—physically, emotionally, intellectually. If you have a given competence that gives you pleasure, that's a far more important measure than your age.

How Do You Want To Be Remembered?

One way to look at the scheme of your life is to write an obituary for yourself. That may not seem like a pleasant task, but in the course of writing it, you spell out for yourself what you want to be able to look back on and what is, in your own mind, your ideal career. Such an obituary should be written as it would appear in a newspaper, including a dateline and the who, what, when, where, and how of life experience. When you are compelled to describe your life retrospectively in 100 to 200 words, the crucial issues toward which one strives will stand out in sharp relief. In effect, the mock obituary, written in the privacy of your home or office, can serve as a personal road map for implementing your plans.

Side Roads

I love stories of people who go astray. They start out studying to be acrobats and end up running for governor. The people I mean are not unstable. They are open to the opportunities around them, and eager to find another aspect of themselves. Jonathan Miller, who strayed from medical school to a very successful career in comedy, theater, and film-making (and who has now gone back to medicine), says, "Everything I've done ... has come about because someone rang me up or appeared at the door and asked if I'd like to come out and play."[2] Most people can't afford to play double or nothing with their careers every few years. But I wish more adults were willing to come out and play. Did anyone ever ask you to go in with them on an invention? Did a friend ever suggest you walk across the country together? Go ahead, do it! Take it seriously, the way you would rebuilding a house or running a charity. You can bet that when Miller comes out to play, he works hard. Some people get more adventurous once their children are grown. But it's a gamble to put it off that long—you might stiffen up like the Tin Woodman in *The Wizard of Oz.* Look what he almost missed.

Fork In The Road

It's in a company's best interest, and the right thing to do, to look after the professional welfare of its managers. But that never relieves managers of the responsibility to look out for themselves. Managers who deserve promotions may find themselves caught in a bottleneck. Budget restrictions may cause promotions to be deferred, or contraction may limit the number of higher level positions. It's not your fault, and it's not really the company's fault. But it's *your* career, your life, and your self-satisfaction that are at stake.

It's important to consider your options—consider them seriously. Changing companies, changing careers, or retiring early may be impractical or unnecessarily risky. But I fear these possibilities are never even given a fair hearing by many managers. Try this: instead of asking yourself, "If I got squeezed out of my job, where could I go and what could I do?" ask, "If I were suddenly free to start something new, what else have I always wanted to do with my life?"

The next question is: "How could I get there from here?" What must you add to your present skills and knowledge to start your own business, develop (and possibly patent or publish) a good idea, reduce crime in your community, improve the school system, or start an opera company? What does it take to run for political office, or to teach?

If you are in your career and your organization by choice, of course you want to hang in there. And being passed by for a promotion once isn't the cue to jump ship and start over. But there's room for more than one achievement in your life. Your career should be something you do with your life, not life itself. Your career may stall or run aground, but your life need not founder, nor need it languish like an unfinished book on a bedside table.

Getting Started

"Getting started is the hard part," as they say. It's as true of a career as a single project. Finding the right job, establishing a record and a reputation, requires serious effort and psychological consideration. The uncertainty is tremendous—but so is the opportunity, because your whole life is ahead of you.

Shooting Blind

The importance of a good cover letter when applying for a job is a cliché, but what makes a cover letter good is information that's hard to come by. It's clear from the letters I receive that assertiveness training has had its effect, because people are perfectly willing to say all the wonderful things they have done and can do, and are quite sure I will be pleased with their services. What these letters generally lack is any evidence that the person knows who we are, what we do, how we function, and what kind of people make up our staff.

If you want to capture the interest of a prospective employer, or present yourself as a candidate for a higher role in your own organization, you have to know what the prospective employer's interest is. A letter which essentially says, "I can do all these things," is likely to provoke a "So what?" response. A letter which says, "The work you do interests me, and I can be useful to you because I have done these things which are right up your alley," is much more likely to spark some enthusiasm for further contact, providing you really know my alley.

A cover letter or other presentation of self must convey a sense of purpose in order to be effective, according to David Hizer, executive vice president of an executive search firm. I agree with him wholeheartedly. He also suggests four objectives for a cover letter:
1. Target your application to a specific person.
2. Direct the reader's attention to specific skills he or she may find valuable.
3. State clearly your reason for being interested in that particular organization or job.
4. Designate the time and form of your next communication with the reader.[3]

If you don't make the effort to learn something about a prospective employer's needs, you are shooting blind. Your chances of hitting the mark are minimal, and you might as well not waste your time.

Making It In A Man's World

I've often said that women need mentors to help them climb the corporate ladder. But many work in male bastions and encounter considerable hostility. How can they make it? One woman manager who's been there and has learned the ropes says women need these survival skills:

1. *Competence.* Newly hired or promoted women must first prove they can meet the requirements of their job descriptions. They must meet specific goals, build support for their achievements, and maintain complete records of their activities and contacts. In short, they must be fully on top of their jobs as soon as possible.

2. *Endurance.* Even if you're the best at what you do, it won't matter if you don't hang in and survive.

3. *Awareness.* Watch for who has the power to say yes and no and to get things done. Then figure out how to link your purposes with theirs.

4. *Sensitivity to feelings.* Deal with problems as they occur. If someone is upset, talk to him or her before feelings have a chance to fester.

5. *Self-control.* You can't lose your cool and be effective, she says, adding, "I didn't want people to be able to read my feelings when I was upset."

6. *Overriding purpose.* When women are under extreme pressure and told that they'll never make it in the organization, they need the determination to succeed. "I didn't want anyone to get the best of me, and be able to tell any other woman that she couldn't make it, either," this manager says. When the going got really rough, this purpose often helped her hang in.

This advice holds good for anyone who is new to an organization or a position and is feeling under pressure. All successful managers are skilled at reading situations, understanding people, and then responding accordingly. And the more reasonably and rationally you behave when you're under attack or caught in a political maelstrom, the better you'll survive. But it's still true that once you've proven yourself and have made it plain that you're no quitter, you'd do best to find a more comfortable position—preferably with a mentor.

Stake Out Your Own Turf

While still a newcomer at the U.S. District Attorney's Office for the Southern District of Texas, Michol O'Connor took on a case for the Department of Agriculture concerning illegal transportation of eggs. Her colleagues explained that she was free to reject such low priority cases for more "important" ones, such as gun running or drug dealing. But she continued to handle these unpopular cases because they brought her great satisfaction. Rather than struggle to be outstanding in the glamour areas, she could be outstandingly successful in uncrowded arenas. Rather than get one drug smuggler locked up, knowing that the drug traffic would go on, she could permanently reduce the disease hazard to livestock by getting an international airline caterer to dispose of their garbage properly. And she won the appreciation and cooperation of her clients in doing so.[4]

There is a lesson here for the manager who feels lost in the shuffle. One way to stand out is to tackle a problem that no one else is bothering with, even though it needs to be solved. Of course, the politics of the situation must be considered. Take care not to hurt your chances for promotion by stigmatizing yourself or just dropping out of sight. The right people need to know, not that you work on oddball matters, but that you *solve* problems.

Nothing Ventured, Nothing Gained

The American astronauts were lionized as heroes, and most went on to successful careers—most notably, Frank Borman to head Eastern Airlines and John Glenn to serve in the Senate. But when NASA first described the Mercury Redstone program to a select group of test pilots, it wasn't clear whether, in choosing space flight, the pilots would see their careers take off or fizzle, says Tom Wolfe in *The Right Stuff.*[5]

It's often hard to predict what steps will most benefit a career path. The pilots who became astronauts traded piloting skills for fame and adulation. But they consciously ran the risks that people would see them as guinea pigs, that they'd fall behind the state of the art in test piloting, and that they might never make it back alive. For most of them the risks paid off.

Managers too must take risks if their careers are going to take off. There's no knowing for sure how working relationships will develop, which units of an organization will gain in importance and prestige, or what positions will give greatest visibility to your skills. You can get as much information as possible from peers, superiors, friends, and career counselors before making a job change or a career move. But at some point you'll have to listen to your instincts, make a choice, and see how well it flies.

Making The Grade

A successful career requires commitment—to yourself, to your organization, and to your field of interest. If you leave out any of these, you're likely to find you've headed down a blind alley. You probably will fare better if you also commit yourself to your family—your most likely source of support when the going gets rough. More about that in the next chapter.

Serendipity

One of the long-standing human debates is over the role chance plays in our success or failure in life. But as in so many debates, a strong case can be built for the middle ground—chance has a part to play, but we must take advantage of it. In 1745, Horace Walpole coined a word for that felicitous combination of luck and ability: serendipity. Curiously enough, the "ability" aspect has slipped out of the present-day definitions.[6]

If you're not doing well, it's certainly more comfortable to attribute success to large doses of luck than to the balanced notion of serendipity. But it takes ability to see opportunity and make use of it. It takes a mind that is open and receptive, exposing itself to new ideas and to new perspectives on old ones. One of the traits that differentiates managers from executives is the ability to make penetrating observations. Executives must look at implications of what they see and go beyond the obvious connections, rather than skimming along the surface of experiences and tasks to be done. They need to have quick intellectual perceptions, with good judgment about people and about the appropriate means of accomplishing their objectives. Working harder is never a substitute for that kind of capacity.

How can you know if you're prepared for opportunity? First, think about some of the recent important decisions you made. How well did you do with them? Where did you fall down? Was it data, was it thinking through, was it conceptualizing? Just where were the flaws?

Second, is there a way to fill the gap in your ability? Can you examine with somebody else what you should have considered in making those decisions? Can you take courses on decision making? Can you look at how your manager goes about making decisions? These are all ways of checking yourself out.

And next time you find yourself wondering why Joe has all the luck—think serendipity.

To Make It Big, Invest Yourself

When Akio Morita, chairman and cofounder of Sony, first came to the United States in 1953, he felt that "selling our products there would be impossible." And, he says, "I was shocked at the difference from our technology, the difference of scale, the history." But Morita didn't allow himself to be overwhelmed; he kept coming back, and finally moved his family to New York City. "From the beginning, I tried to learn the American way of doing things," he says. As a result, he made his Japanese company a household word across the United States.[7]

Morita's experience highlights the value of patience, perseverance, and long-term personal investment. Too many American organizations demand immediate action and quick results. They're too quick to see the time spent thinking, testing the waters, or becoming acculturated as time wasted. They often send their best people abroad and expect them to put down roots and reap profits from nearly the moment they step off the plane. True, impatient American managers are worried about protecting investments, but too often they ignore the significant investment of energy, intellect, and emotion they demand of their people. As a result, they too often risk the personal investment as they set their sights on the quick money return.

Do you operate on the Japanese or the American model? When you feel uncertain and out of place, do you find more "pressing" and familiar matters to handle? Truly innovative people get inside situations and subjects they don't yet understand. They have a feel for what's important, and once they're in a situation, they start to shape it. If you want to progress, don't stick with what you've mastered, but invest yourself now and then in ambiguous enterprises. You may find yourself riding the crest of significant success.

From Cradle To Career Path

It's not always true that marriage and parenthood weaken a woman's attachment to work. "Before my son was born, I just had a job," reports one woman manager, "but afterward I thought seriously about my career." And another woman manager agrees, adding that she committed herself more seriously to her career as she settled into marriage.

The experiences of these women may surprise some people. But they're not hard to understand. As these women settled into their adult identities, they became more serious about all their roles. Like most men, they realized that their domestic responsibilities reinforced their career responsibilities. Their ego ideals demanded that they be serious professionals. They could no more feel good about their domestic identities without career success than their husbands could. They devoted themselves to work with renewed energy after marriage and motherhood because they felt they owed it to themselves, their husbands, and their children.

Know Yourself First

When you're a candidate for a promotion, you ought to have a clear picture in your own mind of what you can do and have done well, along with a good idea of what you are looking for in a job. Then you can make a deliberate search for someone who needs what you have to offer—either in your own organization or another. This calls for creative skill in presenting what you do well, and avoiding such trite clichés as "a good manager can manage anything." Too often people merely depend on their superior for promotion. Sometimes they are promoted into jobs that don't fit them.

Their pleasure at the promotion blinds them to the hazards (for them) of the job. They then suffer defeat. It's your life, your career. No one else can or will look after it as carefully as you can.

Fit To Kill

Many managers angling for promotions are hiring PR consultants. They're taught how to give off the aura of success: the consultants choose wardrobes, teach gestures, even plant articles in trade publications.[8] And another hot fad teaches people to "read" the body language of others. Linguist John Grinder and Gestalt therapist Richard Bandler claim they can teach people to get whatever they want out of any encounter with others.[9]

As one of William Faulkner's homespun characters puts it, these faddists are "so sharp they just might cut themselves." They claim that people can achieve lasting success through sham, posturing, and intimidation. That's nonsense. No one can earn a promotion and live up to its responsibilities by being put through their paces by a glorified horse trainer. And hard-boiled training in the manipulation of others won't get you more than a quick and dirty advantage. More serious approaches don't always give clear, quick, or easy answers. But they do teach people how to listen to themselves and others, and how to think about what they hear.

To Move Up, Speak Up

What should a manager do if she thinks her career path is blocked because she's a woman? Talk with her manager, say several women managers. These women have seen men promoted first and fastest; they've had managers who assumed that women don't want more responsibility and pressure. Their managers couldn't know how badly they wanted to move up until they spoke up, these women say. As they cleared the air, their careers got going.

Many managers fear they'll hurt their careers if they speak up. Some are afraid of overstepping. Others, who want to ask for advice or information, are afraid of misstepping. They're afraid they'll look like fools. But knowledgeable people like to share their expertise, and managers notice who's smart enough to ask the right questions to avoid blundering. I'm not talking, of course, about people who can't make a move without their manager's approval. I'm talking about people who know they can show how smart they are by asking the right question at the right time. Managers can't read minds. If you know that you need information—or that your manager needs information—speak up and clear the air. That's the first step toward change.

Nipped In The Bud

One of the routine gripes I hear comes from staff people who want line jobs. They don't see why it's so hard to move in that direction, and they grouse about not being given a chance. Some spend an occupational lifetime discontentedly longing for a line role. Often they are technical staff people who realize the limits of their functions and understand where the power lies in an organization. Recently a man in his late 50s, who has always been in a research role, began looking about for a line responsibility. He hasn't found one, and he isn't likely to. The fact is, such a move must be made early in one's career. Exceptions are rare.

One reason it's hard to move after the first few years is that the person is already being paid too much to go back and start as a lower level manager, yet he or she needs that lower level experience. Another is that, starting late, one is not likely to go as far as a younger person, and it is often more worthwhile for the organization to fill lower level positions with people who can be trained to eventually take on higher level roles. Also, the person's experience in his or her own field may go to waste. The third reason is a matter of personality. Many people go into staff roles in the first place because it suits their personalities to play a support role rather than a take-charge role, or to spend their time independently designing or controlling rather than coordinating the efforts of many people in order to implement others' ideas. This is also likely to be the case with people who have been reassigned from line to staff functions. If one has difficulty taking charge, being proactive, and providing leadership, one is unlikely to be happy or do well in a line role. It's nice to fantasize about being in control and to imagine being able to run things better than the line people do, but the reality will not necessarily be as pleasant.

If you are in a staff function and would like to move into a line role, lose no time about looking into the training, education, or experience you need to be eligible for a transfer. If there is no opportunity for transfer in your organization, begin looking immediately for an organization where your experience might be more applicable to a line role. And if neither is possible, it's time to begin accepting the reality of your situation. In the eyes of most people, you simply are not eligible for a line position, even though you may have competences that haven't been allowed to flower. There's no point spending the rest of the years until retirement being angry or bitter about something that can't be helped and isn't going to change. However, you might want to direct your energy into encouraging young people who enter your department to look ahead and plan ahead a little more than you did.

Keeping Up With The Times

Keeping abreast of the advances in your field is no joke, even in a fairly restricted area such as TV repair. One repairman recently told me he must spend two hours a night reading to keep up with the technical changes in just his branch of electronics. This man is well read, technically knowledgeable, and literate. I can only wonder what this means for people who are not like him—and who service our TVs.

In management, a field so much broader and more complex, the problem is compounded. The flow of information increases, demanding more study time; the complexity of the information increases, demanding higher levels of abstraction. If you're going to make it in the professional management world, you had better be literate to start with and stay that way, or start doing your remedial work immediately.

Middle Age

Ten, fifteen, even twenty years can go by in a flash. Middle age is the time of reassessment—a time to slow down, look at where you've been, decide how you like it, and make new plans for the future. You may not like what you see, but it's best to take stock now, while there's still time to do something about it.

Killing The Messenger

A king who kills the bearer of bad tidings is overtaken by events anyway. And if he will not even listen to the messenger, he is taken by surprise to boot. One of the events that overtakes many men and women is some type of mid-life crisis. The warning symptoms are depression, boredom, self-doubt, hostility toward one's spouse of many years, and impatience with the "chores" (breadwinning, housecleaning, child rearing, sex, going places together) one has done for so long. In an article on Carl Jung's treatment of mid-life patients, Ladson Hinton says, "Jung felt that symptoms were meant to be listened to and not subdued, that the intent of depression on one level is to make one be still and listen, learn to be receptive, rather than try to will that life go on as before."[10]

In Jung's view, mid-life is a time when the major goals of the ego have been achieved: the child has become independent of parents, and the adult has formed the major relationships and accomplished the major tasks of life. To do this, certain aspects of the personality had to be suppressed, such as the childish ability to play, and a man's "feminine" or a woman's "masculine" characteristics. Now that the ego has had its day, these unconscious strivings want to be heard. Depression, moodiness, and estrangement from your spouse can be the mind's way of forcing you to turn inward for a while.

This does not mean you should simply abandon your spouse for a younger lover. Such a distraction probably won't help for long, anyway. Mid-life depression is not a random surface affliction, like poison ivy, to be salved until it goes away. It has meaning. It has a message for you, if you'll listen.

More Than Love Songs

John Lennon achieved success that few ever know. But with it came sacrifices common to many. He lost time and privacy in which to grow and learn about himself. The man who wrote and sang so perfectly of loving lost the chance to love and care for his own family: "I hadn't seen Julian, my first son, grow up at all and now there's a 17-year-old man on the phone." When he remarried and had another child, he was determined not to repeat his mistakes.[11] That he was wealthy enough to simply stop working and become "the housewife" was his rare fortune. But that he chose to do so, that he could admit that he had to learn again how to love and be loved, were worthy acts of a rare man.

Check Your Vital Signs

Sooner or later everybody reaches a plateau. This is not necessarily the same as reaching your level of incompetence. A plateau may be the result of changed perspectives, changed values, or the undermining of your spirit by changed organizational circumstances. But lack of interest is a far cry from lack of ability. It's important to know when you have plateaued, so you can take whatever initiative is necessary and possible to get moving again. That may mean a different kind of job, another organization, a new career, or something else. If you are aware of reaching a plateau, then you can make choices. If you aren't aware of it and do nothing about it, you run the risk of receiving successively lower performance appraisals, being put on a shelf, or being fired.

How can you tell when you have hit this kind of plateau? Here are a few cues:
1. You're no longer interested in doing what you're doing; you just do it out of habit, compulsion, or necessity.
2. You can't seem to keep up with the changes in concepts and technology in your field or position. You feel as if you are in over your head, flailing your arms to keep above water.
3. You feel more worn out than before, even though your job hasn't changed much except for its increasing complexity.
4. Former peers and subordinates are going past you.

5. The prospect of having to learn new techniques and new concepts makes you feel like hiding.

If you think you have reached a plateau, what can you do about it? First, and most important, size up your situation and identify your options with the assistance of someone whose perspective and judgment you can trust. Ideally this should be a professional who can rule out the possibility of depression. Second, talk over your feelings and options with your family. Third, work out a step-by-step plan for following through on those options.

If you feel you must stay with your organization, talk over your feelings with your manager. Indicate the kind of work you can continue to do satisfactorily. If, after considering your situation, you no longer wish to be promoted, make that known. Your manager may be relieved; in many instances managers are afraid to tell their subordinates that they can't be promoted, for fear that the subordinate will somehow be destroyed. If the two of you can get the matter out in the open and come to terms about it, then neither will have unrealistic expectations or unresolved guilt hampering your actions.

Middle-Aged Melancholy

When things turn out badly for us in middle age, we're likely to blame ourselves—and despair of being able to set things right. We're aware of the consistencies in our behavior that have made trouble for us over the years. And we realize that there are many things we can't undo, atone for, change, or amend. By middle age most of us have lost the youthful freedom to blame our failures on the fates, or the optimism to believe that we'll right our wrongs one day. As V. S. Pritchett so beautifully puts it, "It is not always pleasant when events of one's half-forgotten past come back in middle age, bite at the heart and stir up guilt."[12]

Our guilt is more intense in middle age because we feel time running out. We fear that we won't be able to change painful patterns of interaction before it's too late. The experience of one middle-aged man is typical: having taken over his entrepreneurial father's business, this manager has long chafed at his father's endless carping and second-guessing. Their relationship has been defensive, hostile, and bitter. "But what really hurts," says the son, "is my feeling that he'll die before we manage to patch up our relationship."

It's common for people to become so severely self-indicting that they can't take positive, realistic action. In middle age we must come to acknowledge our imperfections, and accept that we'll never be perfect. But if we can use the wisdom of our years to bring our goals and expectations down to a reasonable size, we'll often find that this stage of life does indeed hold opportunities for significant growth.

One Size Won't Fit All Ages

Everyone who fulfills a role begins to feel the chains. One's role can interfere with one's progress through the developmental stages of adult life, warns psychologist Laurence Gould, CUNY, in a paper on "visionary leadership." Though the task of the role may originally coincide with the task of a certain stage of life, it is likely to clash with the task of the next stage. The result can be a conflict which destroys the accomplishments of the first stage, or a failure to reach any further stages. Gould makes an example of the career of King Arthur. Arthur came to power partly through his youthful military prowess. In middle life he sought negotiation and peace rather than warfare. Yet when enemies persisted, he—as leader—had no choice but to resort to an activity (warfare) he now loathed.

It's good to follow one's dreams—that's what makes life satisfying. But dreams must evolve over the decades or they just won't fit. The dream of fulfilling a leadership role is especially hard to reconcile with one's own development over the years, because leadership involves fulfilling other people's expectations. Your needs for personal development are unlikely to influence those expectations. Fortunately, different leadership roles call for different behaviors. You can be a leader all your life, but in different ways at different life stages: as a force for change, as an uplifter of the dispirited, as a good example who can communicate your values publicly, as a mentor and teacher of the young.

When you feel dissatisfaction around the age of forty and again at sixty, when you feel your dream is failing, it may be time to let the dream grow and change. This is not something you can sit down and figure out in a weekend, and it will help to talk with someone else about it. If you've lived a long time with your dream, changing it can feel like betraying it. But most people who have stayed content for a whole lifetime have learned to recognize the evolution of their ideals (such as marriage, parenthood, ambition), and to give the new forms of their ideals a fair shake.

Middle Age And The Creative Process

Some people like to deny that there is a middle-age crisis and that it has significant impact on creativity. But the composer Rossini recognized it as he approached mid-life. He stopped composing at the age of 37, "a thing that has always puzzled scholars," according to Gary Wills. Rossini's contemporaries were struck with amazement—it was as if he had stopped breathing. Rossini, one of the most natural composers of his time, had no more miracles of composition to serve. He called his last solemn mass the "Monkey's Last Trick." He had no more tricks left—there was a depletion of his creative wellspring.[13]

Spontaneous, brilliant, insightful creativity occurs before the age of 35. It is a kind of controlled craziness that becomes inhibited by our perceptions and knowledge of our world as we approach middle age. At this period in life a new kind of creativity evolves based upon a reworking of our intellectual and emotional soil. This type of creativity rarely involves radical departures from accepted fact. It comes about as a result of integrating our knowledge within our personal frame of reference.

Rossini could have continued writing his operas and orchestral works, but he would have been reworking material that his early creative genius had forged into new musical forms, with none of the spontaneity of his youth.

Mid-Life Renaissance

Many of us fear we've accomplished all we're going to by the time we're about 35. But while many people do hit a plateau in their skills and performance when they reach middle age, others find that creativity blossoms late. A look at Nobel laureates gives room for hope: most Nobel science laureates do their prize-winning work in early middle age. And some winners are considerably older when they make their breakthroughs. Oswald Avery was 67 when he demonstrated the genetic importance of DNA.[14]

The mid-life crisis may be a less painful experience if we don't assume it means a decline in our powers. People who are engaged with their work, families, friends, or communities may find this an especially generative time of life. They no longer have to worry about starting a career, making it financially, or settling into the responsibilities of family life. They can give more rein to their creative impulses, and may find themselves developing new facets of their jobs. Other middle-aged managers start successful new businesses late in their careers, while still others develop serious avocations or take on important roles in their communities.

Prejudice Against Older Executives

Is decision-making performance related to age or to experience? Ronald N. Taylor, U.B.C., Vancouver, found that older line managers tended to gather more information and to diagnose the value of the information more accurately and quickly than younger line managers, regardless of previous experience, but that they had some difficulty in coming to a decision. They showed less confidence in their decisions and more flexibility in altering them.[15]

This shows that impairment of processing abilities is not relevant in the working age group. The difference can be explained in terms of life stages. Young managers can successfully deny both their dependency on others and their mortality. They are growing and doing things. They can feel more confident with no more reason to feel that way. As a person grows older and physically less capable, he becomes more dependent on higher authority not to throw him out. He may recognize new techniques in which he is not adequately schooled, and he may have had enough experience to know that seemingly perfect answers don't always turn out that way. Hence the older person's greater insecurity in the face of a decision.

Older managers should meet regularly to share experiences with each other. The heavy emphasis on youth in our culture constantly threatens them and acts as a damper on their potential contribution to an organization. Mutual reinforcement can counteract that cultural force and bring out the benefits of their greater depth of experience.

Past The Peak

Movie stars who have passed the peak of their stardom often become character actors. Sometimes they portray lovable old souls and sometimes Frankensteins, but they play a rich and supportive role which puts them in continual occupational demand. A similar thing can happen for managers. After reaching a peak of activity and advancement, you may plateau. Then it's time to take on a character-actor role. You may be a fountain of information on your specialty, or one to whom people can turn as a sounding board, or you may play some other developmental or guiding role. If you try to continue being a star, you'll be fighting to regain a path there's no chance of regaining. You're more likely to slip and slide into oblivion.

When we think of second careers, we usually think of going outside the organization and doing other things. But it's also possible to redefine yourself and your functional contribution within the organization, and to be recognized as an authoritative, helpful, informative person who is a rock of stability for the organization and a guide for others.

There are movie stars who can't act, but rise to great heights because of their beauty or a cultural fad. They don't last long once they peak, because they have nothing else to offer. But real actors, such as Shelley Winters and the late Melvyn Douglas, have a continuing and valued contribution to make. It's the same in management. One man who is retiring from a salary administration role will be greatly missed, because his knowledge and ability are highly regarded. He has not given a spectacular or meteoric performance; but he has seen some of the meteors in his organization die out or fall with a thud. He has the satisfaction of having earned the respect and affection of all the people he's worked with, both for himself as a person, and for his particular skills and competences.

Retirement

It's only the end of the line if you think of it that way—or if you don't think of it. Practical arrangements are not nearly enough. How do you want your life to go on?

Not Of An Age

With new laws allowing people to stay in the work force past age 65, is business going to be burdened with many employees who simply can't function as well as they did when they were younger? Not necessarily. There are two factors involved: 1) the level of functioning of older people; and 2) whether people make use of the option to keep working longer than they would have otherwise.

Level of functioning past age 65 depends on level of abstraction. Elliott Jaques' work indicates that the levels of abstraction of people in the first three strata peak between the ages of 50 and 65, and then begin to decline. (Stratum III is the plant manager level.) But in the higher strata, capacity for abstraction is still increasing at 65. Many people in the lower strata will begin to feel overwhelmed by the demands of the workplace, and will choose to retire. Others will have certain skills which they have maintained, which are second nature to them, and which they will be able to continue to perform as long as they are physically able.

Those in the higher strata will not feel overwhelmed by work demands, but as their perspective broadens they may find the concerns of their work too narrow. They, too, are likely to retire, and to take on tasks that make use of their breadth of understanding. Whether they choose to stay in the organization or go on to something else, they will need to keep up with the changing world. This means finding ways to stay in touch with the thinking of younger people, once their own children leave to establish their separate lives. It's too easy to live in the past, to become frozen in place and unable to adapt.

At any level of abstraction, it is possible for people to develop new or different career activities which they can carry on at their own pace. The ones who don't, who have nothing else to do, are the ones who will want to stay in the organization. When they reach the point where they can't measure up, they will have to be told. If the information is sprung on them out of the blue, they will get their backs up and insist that they can still do the job as well as ever, or at least well enough. So continuous feedback on performance is necessary. If people are provided with specific information about how they are doing on a continuing basis, they will gradually see that they can't keep up, and pull out.

You can prepare yourself for aging, and recommend that others do so as well. Look around at the older people in your profession and see what they are doing. Where does age first begin to show? What do you see people doing in order to cope with the effects of age? What works and what doesn't? If you have some idea of what it will be like and how you might adapt, you won't be at such a loss as it begins to happen to you. Aging doesn't have to come as a surprise.

Changing Courses In Midstream

A highly competent and intelligent retired senior executive who has not made plans for his or her own retirement is a demoralizing sight. I've seen a significant number of men who have overinvested themselves in their own organizations, often over a period of years, and who have no other roles outside of them. They persist in trying to hang on to the organization through board membership and continued interference in the operation of what was once "their" organization. They also feel guilty about their interference, but they can't let go nor can they really take part. Those subordinates who must shut them out or cut them off feel guilty. Such retirees frustrate their successors who have difficulty handling them. They arouse tremendous anger in themselves because they feel nobody wants them and they don't know what to do about it.

The methods they propose in board meetings or in public and governmental relations often have become obsolete. Their conceptions no longer fit current realities. They can't even head charitable campaigns because, to do so, an executive must be in a position to contribute his or her company's money to others in similar roles.

Every executive and manager owes it to himself or herself and to his or her company to prepare for the eventuality of retirement. Those who have prepared themselves for this different phase in their lives find it a new and invigorating experience—a time for exploring new ground, a period of utilizing their vast knowledge in different and creative ways.

The responsibility lies with the person. He or she cannot be like the martyr-mother who, by her behavior, says "Love me. Look how much I have done for you!"

No Crystal Ball

Reflecting on a past Presidential election and the man on the way out, columnist August Heckscher noted that "the loss of power is one of the most painful experiences that can afflict a person."[16] Every executive and manager wields power. And, barring an untimely death, each will have to lose it, by retirement or by leaving the position for any number of reasons.

Every manager should give this some serious thought in the years approaching retirement. It takes time to get past the glib characterizations ("Oh boy, I'll never get out of bed!" or "My husband and I will drive each other nuts!") and start imagining how you'll really feel. This sort of mental rehearsing is very important. Of course things won't be exactly as you imagined them, but you'd be surprised what insights will come if you let your imagination go. One of the reasons widows do better than widowers is that women rehearse this way for the probable loss of their husbands. Men rarely do. The more different situations you daydream yourself into, and the more different reactions you can imagine having, the more complete a picture will emerge of what retirement will mean to you. And the meaning *will* be complex, with conflicting aspects and alternating feelings.

Use all your powers of fantasy and imagination when major changes are on the way: retirement or promotion, marriage or divorce, the death of a parent or the birth of your first child. This is not escape, it's investigation. You can't know the future, but you can try to know yourself. That will tell you more than any crystal ball.

Retirement Shakes Up The Movers

A major problem in retirement programs has to do with executives and managers who have been moved around so much that they have no permanent home. This is complicated by the fact that most preretirement programs have no adequate psychological process to help people cope with the transition. There are essentially two kinds of groups for whom preparation must be made: those who are locals—who have stayed essentially in the same areas for most of their working lives—and those who are cosmopolitans—people who have been highly mobile, who have not anchored themselves in a given location. There is an important need to keep retirees as part of the corporate family and to sustain their identification with that family. Otherwise they are frequently left to their own devices. If they have been highly mobile without any roots, they may find themselves with groups of "alumni" of the same company and certain geographical locations but they are still stuck with the questions of "how do you find a new way of life" and "where do you go to live." This problem will continue to be with us. It requires more active involvement by corporate management.

An Argument For Retirement

Executives who dread retirement are often so career-obsessed that they can't imagine the vistas which leisure can reveal. Such managers can learn from the experience of retired IBM executive Robert Hubner, who writes:

"The easiest thing to do at 60, or 65, is to *keep* working. Habits are ingrained. . . . The status quo can continue precisely, and nothing need *change*—just keep plugging away, until death do you part.

"The much more difficult thing to do is to take up new pursuits, new schedules, new projects, new acquaintances, new business problems, new family relationships, new everything....

"I've had projects piled up for years now that I've been wanting to do. I feel the same gnawing urge to get at them that I did to solve a business problem for 37 years at IBM. The difference is, I've got to acquire some new skills to do some of them. *Profound* skills, mind you, like making a souffle, properly using a sketching pen, avoiding dismemberment on a band saw, celestial navigation, the perfection of parallel skiing, to name a few. Serving on several profit and nonprofit boards and consulting with IBM, et al., is *interfering* with these interests, and how I ever found the time to go to work each day now escapes me....

"Life is so incredibly rich, time is so incredibly short, the opportunities are so incredibly numerous, that the loss of their full exploitation is incredibly sad."

Bob is right. There is no special virtue in continuing a career for more than 40 years. There's more to life, as Bob so amply illustrates, and managers who have earned the opportunity to retire comfortably do well to explore their options to the fullest. Organizations also do well to give older people, as Bob says, a "gentle push into the water"—both for their own sakes and for the renewed vigor of the organizations. I'm not saying that older people can't perform well, but that people and organizations need change or they go stale.

Every manager should stop from time to time to ask, "What would I like to be doing if I weren't heading for work? What 'profound skills' have I always wanted to develop and never found time for?" With some thoughtful preparation, you can make your retirement a renaissance.

Aging

According to Erik Erikson's stages of development, the last stage is the age of ego integrity vs. despair.[17] That means this is the time when you look at your life as a whole, you put it together in a way that makes sense— and if you can't make sense of it, you are vulnerable to despair. What counts is not so much what you have or haven't done, but whether you have come to a place where you can make peace with whatever has been.

Twelfth Round

"By the time you reach your sixties, you feel as if you're in the twelfth round and you're battered," says Norman Mailer. "Your powers to protect yourself from distraction are much smaller. You really have to concentrate on those last few rounds.... You tend to isolate yourself because the odds that a young writer would come along and write something that can teach you something is not likely, although it might delight you, and you might say, gee, what talent."[18] This is why the best time for mentoring is between the ages of 35 and 55, the age of generativity. Beyond 55, one reaches the age of integrity—a time when many achievers are preoccupied with keeping their own efforts going. Thus preoccupied, they have less energy to invest in other people's growth and development. It's better if older people don't close themselves in too much, and can keep in touch with what younger people are thinking and doing. It keeps them younger and more alive. But if you aren't content that you've achieved what you wished to achieve in your lifetime, the emphasis has to be on getting your own job done, using your last years for yourself.

Keep In Touch With The Young

We have all encountered the aging person who cannot remember what happened last week, but recalls with vivid clarity an experience of many years ago. While brain damage due to the aging process has often been cited as the cause for this behavior, Dr. Tobias Brocher offers another explanation. He suggests that as a person ages she is increasingly surrounded by young people with whom she has little in common. She also experiences the losses of friends, social contacts, and other cues which reaffirm her identity. As a result she begins to lose her identity and retreats to her previous world, acting as if her environment had not changed.[19]

This is why aging leaders who continue in their leadership roles are apt to become quite rigid, and insist that their younger subordinates do things the way they've always been done. This withdrawal from younger people means that those in older age ranges become increasingly obsolete and go off in directions that are less and less relevant to the organization.

Older managers who are satisfied with their achievements may be able to shift the emphasis away from their individual efforts, and avoid the tendency to withdraw from younger people. Such managers may continue their mentoring activities into the age of integrity (55+), using them as a vehicle for integrating their life's experiences. This will enable them to be engaged with younger people, to hear what they have to say, and to learn about new techniques and skills they bring to the organization. And this will give younger people an example to inspire their own efforts, plus the benefit of the older manager's accumulated experience.

Trials Build Survival Muscle

It's an old story among seamen that older men survive under conditions of severe physical and psychological stress while younger, stronger men often perish.[20] What that experience seems to mean, according to those who have studied it, is that those who are determined to live sustain hope, when others give up. Much of that determination to live has to do with having experienced hardships and difficult times before and having survived them. There is an advantage to aging.

Living To A Ripe Old Age

Many old people are called senile when in fact they have physiological ailments, says Richard Besdine of the National Institute on Aging. It's easy to assume a psychological malfunctioning, he says, because aging brains are "particularly vulnerable to insults occuring elsewhere in the body." Among the commonly missed diagnoses: tumors, vitamin deficiencies, infections, tuberculosis, anemia, hyperthyroidism, and chronic renal or liver failure.[21] This kind of misjudgment also reflects our preconceptions. Americans fear old age and underestimate the abilities of the old. But we're starting to change, and Besdine's findings are part of a new trend. More of us are living longer and healthier lives, and more elderly groups are developing political clout. Largely because of their efforts, the mandatory retirement age has been moved up. With more older people working, more Americans will see the potential for productive old age. These new attitudes will make it easier to spot and treat physiological ailments that have been confused with senility. And that in turn will make more old people even more productive. So if you have elderly parents, don't assume their symptoms mean senility. Make sure they have a thorough medical examination before you draw any conclusion.

"One's-Self I Sing"

An important book gives us a whole new slant on mental health in old age. Morton Lieberman and Sheldon Tobin studied over 800 people, ages 65 to 95, most of whom were in very stressful situations. They present their findings in *The Experience of Old Age*. They conclude that:
1. There are life stages, and the long period of adulthood is "marked by as much change as continuity."
2. This means that different definitions of mental health must be applied to different life stages, just as different standards of physical health would apply to teenagers and their grandparents. In earlier stages, the primary tasks reach outward: formation of relationships and mastery of the environment. In old age, the self is under attack—as the body weakens and as contemporaries die— and the primary task turns inward. The authors conclude that the basic psychological task of the elderly is "the maintenance of an integrated and coherent self."
3. With a different psychological task challenging the elderly, strategies and characteristics that were maladaptive in earlier stages of life can prove to be beneficial to mental health in old age. One example is aggressiveness. To survive the crises of old age, it can be very

helpful to have a "tough old codger" personality that, in the crises of earlier stages, would have been a real albatross. Another example is what the authors call "myth-making"—the rewriting of memory and history that is often seen in old people. In a younger person this would be seen as mentally unhealthy denial or grandiosity; in older people it might also be seen as senility. But Lieberman and Tobin believe that, in order to fulfill the basic psychological task, "a great amount of 'bending' of reality is acceptable, or even essential, necessitating modification of our definition of mental health."[22]

Most of us will face the aging process twice: when our parents get old, and then when we, our siblings, and our friends get old. I expect this book, and the research it will inspire, will have a lot to do with how we view these processes, how we judge how well we and those we care for are doing. We may have been wrong about a lot of things before now.

Voices In The Night

The prospect of growing old, for many people, is not a pleasant one. Yet it can be, as Frederic Prokosch shows us in *Voices: A Memoir.* At the age of 75 he is still productive, still writing, in his "ceaseless effort to produce a masterpiece." He still approaches each day with freshness and wonder, absorbing its beauty and anticipating "what strange new excitement the day will hold for me." This is not denial that it is the end of his life; he seems to accept and even relish that fact. "My voyage is at its end," he says. "I think how glorious to grow old! . . . I am no longer afraid of loneliness or suffering or death. I see the marvelous faces of the past gathering around me and I hear once again the murmuring of voices in the night."[23]

In Summary

1. *Unlike children, adults have a lot of control over how they spend their lives. If you think about where you're going and how you'll get there, you're more likely to be satisfied with the end result.*
2. *Knowing yourself and your needs, and being able to present both of these to others, makes it more likely that you'll get where you want to go.*
3. *The early years of adulthood usually are devoted to your own growth and development, somehow proving yourself as an adult, moving out into the world.*
4. *Middle age is a time for turning one's attention to the development of others, assuming the efforts of your early years have been successful. If they have not, then this is the time to correct your path.*
5. *In later years, your attention is likely to turn inward, in an attempt to integrate your life's experience and be satisfied with what your life has been.*

Family Matters

The closest relationships we have are with family—the family into which we are born, and the family we create for ourselves as adults. These relationships are likely to be the most stable over time, yet they may be the most stormy, emotionally. And they are likely to be the source of the stormier parts of our relationships at work. Ideally, family members are the ones we can call on when we are in need. They are the people we can count on when things are difficult at work, to restore us and send us back refreshed. But they can only function that way for us when we keep our relationships with them open and honest, and when we are committed to helping them just as they are committed to helping us.

Career And Family

It's the great balancing act of the twentieth century—how to have satisfying work and a satisfying emotional life. The greatest career demands coincide with the time when the demands of child rearing are likely to be greatest. Something has to give, whether it's one career, the other career, or the children. The hard lesson is that you can't have it all, and if you don't make the choices consciously, you make them by default. Decisions made by default feel like they're imposed from the outside, and you're likely to resent the burden, the loss, or the person you think made the decision. When you make a conscious choice, you know what you're getting in return for what you're giving up. You're more likely to appreciate it.

Keep The Home Fires Burning

Have you been putting in long hours to establish your career or to improve your chances for promotion? If so, your spouse may be experiencing the classic symptoms of grief in your absence, according to Dr. David Owen Robinson, who studied the spouses of medical interns. The interns' long and frequent absences from home caused their spouses first to deny the separation and feelings of abandonment, then to protest them, and finally to detach themselves psychologically from the absent spouse. These responses correspond to the process of mourning.[1]

What can you do when your work makes unusual demands on your time? Talk with your spouse—in advance if possible—and explore your feelings of loss, grief, anger, and guilt. Understand that these feelings are natural responses to loss. When you can anticipate and understand your feelings, you can better cope with them. Ask your spouse how you can help him or her adapt to the change. You can help your partner find a replacement occupation—perhaps taking a job, enrolling in a course, or joining an organization. Most importantly, assure your spouse that though the increased separation is necessary, it is not a rejection. When couples can squarely face the implications of separation together, they can later reestablish intimacy more easily.

Come Away, O Human Child . . .

The worst problem with workaholics is that so many of them are married. They're trying to fulfill two contradictory psychological contracts—one with themselves, and one with their spouse and children. With a workaholic, the first one wins. They give most of what they have to the satisfaction of their professional ego ideal, and too little is left for the satisfaction of their families.

What can the spouse of a workaholic do? There's very little chance that you can totally overhaul the workaholic's personality, but you may be able to change some of his or her behavior. According to Dr. Alan Sostek, a Boston psychologist, the main thing you need to do is stand up for yourself. You must act, not just react. This means telling your spouse calmly and coherently what the situation is and why it is intolerable to you, instead of waiting until the last straw makes you explode. It means making arrangements to do things together, rather than waiting for your always-too-busy spouse to be available. It means knowing what you need and want in your marriage, rather than taking what comes and hoping somehow it'll improve. The odds of a positive response to your requests for time and attention can be improved by making them sound like options—and the better part of the bargain, to boot. For example: "You don't have to make a million bucks this week; we'll think you're hot stuff if you spend the whole weekend with us."

Not knowing what your workaholic spouse does all day can leave both of you feeling isolated. But your requests for information may be greeted with evasions like, "You wouldn't understand," or "I don't want to talk about it when I get home," or "Never mind—it's buying your food." Don't give up trying—your need for information is real and important. That's one of the reasons I routinely invited spouses to take part in the AT&T-Pace U. course I taught for ten years on Human Behavior in Organizations. And that's why I urge organizations to include spouses in the meetings my colleagues and I are invited to address.

Cutting Back To Full Time

The articles about women who are trying to combine careers and motherhood are full of horror stories about women who have become nervous wrecks, whose children feel lost or abandoned, whose marriages have fallen apart, or who quit working just in time to prevent some disaster of that sort. The message is that career plus family is too much for these women. But as I read these articles, I am amazed at how much these women think they have to do in order to have a career, and how much they think they should be doing as mothers. They need to cut back, certainly. But they have plenty of room to do so! They don't need to give up their careers, they just need to cut back to a 40-hour work week.

The women who are happy with both career and family are willing to do each less than 100% of the time. "I enjoy watching my son grow, but I don't have to be there for every scraped knee," says one woman. The women who are happy doing both tend to agree that career plus family *is* too much for one woman—but maybe not too much for one woman, one man, and possibly a housekeeper or other paid help. "The role of the father is particularly vital to the successful two-career family, and it is clear that, across the country, the definition of 'father' is beginning to change. No longer the shadowy absentee authority figures of a previous generation, men are falling in love with their babies and becoming more comfortable with nurturing."[2] That sounds as if it will be good for the children and the fathers, as well as the working mothers. It's too bad that many fathers still have to tell fibs when they have to stay home with a sick child. That's a place where business could change—by recognizing fathers as parents, too.

What Silences We Keep

When facing unusual pressures, many managers try to hide that fact from their families. If there are serious problems in the organization or your own work which arouse your anxiety, or if you have suffered a severe injury or illness, you might assume that you can and should take care of your own problems. Besides, it might seem that telling the family will only worry them unnecessarily.

It's far wiser to tell your family as much as you can about what's going on and incorporate them into your concerns. They'll probably know something's amiss anyway, because your tension is bound to show up one way or another. If you say nothing, they'll probably jump to the conclusion that they have made you angry. But if you share your burdens, they will usually rally around you, strengthening family bonds as the whole group faces the outside world together. They can help you think through your options. Having done so, they'll be prepared to support you in your decision. It will affect them, too—even if only by virtue of that family bond. Let them help you. And don't underestimate your children. They can be wonderfully supportive in a crisis.

How Could You Do This To Me?

When someone in the family gets sick, of course others rush to help. They are concerned, perhaps anxious, and sorry that the person isn't feeling well. People also feel angry. A sick person makes demands on you. You have to help him or her, run errands, do special things to cheer and comfort the person, and sacrifice your own appointments or dates in the process. Inevitably there is some anger, but it's very hard to express it, or even to be aware of it. After all, the person is sick, and the reason for the demands is beyond his or her control. You know that anger is irrational under those circumstances, and make an effort to deny the feeling.

It's important to recognize that both sets of feelings can be present: the negative feelings of anger and perhaps abandonment, as well as positive feelings of compassion, sympathy, and altruism. And if you recognize the negative feelings, they tend to dissipate more easily. If you don't, they remain an unconscious drain on your energy without your being aware of what's dragging you down.

Rock Of Gibraltar; Garden Of Eden

How do people stay married forty, fifty, sixty years? It's beginning to seem incredible, and popular wisdom would have it that people just don't believe in marriage anymore. They do, but the ideal has changed, from permanence and stability to happiness and understanding.

Counselors Judy Todd and Ariella Friedman interviewed couples who had been married 50 years or more. "What they learned . . . was that for these people the marriage, not happiness, was important." The marriage could be preserved by avoiding conflicts rather than confronting them, and by simply refusing to give up.[3] But happiness and understanding cannot be ensured by sheer perseverance. For this reason, says sociologist Gary Lee, Washington State U., "Our high divorce rate is . . . not particularly surprising. Much more surprising is our high remarriage rate: the substantial majority of people who divorce remarry, and do so fairly soon after the divorce."[4] People still believe in marriage very strongly; so much so that if one marriage fails, they soon want to try another.

It's good that people are willing to keep trying. But apparently many of them aren't trying hard enough, or aren't making the right kind of effort. People with more than one divorce are frequently repeating their mistakes. Often they choose the same kind of person, who turns out to be incompatible with them in the same way, such as: strong people who dazzle them and make them feel secure, but in the end abuse them or do not give them affection; troubled people who are grateful for help and affection, but in the end are too demanding and dependent; people who promise to give up alcohol, gambling, violence, or other lovers—such promises are flattering, but unlikely to be fulfilled.

It's not that you ought to wait around for the perfect mate. In fact, if someone seems absolutely perfect, something is being ignored or denied. Wisdom is choosing not only the qualities one values, but also the faults one can live with. Of course this is hard to know in advance, but it should be considered seriously *before* marrying, especially if one has been married already, and has some solid evidence on the subject. Wisdom is also knowing one's own troublesome ways and unrealistic expectations, and trying to temper them.

There's nothing new or modern about bad marriages. What's new is the freedom to chuck them. But the freedom to correct mistakes is also the freedom to repeat them, thereby wasting your life, wearing away your self-esteem, and making life miserable for your children.

Work/Home Compromise

Successful professional women need privacy in order to work, and it makes them feel lonely. That's the finding of Sara Ruddick and Pamela Daniels,

who interviewed women in many fields for their book, *Working It Out.*[5]
Though the conflict between work and personal life is often seen these
days as a women's issue, it isn't really. Anyone with a powerful ego ideal,
who is driven to perform, learn, and achieve, inevitably feels a certain
loneliness. These people don't socialize freely because there just isn't time,
and work takes them away from families or friends more than they'd like.
But most important, such people are so preoccupied in their own heads
with what they want to achieve that they necessarily experience a certain isolation and loneliness. The conflict is part of the psychology of
achievement.

Men are subject to many of the same feelings that women are more
likely to put into words. Managers who work long hours, or who travel
frequently, often blame themselves for neglecting their families. They miss
those ties, particularly because men tend to learn about feelings from
women, and are more likely to express their feelings with women than
with other men.

Some suggestions on how to think about the balances between work
and family life, between achievement and sociability, are offered in
Tradeoffs: Executive, Family and Organizational Life by Barrie Greiff
and Preston Munter.[6] The subject deserves careful thought and planning,
for the well-being of all concerned. The answers and compromises certainly aren't easy. But people who don't expect them to be will be better
prepared to make choices than those who naively assume they can have
their cake and eat it too.

Traditional Roles For Executive Wives

The new managerial woman is a reality, but the fact remains that many
organizations still expect executives' wives to fill traditional roles, such
as presiding at social functions and volunteering for community service. In effect these wives are social leaders who represent the company
to the community. And in some organizations, the husband simply won't
make it unless his wife is his partner. Whatever you may think of this
practice, it's the better part of wisdom to recognize where it exists and
avoid costly mistakes by bucking a solidly entrenched tradition.

The role of the corporate wife hasn't changed in many instances since
William H. Whyte described it more than 30 years ago. Companies often
interview the wives of executive candidates, he wrote, to make sure they
don't get anyone who would upset existing social balances and embar-
rass the organization.[7]

Young couples do well to face this issue squarely early in the husband's
career, and, if possible, before marriage. What are their individual needs
and expectations? What conflicts are they likely to encounter? What areas
of compromise do they see? Some husbands, for instance, will most need

their wives' support early in their careers, when they're least sure of themselves. Some wives will thrive in company towns where they enjoy a special measure of prestige and influence. Other wives will do best in large cities, where the husbands' organizations tend to make fewer demands on them. There is some room for maneuver, in other words, but only when people face the facts, and base their decisions on solid information.

In addition, managers who assign male subordinates to roles where the wife is important should be sure to talk the assignment over with the wife before making a final decision. If the assignment is a real problem for her, you can be sure it will soon be an organizational problem as well.

It Takes Two To Transfer

Company transfers are becoming increasingly difficult. When people stay longer in grade in various places, they form stronger attachments, which makes it harder for them to leave. Their age and stage conflicts are magnified. In the early years of marriage, wives who are not employed outside the home are often preoccupied with bearing and rearing children to a certain exclusion of the outside world. Since their primary investment is inside the home, moving is not excessively difficult. When children have grown into adolescence and begin to leave home, however, those wives begin to deepen their attachments to their community, their friends, and sometimes to a job. Many women have achieved considerable social stature in their local community by this point, and, unlike their husbands who can transfer status through the structure of the company, those women lose their position entirely when they move.

When companies contemplate moving male managers, especially those at higher levels, they should inquire about the interests and activities of the wives. When wives become involved in planning and in advance scouting, they can prepare themselves for making an adjustment which is quite different from that which is demanded of their husbands.

To Be A Man

What does it mean to be a man? That's a big question, but Mark Gerzon takes it on in *A Choice of Heroes: The Changing Faces of American Manhood*. As the subtitle suggests, his answer is that the answer is changing. The archetypal heroes are poorly suited to today's reality, and the men who pursue and approach the ideals of their youth may find themselves unhappy and even ineffectual in today's world. Gerzon sees five traditional models, each being transformed into a new, emerging model:

1. The *Frontiersman*, the conqueror and exploiter of new lands, is becoming the *Healer*, who recognizes his dependence on the earth,

husbands its resources, is considerate of and sensitive to others' needs, and sees gentleness as strength, not weakness.

2. The *Soldier,* the protector and defender by means of violence, is becoming the *Mediator,* who protects and defends by preventing violence, finding common ground, and working out solutions in which all parties get some of what they want.

3. The *Breadwinner,* the provider, measuring his manhood by how much material wealth he provides, is becoming the *Companion,* who eats bread together with another; one who shares his life, not just the fruits of his labor.

4. The *Expert,* the hoarder of knowledge as a means to power, is becoming the *Colleague,* who is willing to give over the power of controlling specialized knowledge in order to enjoy the mutual benefits of sharing knowledge and combining skills.

5. The *Lord,* the entitled, the served, denying his human needs while demanding that they be met, is becoming the *Nurturer,* capable of caring for others in return for the care he receives.[8]

This book isn't the last word on masculinity, but it's a good thought-provoking first for anyone who's interested in the male side of changing sex roles. Some of the pressures of change are already being felt in the business world, where managers are being called upon to share information and decision-making power with their subordinates; where increasing numbers of managers turn down transfers that require relocation; where computers are equalizing access to information; and where some men are beginning to change the balance between hours spent at work and hours spent with their families. As two-career families become more common, men receive less nurturance from working wives and are called upon to give more nurturance to wives and children. The need for men to balance their work and home lives differently will grow. Organizations will feel the pressure eventually, although that may take a long time. For a while, the men who want a different lifestyle will be few and they will work out special arrangements, give up promotions, or leave the organization. But the evidence is growing that the current managerial lifestyle is hazardous to both physical and mental health. Something is going to have to give.

Being A Parent

Children react to everything you do. They're even more sensitive to your behavior than subordinates are! That can be a good thing—it provides them with ideals, values, and conscience. It can be a bad thing, when you don't have time, don't feel you can share what's on your mind, or bring your frustrations home from work and pass them around. As the most powerful influence in your children's lives, you want to think about the effect you have on them, and make it a positive one.

Test-Tube Trauma

Will test-tube babies, if they should ever grow to term in the lab, bring us a brave new world? Albert Rosenfeld argues that this advancing technology will bring many advantages: physicians can watch the baby develop and surgically correct deformities; the baby can grow in an "ideal" environment, free of viruses, nicotine, alcohol, and even unnecessary jostling; parents can develop strong attachments to their baby before "birth" by watching it grow.[9]

Psychologically this assessment misses the boat. We're not going to develop better babies or better parents by trusting technology and regularizing as much of the birth process as we can. Physicians have tried with drugs and monitors to control the birth process, and many women have rebelled. They point out that drugs often do more harm than good, and that distrusting the natural birth process disrupts the mother's and baby's initial relationship. There's no reason to think that a silent, sterile glass jar is a better prenatal environment than the womb. If we ever see test-tube babies, we'll undoubtedly discover that because they were deprived of the jostling, rocking, and muffled sounds that are our earliest experiences of mothering, they're emotionally undernourished. Nor is peering into a glass jar any preparation for parenthood. We learn to be parents by nurturing and teaching our children, by developing attachments, and by growing with them. We don't become better parents by foisting our kids off on professionals. Test-tube babies may be a scientific advance, but they're a human loss: they sever the most basic bond we know.

The Silent Observer

Infants between 12 and 21 days of age can already imitate both facial and manual gestures, according to Andrew N. Meltzoff, Oxford U., and M. Keith Moore, U. Wash. They conclude that the imitation implies that human infants can equate their own unseen behaviors with gestures they see others perform.[10] This underscores the crucial issue of modeling behavior on the part of parents and managers since unconscious modeling processes are going on all the time. Perhaps this is the reason people use the saying, "Actions speak louder than words."

No Language But A Cry

Many parents are afraid that responding right away every time their child cries will encourage the child to cry more, and they will end up with a spoiled brat. This is simple reward-punishment thinking, and there is good evidence that it is incorrect. Mary Ainsworth, U. Va., observed the interactions of mothers with their infants in their homes for several hours every third week during the first year of the infant's life. At first there was no correlation between the babies' crying and their mothers' actions. But by the time the babies were a year old, the ones whose crying was promptly attended to cried less.[11]

This isn't so surprising when you stop to think that crying is an infant's way of communicating its distress or need for something. If the little darlings could just say, "Excuse me, Ma, but I think I could use a change," they wouldn't need to cry as much as they do. If they could understand the world around them, they wouldn't have to be frightened. But those things are yet to be learned. In the meantime, children need to signal the need for comfort, whether physical or emotional, and crying is the only way they have. Babies and children need the attention of adults in order to grow emotionally. Let's give them credit for knowing enough to ask for it.

As for spoiling, we spoil children when we let them manipulate us or when we make them stay dependent. We make children stay dependent when:

1. We do for them what they can readily do for themselves.
2. We overprotect them, not letting them take risks and encouraging them to attach too much to adults.
3. We try to overwhelm them with toys and material things as a substitute for our presence and attention.
4. We don't provide adequate and reasonable structure and controls for their age.

We let children manipulate us when we are overanxious, overcontrolling, or guilt-ridden. Children sense these feelings and play on them to get what they want.

In Child Care, It's The Quality That Counts

Authors of child care books have been reluctant to give approval to mothers who go to work before their children reach the magic age of three years. Is it true that infants and young children are harmed by being left in someone else's care? Apparently not, provided the care is of high quality. According to a review of the research evidence, nonmaternal care does not, in itself, have adverse effects on the child's attachment to the mother, intellectual development, or social-emotional behavior. The mother's attitude about working instead of caring for the child full-time, plus the quality of child care, is more important than who gives the care and in what setting. Fortunately, attitudes in the popular press toward working mothers and nonmaternal care are gradually becoming more positive, easing the burden of guilt society has placed on women who take on this dual role.[12]

There are several things parents can do to ensure that the mother's absence has no detrimental effects on their children. They can select a caregiver who will play with the child and give loving attention, not just satisfy physical needs. It is also important to have a continuing relationship with the caregiver, whether in a day-care center or at home, so that he or she is a constant in the child's life. If the child repeatedly becomes attached to caring figures, only to have those attachments broken, the child will eventually stop forming attachments. So the key is good, consistent mothering care, regardless of whether it is given by the mother or someone else.

Working mothers themselves need to spend time with their children, time relatively free from distractions. Beyond that, the best thing they can do is to have confidence in the decisions they have made.

And How Do Little Girls Grow?

Anything that will encourage a woman to become a fulfilled person will be good for her daughters. When a mother is dissatisfied with herself as a person, the daughter's identification with her is undermined.

A girl's first love in life, just like a boy's, is her mother. She must give up the mother as a love object in order for the identification process to proceed. If the mother is not happy, the girl's development may stall at the point where she herself tries to take on the job of making her mother happy. Eventually, however, she will sense that she is not naturally equipped to do that. As a result, her forays into the world of achievement may be driven and compensatory instead of natural. Further, she will not develop the respect for, or trust of, men that comes easily to the daughter of a well-satisfied woman.

Women need to keep perspective in the face of pressure from women's lib and learn to balance their roles in the family, community, and work world according to their personal needs. In addition, they should prepare actively for their retirement from the role of mother so that they can anticipate that part of their lives with equanimity.

When Daddy's Not Home

Not having a father around inhibits the development of a child's conscience, reports Dr. Fitzhugh Dodson, author of *How to Parent* and *How to Father:* "Conscience . . . is not innate; it's learned. If father isn't around in those early years, the child, particularly a boy, gets the idea that ethics and character, a sense of right and wrong, are feminine. When he becomes an adolescent, he wants a male gender identity and, so, casts off those characteristics he associates solely with his mother."[13]

Dodson is right about the importance of fathers but inaccurate about the reason. Conscience is not entirely learned. A child forms a conscience in part to counteract his early aggressive impulses. He wants to make himself so good that nobody would ever suspect him of being bad.

The real significance to a boy of a missing or frequently absent father is that rivalry cannot take place day by day and be tempered by the father's gentleness and affection. If the mother lavishes attention on him and brings him closer, the intensity of his rivalry with his father is increased—his guilt and fear of retaliation along with it. The boy projects these feelings into the void when the father is not there.

A girl tends to idealize the father in his absence, and this is what intensifies her rivalry with the mother. If she gets extra attention from her daddy at the expense of the mother when he is around, or if the mother puts him down and treats him as a weak person, her problem will be exacerbated. She can easily manipulate the relationship, and the father may not see that, if he is intent on not upsetting the relationship or spoiling the weekend. Especially if discipline has been turned over to the mother, a girl can get the idea that everything is going her way with her father, and that she has it all coming. This is the root of seductive and manipulative behavior.

Since many managers are not home as much as they would like, it is important for them to use their role wisely when they are. Girls need appropriate control and discipline as well as loving, and boys need lots of affection, especially in the early years when the issue of rivalry is prominent.

A Frail Reed To Lean On?

Young babies can mother their parents, says psychologist Marian Radke Yarrow, National Institute of Mental Health. Yarrow, who studies children aged 10 to 30 months, says, "Babies have amazingly generous impulses." They offer upset parents their bottles, favorite blankets, or toys, and spontaneously hug and reassure them. Young children simply aren't as self-centered as many psychologists have thought.[14]

Children imitate the significant behaviors they observe. When parents are sympathetic and comforting to hurt or unhappy children, their children learn to comfort as well as be comforted. But these findings raise another issue that more parents would do well to take to heart. That is, parents don't help their children by hiding all their stressful and unhappy feelings from them. Children need to see that adults get unhappy too—and get over it. Children need to give comfort and support as well as receive it. That's one important way that they learn to control what they can in their worlds, and live with what they can't control. It's a way of internalizing and acting on some of the most important attitudes they see their parents express. Your children won't fall apart if they hear you sound upset or see you cry. They'll know you have something in common, and they may be able to comfort you more than you'd ever guess.

Where's Mommy?

What happens to the rest of the family when one parent is hospitalized for mental illness? In most cases, nothing—in the way of help from mental health professionals. But help is needed. The absence of a parent or spouse is difficult enough under any circumstances. When the absence is due to a situation that is not well understood and bears many negative and frightening connotations, the stress can be great. And there's usually no way to predict how long the hospitalization will be.

The well parent needs to recognize that he or she *is* in considerable distress, and it is not a sign of emotional weakness or instability to need support. If it is not offered, the person should ask for it—from the hospital, and from friends and relatives. The children will be needing extra support, and it will be hard to give it if the parent is not getting much. What kind of support do the children need? Mainly they need information and reassurance, just as the parent does. Even if they don't ask, they are wondering: Where is mommy (or daddy)? When will she (he) come home?

Research sociologist John Clausen says children should be told as much as they can understand about what is happening. He advises against putting it in terms of physical illness, even as an analogy. "At the very least, children should be told that all the screaming and shouting and threats in the home before hospitalization were brought about by emotional upset. The children should be made to understand that they weren't responsible for it."[15] The people who stand the best chance of making them *believe* that they are not responsible are their parents.

Feels Like Square One

One of the most painful dilemmas of divorce for men is this: How do you abandon your kids and still convince them that you love them? In a study of divorcing families, Drs. Judith Wallerstein and Joan Kelly of U. Calif.-Berkeley found that men didn't visit their children as often as they said they would or wished they would for a variety of reasons. These ranged from depressions brought on by visiting the old house, to humiliation at the possibility of encountering the ex-wife's new lover, to fear of rejection by the children.[16] But it's unlikely that the children would be aware of any of this, or understand if it were explained to them. What they *do* know is that their father left them and didn't come back. Younger children may even conclude that mother, too, will disappear one day. Young children can also be worried about how daddy is being taken care of. If he's not here, where does he sleep? Where does he get his food? Children who visited their father in his new residence "took particular comfort in observing that the father had both a bed and a refrigerator."

Drs. Wallerstein and Kelly conclude that father-child relationships are subject to considerable change after a divorce, and that the crucial period is "immediately after the father has moved out of the household." Unfortunately, this is when everybody concerned is under great stress and feels least able to cope with such difficult emotional issues. Fathers may begin to realize how little they understand their own children as they try to reach them from outside the family structure.

But the hard work can't wait. If you hold off explaining these threatening and confusing events to your children, they will explain them to themselves—in ways that may frighten or damage them permanently. If you don't make your love and care tangible, you cannot expect them to assume or deduce it. Your explanations and demonstrations of affection must be understandable and honest. You must be willing to offer them over and over—the confusion and insecurity won't be dispelled by one big talk or one tender episode. And you must listen carefully to discern what your children really want to know. It may be very frustrating. But some fathers who made the effort found themselves closer to their children than when they lived together.

Parent Loss

Prolonged marital discord is harder on young children than the death of a parent. It has long been known that young children separated from one or both natural parents are predisposed to depression and attempted suicide in later life. But a more discriminating study by Thomas Crook and Allen Raskin, National Institute of Mental Health, shows that the manner of separation is far more important than the fact of it. "A childhood characterized by parental discord and the intentional separation of parent from child *is* associated with attempted suicide in adult life, while a childhood characterized by the loss of a parent through natural causes appears unrelated."[17]

A child is not yet mature enough to feel herself a wholly separate entity, so she will feel mixed up in whatever happens in her family. Also, the feeling of magical omnipotence that is a natural part of every childhood is still close to her. She is likely to reason that she ought to be able to resolve the situation. If she can't, she will conclude that she has therefore caused it. This leaves her with a residue of guilt that will underly all the normal experiences of failure in later life. A child whose parent dies may also feel as if she caused the event, but if the environment around her does not further stimulate and develop that notion, she has a much better chance of supplanting it with a more adult perception as she grows up.

Sex Talk—Still A Dirty Word?

Parents are still inhibited about discussing sex with their children, according to a study of 1,461 parents by a Harvard-based project. Why? Because attitudes have changed so much. Parents are confused about their own sexual roles and identities, and they don't know what to tell their kids. Many fathers, for instance, say they'd like their sons to feel free to cry— but the fathers themselves don't cry. And few parents who want their kids to be comfortable with their sexual feelings can discuss erotic behavior with them.[18]

Whether or not we talk openly about sex with our kids, we're still communicating. If we're confused or ashamed or embarrassed, they'll know it, and they'll feel uncomfortable, too. We help our children most by giving them the factual information they need, and letting them know we welcome their questions. Then if we don't know how to answer, it's best to say so. When parents and children can voice and explore their attitudes together, they can come to terms with their feelings. It's the same old story—it's always best to talk out powerful feelings.

A Day In The Life

Every day Mr. Banks went to work, "and while he was there he sat on a large chair in front of a large desk and made money. All day long he worked, cutting out pennies and shillings." You go to work every day. Do your children have as clear a picture of how you "make money" as Jane and Michael in P. L. Travers' *Mary Poppins?* A huge portion of parents' lives is often little more than a name to their children. This mystery may not trouble them, but it sets unnecessary limits on their understanding of their parents.

Perhaps children would not so readily come to regard their parents as givers and withholders of money if the earning of that money were not some invisible process. Working parents, especially fathers, might avoid potential second-string status if that missing part of their lives were real to the children. It wouldn't be so hard to let your kids in on it. Here are some things you can do:

1. Explain exactly what it is you do. Why is it useful? Who pays you and your company to do it? Who tells you what to do?
2. Take them to work from time to time if you can. And don't just show them the nifty machines and take them out to lunch. Let them see you doing your job.
3. Tell them what happens to you at work. Do they realize that your day is as full of events as theirs? That you have friends, write reports, meet new people, get yelled at?

This has nothing to do with preparing them for a career, or introducing them to the world of work. I'm talking about sharing lives. And about setting an example that will help your children share their lives with you in the difficult years when their peer culture pulls them away.

Which Costs Are You Counting?

If you've got money, give everything you can to your children, advise many. And you want to. But an affluent manager must count other costs. Children whose parents shower them with too many gifts prematurely tend to have special kinds of emotional problems. Parents naturally feel good about giving things to their children, and those who have worked themselves up often develop a strong wish to save their offspring from a similar struggle. But if they do, they often also save them from growing up. When children don't have the chance to demonstrate to themselves that they can master problems in life step by step, that they can move on their own from one signpost to another, they gather no sense of the movement of life, or of growth. For instance, if a young couple in graduate school is supported by their parents at a solid salary level, they have no motivation to get on with things, and they can experience no great thrill when they finally begin earning on their own. They have been denied certain emotional experiences that children of the less affluent can hardly avoid. It is the timing and the meaning of a gift in the child's development that matters ultimately, not its monetary value.[19]

Yet the idea of not giving children whatever they can afford raises guilt in many parents. Often, talking over what you are really doing for your children and considering whether you might be making them too dependent will counteract the irrational guilt.

Tell Them The Facts Of Life

John Gardner, former head of HEW and founding chairman of Common Cause, writes: "We are not very good at communicating to our children that life has always been hard and always will be."[20] Kids suffer when parents can't give this message. First, they expect to find gratification everywhere; second, they judge themselves harshly for failing to be perfect. We need to help our kids understand the phenomenon of the exaggerated ego ideal—how we set impossibly high goals for ourselves and then criticize ourselves harshly for failing to fulfill them. Children who understand this phenomenon can learn better to balance their expectations of themselves against the realities. This is an especially hard lesson for children. When they're very young they see their parents as perfect, and think that one day they'll be perfect, too. And even when that view fades, they're used to growing, maturing, and developing new skills quickly. Realizing that that process doesn't go on forever comes as a jolt.

When Boys Will Be Boys

It's still mostly a man's world, but schools discriminate against boys, says Diana McGuiness, U. Calif.-Santa Cruz. Schools reward skills in which girls tend to excel, she says. Among them are: reading, writing, abstract thinking, fine motor tasks. Boys, on the other hand, tend to excel in visual perception, construction, and gross motor tasks. The result? Boys are far likelier than girls to be labelled hyperactive, learning disabled, or dyslexic.[21]

If your son is cited as a learning or discipline problem, get all the facts before you assume he's at fault. He may have trouble sitting still but be a whiz at setting up experiments. He may be slower to read than your daughter, but quicker to figure out things for himself. Sometimes, for efficiency, schools pressure kids to conform to the needs of the group. But schools can also change to accommodate kids. Parents who help teachers assess their kids' strengths and weaknesses and find productive outlets for their particular energies do everyone a service.

It's important, of course, to treat boys and girls equally. But you can't treat people equally by treating them all the same. Whether because of biology or socialization or both, boys and girls do *tend* to be different. Boys are often active, impatient, messy, and energetic. Many of those traits are creative, and serve them well later in life. It doesn't help to ask active boys—or girls, for that matter—to bottle up their raw energy. They need to learn how to channel it and use it productively.

Learn Right By Wrong

Schools don't merely discriminate against *boys*, argues psychologist Margaret Donaldson, U. Edinburgh; they discriminate against *children*. Too much teaching is geared to the ways adults think, and teachers often fail children without trying to understand the reasoning that led to their mistakes.[22]

It's easy for adults to forget how differently children and adults perceive the world. Magical thinking is very real for children, as Selma Fraiberg beautifully illustrates in *The Magic Years*. Children replace magical with more logical and empirical thinking very gradually, she says, learning to think as we do only after much trial and error. In fact, she says, infants and children are like scientists, testing and sorting vast amounts of data.[23]

Of course scientists don't hit on the right answers immediately, and kids don't either. But both scientists and children—like the rest of us—learn from mistakes. Mistakes both correct our facts and teach us how to think. That's why parents and teachers need to reassure children that everyone makes mistakes—that mistakes are part of all creative thinking. Helpful parents and teachers know that much of the best thinking is rethinking, and they help children retrace their steps from error to insight.

Preparing Your Child For The Move

It's easy for parents who are working out the details and problems of relocation to forget that young children also have anxieties. A child's anxieties develop from a very different perspective than an adult's. If children haven't moved before, they won't know what will change and what will not—that they'll leave friends but not siblings behind, leave their rooms but take their possessions. If you're planning a move (or some other major change) you can help your children cope with the stress by doing the following:

1. Make time frequently to talk about various aspects of the change. Children can't assimilate a lot of information at one sitting; they need to go over the same information again and again. Make this discussion part of your daily routine.

2. Encourage children to ask questions and express their feelings. Young children may worry that their parents will no longer be with them, or that they'll lose a favorite pet or toy. Older children will worry about making new friends and taking up favorite activities in the new place. Don't assume you know what's on their minds, but encourage open-ended discussion that helps you learn where they need help.

3. Share your feelings about the move. Children need to know in terms they can understand why you expect the move to be good—and what you will miss. They need to be allowed to feel sad about the things they'll lose that you can't do anything about, while being reassured of your basic support and confidence.

Other things that often help are to find stories about children who move, and to encourage your kids to make up stories or draw pictures about going away to a new place. In these ways children anticipate and rehearse the experience, and master feelings that might otherwise throw them off balance.

Parent Burnout

Burnout can affect parents as well as managers. What does it look like? Joseph Procaccini, coauthor with Mark Kiefaber of *Parent Burnout*[24] describes it as "a state of physical, emotional and sometimes spiritual exhaustion" accompanied by "a failure to recognize one's limits" and by feelings of anger, guilt, depression, and self-doubt. All this results from a sense of having an enormous responsibility and being unable to meet the demands of being a good parent. The parents who burn out, according to Procaccini, are generally highly motivated, educated, middle-class, idealistic, and perfectionistic.[25]

If that sounds a lot like managers who burn out, it should. It's essentially the same phenomenon in a different area of life. Those who burn out have such high expectations of themselves (ego ideals) that it would take a superhuman being to meet them. Naturally they get frustrated, then angry, and finally give up.

Responsibility without control is one of the major causes of burnout, and the source of one of the major differences between manager burnout and parent burnout. Managers can conceivably have control over what they are responsible for, although they don't necessarily. But parents really can't have control over their children—or if they do, it's through the psychological devastation of the child. Thus parents who feel responsible for their children's actions (as if they were their own) are setting themselves up for burnout. Parents who have high expectations of themselves as parents and of their children need to recognize that they can't always do everything they think should be done, that they can't always do everything as perfectly as they would like to do it (nor can their children), and that disappointment is part of life. Parents can do a great service to their children by accepting their own limitations and thereby providing a model of self-acceptance.

Success In The Family Business

Should you bring your son into the business? My usual answer is: "No, unless . . . . "

Family businesses are the most difficult of all businesses to be in. A good part of the reason for this is that the rivalry between father and son continues unabated around a prize which the father usually has and the son wants—the company.

In the father's eyes the son will always be a child, less than adequate, and with less experience. However, if the son earns his own spurs elsewhere and in the process demonstrates his competence to himself, he brings his independent skills, his experiences, and his reputation for successful attainment if he returns to the family business. This creates a different relationship with his father and with others in the company. As a result, the son is likely to feel better about himself, and to carry himself with greater authority. Daughters don't have the rivalry problem, but the same issues of self-image hold.

Our Parents' Children

Though we become adults, we are always our parents' children. The effects of our early experiences continue throughout our lives. I've described many of the ways this affects our work lives; it affects our family lives, too—probably more so. And because we are always children to our parents, it is difficult to see them grow old and become increasingly helpless, as we once were with them.

From Generation To Generation

Couples who think they're ready for the divorce courts are often relieved to discover they're really mad at their parents. That's because many people unconsciously choose spouses who are "like the loved or unlike the hated parental figure," say psychiatrists Milton Berger of SUNY-Buffalo and Lynne Flexner Berger. When these people learn to separate marital conflicts from unresolved childhood conflicts, they see their spouses more realistically—and often more positively.[26]

They're right. Our parents have such a powerful impact on our early experiences and our personalities that we carry versions of them within us for the rest of our lives. We then superimpose these internalized parents on our spouses, managers, and others. We replay old, unconscious conflicts in new and often inappropriate situations. When we then can't control or rationally understand our feelings, we feel confused, ashamed, and helpless. In effect we become again the children who first faced those conflicts.

Anyone who experiences marital conflict (or conflict with a manager or other key figure) might ask how the present problem resembles past conflicts. Spouses can feel angry and betrayed when their partners resemble a hated aspect of a parent—or when they fail to live up to a similar but highly idealized parent. But conflicts are easier to manage when you can see past history replaying itself in the present. It's best to be struggling with only one person when you argue with your spouse.

Then You Can Forgive

Actor James Earl Jones, shortly after becoming a father himself, reflected on his relationship with his own father on the *Tom Cottle Show* on Boston TV. Jones was reared by his grandparents on the family farm in Mississippi, while his parents went after jobs in Northern cities. As an adult, Jones joined his father in New York, only to discover that they didn't feel comfortable with each other. Both were actors, and knew the difference between acting and real life too well to be satisfied with acting the parts of father and son, said Jones. Beginning with their common career interest, they learned to like each other. Eventually Jones was able to acknowledge the void he felt as a result of not having his father around while he was growing up. Then, he said, the healing process could start. "Once you accuse," said Jones, "then you can forgive." You may not have any specific accusations to make, he noted, but it is important to make them.

We all are disappointed by our parents, because no parent could possibly meet all the wishes of an infant for love and attention. Fathers are especially likely to be relatively uninvolved with their young children, because of work demands. As adults we may realize that our parents did what they thought was best for us, and we may even agree that they chose the best course of action, as Jones did with his father. That doesn't change the disappointment we felt as young children. Until we can acknowledge that disappointment, our anger remains and keeps us apart from our parents. Once we see our anger and disappointment as legitimate—make our accusations, as Jones puts it—then we are free to let the anger go, forgive our parents, and love them for what they *did* give us.

Be Open-Minded And Close The Generation Gap

Adolescents frequently complain that their parents don't understand them; in the same vein, elderly parents often lament that their middle-aged children don't understand them. Old people frequently feel walled off and shut out; they want to participate more fully in life than younger people are prepared to accept. If you sometimes find yourself baffled by or at odds with your aging parents, you might have a look at Ronald Blythe's *The View in Winter: Reflections on Old Age.* Many of the elderly people Blythe interviewed said they feel unloved and unlovable. They're also pained when younger people perceive them as unsexed or beyond sex—and see the sexual needs of the old as somehow ridiculous. As Blythe points out, homes for the aged are run in ways which reinforce this notion and thus deny their residents an important aspect of their lives.[27]

People with aging parents can best help them by supporting their efforts to be independent for as long as possible. If you don't understand your aging parents, and feel distressed by the changes you perceive in their behavior, first talk with them about how they feel and what they want. It's often a relief for older people to be given the opportunity to talk out their feelings about growing older and approaching death. People who can share that experience with their parents are immeasurably enriched. And it helps them face that stage of their own lives with increased understanding and acceptance.

In Summary

1. *It takes a concerted effort to maintain solid family relationships in the face of career demands. You need to make time for relaxed and open discussion of the things that matter to you, to your spouse, and to your children. This in itself is a source of mutual support, and it provides the context for increased support in hard times.*

2. *The main things children need from their parents are their attention and honest communication. Children are very good at picking up their parents' feelings, even the feelings that are supposedly hidden behind silence or evasions. An overt message that contradicts the covert message is more confusing than convincing.*

3. *The influence of parents continues into adult life, when feelings may be transferred to spouse, manager, and other associates. We need to separate current conflicts from past ones; settling old conflicts is sometimes possible and always useful in clearing the confusion.*

Manager As Citizen

Business always acts in the context of society, whether or not it actively takes into account its effect on society. And even when organizations try to act in the interest of society, doing good is not necessarily a simple task. Society is complex—at least as complex as the human beings who create it. We may try to feed starving populations, only to find the food cannot get there, or that people survive another year only to be faced with the same problem again. Careful diagnosis and planning, an understanding of human behavior and motivation, and evaluation of the results of our efforts are, once again, the keys to making the kind of difference you want to make.

A Long-Term Investment

Social responsibility of business is just a fad, claims J. Clayton LaForce, dean of UCLA's graduate school of management; businesses exist simply to make profits.[1]

This thinking is way out of touch with the times. Social responsibility isn't a crank idea imposed on businesses. It grows out of their power to affect their communities for good and bad. When organizations deny their social responsibilities, they can create powerful community hostility. That's what happened, for example, to a New York chemical company whose waste disposal had noxious consequences. The company denied the problems and showed little concern for the human suffering it had caused or precipitated. As a result, many people found themselves locked into an adversary role with the community's major employer.[2]

Because companies have the power to despoil the environment, shape the local economy, affect the health of the community, and in general make people dependent, they have social responsibility—whether they want to own up to it or not. People affected by a company have a stake in how it operates, and they know it. They distrust businesses that are quick to pull out the political stops to fight regulations or win tax breaks, but won't act to protect consumer or community interests. And no organization can afford to write off community trust—it's a long-term investment that may have inestimable worth. It wasn't until Chrysler's survival was threatened, for instance, that people inside and outside the company fully appreciated the company's and community's mutual ties and dependence. Organizations deny those ties at their own risk. And when they do, there's hell for everyone to pay.

You Get What You Ask For

Should a drug that's been found unsafe be taken off the market? The answer you get to that question depends on how you ask it. When J. Scott Armstrong, Wharton School, asked a group of management students what they would do if they were on the company's board, 79% said they would keep the drug on the market. But when he asked another group what they thought of keeping the drug on the market, 97% said it was socially irresponsible.[3]

People's actions say a lot about what they think is expected of them. When managers take a narrow view, putting their unit's or company's short-term advantages ahead of safety, social responsibility, or long-range consequences, they think they're being businesslike and responsible. They think that when they're at work, what they believe the company expects of them should come first, last, and always. But as Armstrong's example shows so dramatically, that just won't do.

If your subordinates are interpreting your assignments more narrowly than you'd like, take a look at the way you present situations to them. Do you emphasize company loyalty but not social responsibility? Do you speak as if someone's work role is divorced from the rest of his or her identity? Scan the horizon before jumping to decisions that could have unhappy repercussions.

The Effect Of Our Causes

Where do our political motivations come from? There are many psychological answers. Harold D. Lasswell, a Yale lawyer-psychologist, points out that we tend to project or attribute our own hidden motivations to causes and projects. Then we rationalize that cause as being in the public interest and need. Lasswell says we are concerned with power relationships in political activity. As a result, it becomes crucially important to separate legitimate *issues* from the *causes* they become in the self-serving interest of people who need causes.[4]

This is particularly important for managers because so many people go into organizations to serve such political-power needs and rationalize their decisions on the basis of organizational purpose and requirement. You must be clear about your own needs so you will not be corrupting the organization to serve those needs or allowing your subordinates to do so. It is important not to rationalize destructive behavior as being in the corporate interest.

Where Are The Leaders?

People feel helpless to deal with the complexity of social problems for many reasons. We can't trust our leaders the way we used to. The old ruling elite operated with a clear-cut value system, but now politicians pay more attention to what is expedient. Those wielding power can't be experts about everything. They are nominally in charge but heavily dependent on specialists and advisors as well as their constituents. Broad media coverage prevents ordinary citizens from remaining securely ignorant of major social and political problems, and we know so much about the interrelation of events that our problems seem almost too big to tackle. The traditional mechanism for controlling power—namely military force—doesn't work anymore, as Vietnam demonstrated. Nobody has answers. Since all the variables can't be controlled, we are increasingly compelled to interact with each other in the face of ambiguity and continuous compromise.

Many have responded by battening down the hatches—often more than the situation requires. In doing so, we tend to become prisoners, not of reality (though that can be frightening enough), but of the models we use to think about reality. If the current situation really is like a terrible storm that we can do nothing about, then holing up and waiting it out is appropriate. But if it's like a fire, quick action would be more suitable. And we know from the process of psychotherapy that no matter how impossible a problem seems, once a person begins to work on it, anxiety goes down and solutions take shape.

Businessmen can help prevent social panic by mobilizing people to start attacking problems on the local level. This doesn't need to be a do-gooder effort. Businessmen have access to certain kinds of power and resources. If they take hold imaginatively, often a whole community will respond. Consider what happened in Minneapolis. It has a lovely downtown area, a symphony, a ball team, a theater—all because local businessmen decided they cared, and made that town come alive. Likewise, businessmen can demand community action on zoning, education, crime, prisons, and environment. There should be as many models for handling each of these problems as there are communities. Each one should work out its own. Managers can provide the leadership for the necessary interaction, which is the new requirement of our era.

If Only They Knew

"We enjoy and welcome the changes which are technical in character," says George Odiorne, U. Mass.-Amherst; but we "dislike and resist formidably the changes which are basically social and cultural in character."[5] That's a broad generalization, but there's a lot of truth in it. Technical adaptations are easier to make and one can reap the rewards directly. Social changes—overcoming prejudice, for example—are neither simple to learn nor immediate in their effects. And they often challenge our unconscious feelings. The irony is that all important technical changes also bring social changes. They don't come packaged together, so one can embrace the technical change while resisting the social one. One might never even face the social consequences in one's lifetime. Yet in the long view of history, can there be any more radical social reformer than Henry Ford or Thomas Edison?

Antibusiness Sentiment

Bad feelings about big business are more pronounced at some times than others, but they are always there to be aroused. If you identify with your leadership and commit yourself to its purpose, the criticism of your organization feels like criticism of you. That's why you need to do what you can to foster ethical behavior and encourage the good citizenship of your organization. When people make accusations, you need to know what there is to defend.

Tell The Truth

How come nobody trusts businessmen these days? Some blame the press, always ready to stir up a storm about evil businessmen exploiting the public. That may be so, says management consultant David L. Hunsicker, but if it is, it's because businessmen have done such a poor job of dealing with the media. Because they fear the media, and generally have no experience dealing with them, businessmen have avoided explaining their behavior in public.[6] Naturally, when an accusation is made, and all that reporters—and thus the public—can get out of company executives is variations on "No comment," it looks suspicious. It's easy to see the big guy as the bad guy. That's not always fair, but it's a natural channel of thought, and companies ignore it at their own peril.

People and communities are dependent on business in many ways. Because businesses have more power than individuals, people fear betrayal, and hostile feelings are easily aroused. And there is plenty to fear and resent: plant shutdowns and layoffs; shoddy or even unsafe products; manipulative advertising and public relations; lobbying power used to the public's disadvantage; exploitation of certain areas, leaving such monuments as the slag heaps in West Virginia or the "buried treasure" in Love Canal. Many people are affected by these activities, and the public resents feeling powerless or being kept in the dark.

Hunsicker's advice: 1) have someone in your company who is prepared to speak to the public, and who has all the facts and can explain them to people who aren't in the business; 2) defend yourself openly and intelligibly when you're right, and admit openly and intelligibly when you're wrong.

From many years of coping with such problems before getting involved with business, I can confirm his points. The difference between honesty and a slick public relations campaign is one of attitude. Where dependency is created, a sense of obligation should be felt. Honest communication is the best means by which obligations can be turned into useful and mutually satisfactory actions.

Who's Afraid Of Big Bad Business?

People attribute malicious motives to business, even when business may not have such motives. One reason for this is the human tendency to project hostility outside oneself. Anybody who has an adolescent, or who has been in a position of authority, has experienced projection. People who judge themselves harshly expect that the outside world judges them in the same way, whether or not it actually does. And they react to individuals and organizations as if they were indeed judgmental and threatening. So of course they are concerned about anything that's bigger than they are (like big business) and has the potential to do them harm. When the fears are reinforced, as they sometimes are, by actions that legitimately can be criticized, the reactions become that much stronger. In dealing with both subordinates and the public, managers must take projection into account.

Price Isn't Everything

When Mercedes came out with its model 450, Jaguar matched it with the XK12. *Road and Track* evaluated both cars and indicated that the Jaguar, for half the price, had essentially the same qualities as the Mercedes.[7] Why didn't Jaguar clean up? Because customers couldn't get parts and service as easily. The XK12, like many other beautifully advertised products, failed to overtake the 450 for lack of backup.

When you sell a product, you are usually selling a whole function. When that function can't be maintained, an implicit psychological contract with the customer is violated. Failure to recognize this is exactly what precipitated the consumer movement. Now such matters are becoming legal issues. Railing about the evils of governmental controls makes sense only if companies simultaneously begin to assume some responsibility for backup.

Shady Practices Flourish

If white-collar crime continues to be steadfastly ignored, the problem could get worse, said Prof. Donald F. Morgenson, Wilfrid Laurier U., Ontario, in 1975. It did. He saw three forces contributing to a shady climate:

1. Greater complexity of organizational structure and policies leaves individuals more isolated. Therefore increasing numbers of people know that their misdeeds won't be noticed.
2. Job dissatisfaction rises as promotions are longer in coming and more people have to take second- or third-choice jobs. A disgruntled employee is a potential embezzler.
3. The "rip off" mentality thrives when companies seem big and powerful, while families feel at the mercy of the economy. "This is chicken feed to them," the saying goes. Others carry their rationalizations further and pretend to themselves that "It's only borrowing," or more commonly, "It's common practice."

Morgenson urged companies to clear the air by calling every form of stealing by its proper name. In addition, he advised closer employer-employee relationships as a way of reducing avenues of temptation.[8]

Companies that raise a righteous cry about employee dishonesty without examining how their own actions look to employees could well fall flat on their faces. It's true that many companies are caught up in the process of fighting against or lobbying for various controls or regulations. But employees have a right to question the company that spends its money on court suits instead of attacking the problem that the suit concerns (for example, pollution), or the one that stalls in complying with some regulation because a good legal staff can find loopholes in its wording. Only if a company can demonstrate that it honors the spirit of the law, as well as the letter, will it have the integrity to allow it to expect the same of its employees.

Leadership And Ethics

Many organizations don't specify a code of ethics under which they operate. Sometimes they have unwritten or incomplete codes that contain many exceptions. If people are to know what is expected of them, the organization must specify its code of conduct in writing, offering examples in the gray areas. Managers should explain the ethical position of the company to their subordinates, and tell them how they can get answers when they have questions.

If a code of ethics is to have meaning, it must apply equally at all levels. It must be very clear that high-level people who violate it will be penalized severely and appropriately; otherwise the message is that only low-level people will be sacrificed, and one really doesn't have to pay any attention to these things anyway. When the leadership is not ethical, its voice becomes one of hypocrisy, and the effect on the organization is demoralizing. Employees may begin to feel they have a right to do whatever they can get away with, in their dealings with both customers and their own organization. Under these circumstances, cynical skepticism and manipulation can eventually become an organizational way of life.

The Power To Do Good

"The defense of the great corporations rarely, if ever, is that it uses its power to good purposes," observes John Kenneth Galbraith. "It is always that it has no power."[9] But everyone knows that corporations have power. That's why it's important to demonstrate how they do good.

Engaging Women And Minorities

Many people have struggled long and hard with the issues of equal opportunity and affirmative action. We still have a long way to go. It's hard to know what's fair, especially if you feel you have something to lose when someone else gains. As with any long-standing conflict, past injuries keep coming back to haunt us—until we find a way to put them to rest. When people grow and change as a result of new experiences, it's hard for others

*to see, let alone accept, those changes. Progress is being made. We just
have to make sure that we can still say that, ten, twenty, thirty years
down the line.*

Grab Opportunities To Promote Integration

Pressures for providing equal opportunity weigh heavily on many organizations, but some are neglecting their best avenues for compliance. Any time a whole group of people has to learn new skills from scratch, management has an opportunity to promote the integration process.

At a General Foods plant in Topeka, Kan., for example, management abdicated in such a situation. A new plant opened in which workers were trained for every position. They let each newly trained foreman select his own team. Well, no blue-collar white man in that community would be likely to select a black, an Indian, or a Mexican for his team. So none did, and all minority workers ended up on one team, feeling greatly rejected.

As an alternative model, consider the experience of a bilingual German-English school in Ohio, started by Dr. Guy Stern, U. Cincinnati. He found that "youngsters from white middle-class and black disadvantaged homes, when exposed to the new experience of German, performed equally well, regardless of the gap in their regular educational achievements. The logical assumption was that educational differences faded when both groups started from the same level of ignorance without built-in cultural advantages or handicaps."[10]

If you need to open a new plant somewhere, or to install a wholly new technology, use the situation to mix in minority groups. Even at first-level supervision, where none has been a supervisor before, there is such an opportunity.

Tell Them What The Score Is

In an effort to comply with orders to upgrade women and minority group members, management hires a young black woman in a management trainee role. The managerial group applauds itself thinking, "We're on our way." It may well be kidding itself, because the trainee's perception of her role may be quite different from theirs.

Managers often assume that people who are hired in a management trainee role know it and see what's ahead for them. The trainee, from her side of the fence, assumes she's in the secretarial pool. She notes that there are no women in managerial roles; that the men are intensely competitive and aggressive; that the odds of a woman moving into such circles are powerfully against her.

She also observes that the men are highly motivated to achieve and are compensated for their achievements. These same men put pressures on the women who happen to be the secretaries and complain if the women don't stay overtime or respond to organizational pressures the same way the men do. She observes further that the women aren't being paid to have the same degree of commitment to their work as the men are.

This young black woman, never having been told that she is a candidate for a managerial role, given no formal program to guide herself by, offered no coaching or other help, and keenly observing what happens in the office, can only be looking toward moving out of the organization when her education is completed. It takes more to develop women and minority group members for managerial roles than merely a gleam in some manager's eye. His thoughts are unavailable to them, until he tells them what they are being trained for. In the meantime, the only thing they can do is observe the organization's behavior, and plan accordingly.

Gaining Ground?

Women are gaining ground in the legal profession—one of the traditional bases for moving into business and management roles, as well as a traditionally male-dominated field itself. *U.S. News & World Report* offered the following statistics in 1980: 13% of all lawyers were women, up from 3% in 1971; approximately one-third of America's 125,397 law students were women, whereas men outnumbered women 23 to 1 in 1966; the number of women practicing law jumped from 28,000 to 70,000 between 1975 and 1980; and the number of federal judges who were women jumped from 5 to 44 in five years. And of course, one woman on the Supreme Court makes 11% of that elite group female.

One last statistic bodes less well for women: the number of men applying to law schools had dropped by more than 16% since 1975. The statistic to watch now is the average income of lawyers. If the usual pattern holds, the profession as a whole will become less well paid as the proportion of women in it grows. And if that does happen (as of course I hope it doesn't), it will be a strong indication that women are being accepted into the profession—but not as equals.

Undercurrents In The Mainstream

White psychiatrists who treat black patients need special preparation, says Dr. Walter H. Bradshaw, Jr. of Howard U. His advice is equally relevant to mainstream managers working with minority group members:
1. Continuously examine your own feelings, looking for irrational responses to unfamiliar attitudes or behaviors.
2. Learn as much as possible about the minority groups' cultural backgrounds and sense of normality.

3. Acknowledge the pressure minority people feel, and empathize with the racism they encounter.
4. Recognize the aggressions you and the minority people feel, and accept the fact that they won't entirely disappear.
5. Control your fears and aggressions to mitigate your own racially influenced attitudes.[11]

It's true that the cultural attitudes and expectations of minorities and of those in the mainstream are often very different. It's best for all concerned to acknowledge that fact and bring the differences out in the open. But in business organizations this process is best conducted with the help of a highly trained professional. It doesn't help—and it can hurt—to let people pour out a stream of bad feelings and resentments. People need help understanding the source of their hostilities and fears; they need help listening to what others are saying—and why. A skilled professional can keep frank discussions from turning into no-holds-barred free-for-alls.

Organizations cannot simply ask minorities and women to shed their old attitudes and ways of behaving and adopt those of the majority. These newcomers will adopt some of their organizations' ways—they must. But they'll also change the organizations they enter. Mutual change is truly effective change. That's why managers must understand where minority group members are coming from before they can help them and their organizations get anywhere.

But How Do The Romans Do?

An American manager failed to negotiate a simple matter in the Near East because he didn't understand how many cups of coffee it took to establish trust. That calls to mind the fact that cross-cultural issues are becoming more important for managers for two reasons. One is the trend toward setting up manufacturing operations in third world countries, to take advantage of the low cost of labor. The other is the growing number of managers who are not white middle-class males, as a result of EEO and affirmative action. In the first instance, two things can happen: 1) American managers can go to other countries and learn to work with people of another culture, but this is increasingly resisted by other countries; or 2) foreign operations can be run by local people, who must learn to work with American business culture. The second situation is similar, though more extreme, to the situation with American minority group members moving into the business culture.

In all cases, the manager from the minority culture must learn enough about the majority culture to work comfortably with its members. It is to the organization's advantage to facilitate this process, as it will make the operation more efficient. This can be done by developing ways of orienting members of its culture to the foreign cultures where they will be in the minority, and by developing ways of orienting managers from foreign countries and from American minority cultures to the organization's culture. The manager coming into a majority culture is outnumbered, and that can cause fear and defensiveness. Knowledge goes a long way toward reducing those reactions. The manager needs to know: What is the language? How do people talk to each other? How does one address a superior, a peer, a subordinate? Are there other customs about the quality of those relationships, the closeness or distance expected? What is a manager expected to take responsibility for, and what is he expected to refer to his manager or leave to subordinates? How does one dress? What kinds of gifts are acceptable? What sort of behavior, demeanor, or style will offend, and what will be acceptable? How much flexibility is there in this culture? How much difference from the norm will be tolerated?

The manager who doesn't know these things may inadvertently cause costly communication failures. The manager who is busy trying to figure them out on her own has that much less time and energy for the work she was hired to do.

Some issues must be settled on a personal level. The manager who is in the minority must strike a balance between adopting an alien culture and remaining true to herself. This will depend on how important it is to the individual to feel accepted and included, and what meaning the person attaches to the observance of customs and the maintenance of traditions. And both of these will be influenced by the expected duration of the person's stay in the culture.

The organization that doesn't somehow foster cross-cultural understanding displays an implicit disrespect for other cultures, and its managers can be expected to act accordingly. But undoubtedly the first rule of comfortable cross-cultural relationships—as with all human relationships—is mutual respect.

The Readiness Is All

The apparent lack of feminist consciousness in the young women recently graduated from college concerned Susan Bolotin, an avowed feminist, enough to investigate the situation. Her conclusions were that younger women believe in many of the same ideals that "feminists" fought for and made at least some progress toward gaining; these younger women "just call their beliefs *moderate,* while 10 years ago we knew they were radical," says Bolotin. But she faults these women for being "unwilling to act. . . . How can legislative backsliding be prevented, let alone further advances toward equality be made, if women become lazy about naming the inequalities around them?"[12]

I doubt that laziness or unwillingness to act is the real issue. Labeling a set of beliefs with an "ism," thus making it a cause, attracts fiery adherents—people who want to fight for something. There are generally overtones of anger, hostility, and a certain amount of self-righteousness. That intensity puts a lot of people off—especially those who come late, those who are already reaping the benefits of change. As one young woman put it to Bolotin, "The revolution wasn't ours.... I wish that I had a revolution to go to, a cause to believe in. My life has been lacking in the kind of upheaval that allowed women to become feminists." One might say young women have been co-opted; feminists gained enough of what they wanted to take the edge off the next generation's anger. But the fact is, attitudes *have* changed. And when these younger women (or the women ten years after them) come up against the limits of what has changed, *then* a new push will begin. Whether that push has the revolutionary quality of the '60s and '70s will depend on whether the next push encounters enough resistance to create outrage like the outrage of today's feminists.

Social change always comes in waves. Quiet periods between times of turmoil don't mean the problem has gone away—only that people are catching up with the change that has taken place. When women—or any other group that has fought for change—are ready, they will push again, and if necessary they will join together and fight again.

If those who manage organizations are wise, they too will be catching up with the change that has taken place. They will be anticipating the next wave of feminism. And the next big push in organizations will come at the upper-middle-management and officer levels, when women who are now entering lower-middle-management ranks are ready to move on. If organizations anticipate the readiness of these women to move on, the next wave of progress for women in business will be able to take place with considerably less heat and acrimony. We can hardly expect such an enlightened and civilized turn of events, but it sounds as if it would suit the young women Bolotin interviewed just fine.

Aim For Fairness

Have you ever wondered why, try as hard as you can to be fair, someone is always feeling hurt or cheated? Every manager knows this frustration; so does every parent. What is the problem? In large part it's that our conception of equality is based on two inherently contradictory ideals. That is, if you set up impersonal competition, you wind up promoting inequalities; but if you try to compensate for people's differences, you wind up treating them unequally in order to make them more equal.

This contradiction is at the heart of people's frustration with equal opportunity, explains Yale political scientist Douglas Rae. In a long, carefully reasoned, and eminently readable piece, Rae unravels the logical and philosophical underpinnings of the American ideal of equality. It may be logically pure to treat everyone equally by treating them all the same, but in practice that's like issuing every Army recruit the same size boot, Rae explains. If opportunities are equalized over the average for a group of people, some will fare better than others. And the very act of isolating a group for fair treatment can slight those outside the group. But if we decide fairness on a case-by-case basis, we become inundated, and inevitably treat some more fairly than others.[13]

So what's a manager to do? You can avoid some headaches and grief if you follow these guidelines:

1. Define your goals and establish the limits of your authority. You can't satisfy everyone equally, or provide truly equal opportunities for people with diverse abilities, preferences, and personalities. So don't try. Set reasonable goals that you can explain clearly and defend rationally.

2. Allow yourself to be flexible. Subordinates are more likely to feel treated fairly when their managers don't narrowly follow the letter of the law. It can be the ultimate fairness to take personal needs into account. Simple consistency for its own sake does not promote equality or fair-mindedness.

3. Don't expect miracles. Life isn't fair. People aren't equal in their abilities. You can't change these facts, and you shouldn't feel vulnerable to criticism that you ought to. Managers who learn to cope with their guilt don't necessarily treat their people more fairly, but they often seem to, simply because they're more assured. And subordinates feel more comfortable with managers who take a realistic attitude than with those who agonize endlessly over the splitting of a hair.

ADDENDUM: Men And Women In Management*

The day will come when there are no more women managers. Sure, there will be women managing. But they will be managers, not "women managers." The sooner that day comes, the better. The interim is uncomfortable for everyone.

Much has been written to help women managers adapt to their new surroundings. Not so much has been said about how men can be more comfortable with their new coworkers. To some the need is apparent; others already have considerable support and guidance from their organizations. To still others, it's just something they read about. With surprising frequency, women attending executive seminars hear that they are the first professional women some of the male participants have

---

*This *Addendum* was coauthored by Janet E. Robinson.

encountered. For those men, it's easy to deny the need even to think about whether they are comfortable with women managers. But any man who wants to get ahead must recognize the growing need to be comfortable with women as business associates.

Are You My Mother?

Why the discomfort? Women aren't recently arrived from Mars! Actually, familiarity is much of the problem. We fill in the missing details about new acquaintances with bits of our own experience. Unfortunately, men tend to color their picture of a woman manager with details from their experience with other women, not other managers.

From birth on, men have associated with women—as mothers, teachers, sisters, wives, friends, secretaries, coworkers. Some of those women were in business, but most of them were not. So when men try to make women managers fit their previous experience, the results can be strange. Many of the women they have known were not their equals, so they may try to reduce a woman manager to fit. Or they may, by transference, cast her in an idealized or nurturing role. If a man unconsciously casts a woman colleague as his sister or mother, he may then try to sustain the role he played in the original relationship: obedient son to a dominating mother, or bad boy to a mother whose authority he flouted; leader, protector, or persecutor to a younger sister; follower, fierce competitor, tease, or confiding little one to an older sister.

One woman, for example, reported that a male coworker refused to provide information she needed to do her job. Their manager repeatedly instructed the man to give it to her, but she had to go through that routine every time. She tried various approaches—friendly, assertive, formal—but he always reacted the same way. It sounds a lot like a big brother holding his sister's teddy bear just out of reach.

Each relationship takes its own form. Whatever the individual case, it is this not-so-conscious stance that so often gets in the way of business relationships between men and women. So this screening imagery must be dealt with first. We have said the same about situations where a man's relationship with his father gets in the way of his relationship with authority. But here the effect is magnified for a number of reasons.

First, most men have fewer relationships with women than with men throughout their lives. This gives them a smaller range of experience to draw on when filling in unknowns about women. So they are more likely to fall back on stereotypes.

Second, narrower experience with female authority figures means less opportunity to work out ways of behaving toward women in authority. Most of the opportunities men do have come relatively early in life— mother, primary school teachers, Cub Scout den mothers. At that age they have less control over their situation, and the authority is also a caretaker. When they become adults, an authoritative woman may remind them unconsciously of the helpless dependence of childhood. Feeling echoes of that uncomfortable state, on some level they may fear a return to it. Also, they unconsciously may want or expect to be taken care of by women and may be angered by women who don't fulfill that expectation. The conflict between the fear of dependence and the desire to be taken care of is a difficult one. One way to ease it is to recognize that interdependence—the give *and take* of support—is a human trait.

Third, women managers are few in number, so most men have limited experience with them. The more contact men have with businesswomen, the more they can check their unconscious attitudes against reality. Unfortunately, those same attitudes help limit the numbers of women in management. And there is a tendency, as the numbers increase, for women to be concentrated in certain departments which men begin to shun, according to Anne Harlan and Carol Weiss, Wellesley College Center for Research on Women.[14]

Finally, women managers are often in new situations. With few models to follow, especially at higher levels, they are often improvising new behaviors. Some women have been moved ahead faster than is customary, in order to increase their representation at higher levels. All this may leave them less sure of themselves, and inclined to take their cues from the men around them. It's harder to present a solid, consistent image for men to check their unconscious attitudes and expectations against.

What Do You Say?
How can you compensate for your lopsided experience of women? Take every opportunity to balance it. Talk with women managers in your own and other organizations, at conferences, in civic groups, on advisory boards, anywhere you can.

Unfortunately, this is exactly where the trouble begins. Men have conventional ways of talking to men in business settings, but their routines for women have been largely social. We tend to fall back on routines or rituals when we are uncomfortable. So when businessmen are uncomfortable with businesswomen, the social rituals come out full force. The problem is, rituals that start with opening doors and lighting cigarettes are based on "the chivalric ideal that a man protects a woman, who is his inferior in strength or power," as Kahleel Jamison has pointed out.[15] And a person who will only give, never take, creates insupportable obligations in others. So the effect of outdated social ritual on both parties is to "call up the condition of inequality." This leads to confusion and makes it difficult to carry on as equals.

As Jamison notes, the man usually initiates the social context. Women are well aware that objecting to social conventions will label them "women's libbers": too aggressive or fanatic. So it is incumbent upon the man not to employ such conventions, but to stick as closely as possible to the business rituals he would use with a man. If you wonder whether what you're about to say or do is appropriate, ask yourself, "Would I do the same if this were a man?" If the answer is no, rephrase—or refrain.

Managerial experiences and concerns are your most likely common ground with a woman manager; they are also what you really need to hear from her. Check it out! It may feel funny at first to open a conversation with something you sort of expect will draw a blank. But when the woman responds as if your question were the most normal thing in the world, you'll know you're on the right track. And a few such experiences will take the strangeness out of it. As you talk with women managers you will probably discover, as researchers have, that women who manage come in more or less the same variety of personalities as men. As I pointed out in *Executive Stress*, [16] women work for the same reasons and get the same satisfactions from it as men do.

You may be inclined to ask a woman manager whether she is married or has children, and how she handles the combined responsibilities of work and family, especially if you are in a dual-career situation. While that's a legitimate area of discussion, it slides right over the managerial aspect of the woman and focuses on the traditional wife-and-mother role. This topic becomes appropriate at the same point in the conversation where you would bring it up with a man.

Find The Zebra
Your interactions with women managers will be smoother if you can uncover the assumptions that color your perceptions. That means looking at your behavior toward women colleagues and the feelings it reflects; looking at the assumptions about women reflected in your behavior and feelings; and checking with businesswomen whether those assumptions are valid sometimes, often, or never.

Looking objectively at one's own behavior is never easy, and assumptions are almost by definition invisible to the one making them. Here are some to watch for:

1. Are you treating your woman subordinate as if she were your daughter or wife? When one woman presented her male manager with the $600,000 budget she had put together, he responded, "My wife can't even balance a checkbook." He may have meant it as a compliment, but the comparison is totally inappropriate. His wife undoubtedly wouldn't hold that job, either.
2. Do you automatically put your woman subordinate in a support role, without considering her need to have clout? It's easy to assume women want and will do best in traditional nurturing roles. But without an authoritative political position, the woman will be unable to get things done for her subordinates. She won't be seen as

an effective leader, and without that background, she will be ineligible for higher level jobs.

3. Are you unnecessarily rivalrous with women colleagues? If the first child in your family was a girl, you probably had to compete with her for your parents' attention and affection. It would be wise to recognize that and try not to carry that overintense rivalry into situations where you must compete with a woman.

4. Do you bend over backward to please your female manager (or subordinate!), as you had to please your mother or female teachers? Perhaps you fail to take an adequate stand, for fear of displeasing. Or you may feel that somehow your hands are tied. If you recognize this as a feature of your behavior, try to be less obsequious.

In your attempts to understand your own behavior, you may find it useful to recall particular situations or typical contexts, and write down everything you remember. Who said what? Who did what? Then review what you have written. What attitudes do the words and actions imply? Why did they have the impact they had? Would different ones have had better results?

As Others See Us

You might review such incidents with a woman friend or colleague, or with your wife, to get the perspective of a woman and an outsider on the behavior of both parties. If possible, establish an ongoing relationship, so both parties get feedback on a regular basis. It's important to specify the dimensions and boundaries of such a relationship, so each knows what information the other is ready to hear and what is too difficult at present. It may take a while to reach a level of trust where each of you can say what you really mean. Many women managers are reluctant to say anything directly to a male coworker or manager for fear that it will be taken amiss, after which they will be avoided or their performance appraisals will suffer. Defining the relationship gives the woman permission to speak without that fear. Men also need permission to ask what a woman wants or feels, or to comment on a typical behavior, without worrying about getting their heads snapped off.

Those who are ready to try such an arrangement with a coworker might set up a psychological contract, including the following features:

1. Start with a mutual feedback agreement, as outlined above. Each will keep an eye out for the unwitting use of sex role stereotypes by the other.

2. You might agree to tell each other what the changing of sex roles feels like to you. Women don't know how men feel any more than men know how women feel. Amy Hanan, retired personnel director from AT&T General Offices and an associate of The Levinson Institute, reports that in AT&T's male-female awareness seminars, women

were surprised to hear men's pain. Things were harder for men than they realized.

3. The woman might agree to describe her past experience with male managers—what problems she has had with overprotection, exploitation, lack of recognition of her abilities, sexual harassment or attractions. What would she like to do in her present role to help counteract or compensate for those experiences? What might the man do to help make those things possible?

4. The man might be able to tell the woman how others in the organization have responded in the past to women working closely with men, so she will know what she is up against. Will there be talk if they go to lunch together too often? What would constitute "too often"? What style of dress and manners will be seen as a come-on within your organization? What style will enhance her professional image? Both parties could solicit others' perceptions and share them. And it would make sense to discuss how each would like to handle situations where there might be hints of an extraprofessional relationship.

Such a contract must respect the feelings of both parties. Dealing with these matters in advance in a simple, straightforward way can save a lot of energy that would otherwise be wasted on worry, circumvention, and patching up.

Another important, and less risky, source of feedback is exit interviews. Ask the departing woman what attitudes you conveyed in your supervision of her. Did any particular behaviors of yours make your work relationship unnecessarily difficult? Can she suggest any specific ways to improve your working relationships with women?

Feedback We've Heard

For those who aren't ready to ask for direct feedback, or who don't have much regular contact with women managers, some commonly observed behaviors and commonly experienced attitudes are presented below. These comments come from many sources, including women in a major corporation which has made a concerted attempt to treat women equally and to help men and women adapt to this change.

Men tend to be aware of protective and paternalistic attitudes without seeing them as a problem.[17] But women note that they are not offered springboard assignments or positions which require travel or greater time commitments, especially if they have children, and more so if they are single parents. In effect, the manager decides for the woman that she should not take the assignment. Taking that decision away says that she is somehow not up to making it herself; she is not quite an adult. Even if it feels like a formality, make the offer and let the woman decide.

A similar attitude is reflected in the assumption that a married woman must ask her husband's permission to travel. Such an assumption implies that: 1) the husband has the final say about the woman's actions—that is, she is not fully an adult; and 2) the woman has not had the foresight to arrange with her husband for both of them to meet the demands of their jobs. If a woman needs time to make a decision, the reason is her business. If there isn't time, that's her problem, just as it would be for a man.

Another reason for not offering an assignment to a woman is doubt that she really can do the same kind of thinking and managing as a man. Women report that men are surprised to hear them speak knowledgeably. Some women find that they cannot simply speak authoritatively on the basis of their knowledge, but must build explanations of their reasoning into their presentations. It's as though proof of their expertise and logical faculty were necessary. And research indicates that women must be overqualified to be seen as capable of handling a nontraditional job.[18] In fact, the women who have surmounted all the barriers thrown in their way are likely to be the brightest and most achievement-oriented. That makes it generally safe to accept the validity of a woman manager's expertise.

Accepting a woman's expertise is not always easy. Women sense that some men dislike asking questions of a woman if they know she knows the answer. Sometimes men ask for information indirectly, leaving the woman to figure out what the man wants. When a woman volunteers information for which a man feels he cannot ask, often he has an emotional reaction—a sudden sadness. Apparently, both receiving and requesting information from an authoritative woman can lower the self-image of some men. A man who recognizes this reaction in himself might consider: What do I feel I am losing when I ask for this information, or when it is offered? If the loss can be identified, it can be mourned and let go. And perhaps there is a way to compensate for it.

Women still feel that they have to do twice as well as men to be accepted, and that they are often given double the amount of work a man is expected to do. The message they hear is, "Let's see you fail." If you see yourself doing this, consider what you have to gain by the woman's failure, or what you have to lose by her success. Is it this person's success or failure that matters, or does she stand for someone else, perhaps your wife? Does she represent an idea or phenomenon, such as the women's movement? If she does represent something or someone else, your efforts will be more usefully invested in discovering what you have to gain or lose in *that* situation.

Show Me Anyway

We have trouble seeing our own behavior clearly because on some level we don't really want to see it. We go to great lengths to keep ourselves unaware of ways in which we are too far from our ego ideals. When we ask for feedback, we are saying, "Show me anyway." That's why feedback often hurts. That's why we can't always hear feedback, even when we request it. But we all face blows to our self-images from the time we are very young. Learning to live with our less-than-ideal selves is just part of growing up.

When we say to another person, "I'm uncomfortable," we make ourselves vulnerable. We place ourselves in double jeopardy when we say, "I'm uncomfortable because you are here." In the face of our cultural myth that men are strong and fearless, that kind of vulnerability doesn't come easily. It requires a different kind of courage than has generally been expected of men. But finding that courage will allow men to be themselves in a way that has not been possible before. As clinical psychologist Joseph Pleck points out, "The conventional expectations of what it means to be a man are difficult to live up to for all but a lucky few and lead to unnecessary self-deprecation in the rest when they do not measure up. Even for those who do, there is a price: they may be forced, for example, to inhibit the expression of many emotions."[19]

Traditionally, men have hidden their fears and tried to appear invulnerable. This is usually done by freezing up, taking a rigid posture, creating a hard outer shell surrounding the unacceptable feelings. Unfortunately that shell keeps others out at least as much as it keeps the "weakness" (humanity) hidden. Those who do not want to isolate themselves must take a more realistic look at their own feelings and at the capabilities of women. In the process, they will be living up to our cultural ideals of justice and equality, and helping to create a world in which their daughters will have as much opportunity to work toward their ego ideals as their sons.

It is distressing to see businesswomen beginning to adopt this hard shell and other features of male behavior. Women managers say they are not likely to ask their managers for help managing a man, for fear of being seen as inadequate. Some are as unemotional and cold-bloodedly competitive as any man, more than compensating for any expected emotionality and passivity. They may be simply adopting the style of their male coworkers. They may be living up to the perceived ideals of higher level male managers. Or they may be overreacting to the "let's see you fail" message. Such behavior isn't doing them, their colleagues (male and female), or their organizations any good. "Negative consequences of the traditional male role for men's physical and mental health have been documented. . . . Women . . . are likely to suffer no fewer negative consequences. Furthermore, the efficacy of the traditional male model for

optimal organizational functioning has itself been questioned. Characteristics associated with traditional female sex roles, such as an emphasis on people as opposed to production, might actually produce better
outcomes in certain work situations."[20]

Women have much to offer organizations without mimicking men. The
more women can be comfortable with their nurturing roles as well as their
leadership roles, the easier it will be for men to accept them in both roles,
suggests Dr. Leocadia Burke, an associate of The Levinson Institute. And
the more men are willing to see both leadership and nurturing roles as
appropriate for women, the easier it will be for women to be comfortable
in those roles.

Helping Those Who Help Themselves
Women generally prefer to stand up for themselves, but they can't always
do that without being seen as overly aggressive or "women's libbers."
Men who are ready to support women as equals can do so in a variety
of ways.

In some hotels and restaurants, a woman still finds her male subordinate being handed the bill. She finds it hard to intrude on the assumption that he is the superior, but he can easily turn the bill over to her
or indicate that she will pay.

In the situation where the male coworker withheld information the
woman needed to do her job, their manager is a key figure. The charade
could not continue without permission from above. The manager could
support the woman by making it clear to her coworker that he was not
fulfilling his duties. The manager might talk to the man about why he
was not cooperating, while making clear the consequences of failing to
do so.

Women find moving difficult. Establishing ties and an information network is hard enough the first time, but it doesn't get much easier if you're
a novelty in each new department. When sending a woman subordinate
to a new location, try to provide her with introductions and information.
When a woman comes to your part of the organization from another, make
an effort to introduce yourself and others, and help her learn her way
around. Women find they are not as readily asked to lunch or included
in informal gatherings as men. If it's too risky to ask her by yourself,
get a colleague to join you—when you ask, as well as when you go, if
that makes it easier. When people feel isolated, they get defensive; then
they are more inclined to misinterpret remarks or actions, and you get
into a spiral of deteriorating relations.

There is no need to single out a woman in a group *as a woman,* and
usually she will prefer that you don't. Presumably she is there because
she has the proper credentials. Singling her out tends to call that assumption into question. Rather than increase acceptance of her, it sets her

apart. If you feel a need to apologize to her for your language, resist doing so. If your language is inappropriate, you owe an apology to the whole group. If not, she's probably heard it before, and possibly uses it.

Higher level managers who are serious about easing the acceptance of women managers can do so by authorizing and encouraging the formation of support groups where people can share feelings and information about men and women working together. And they themselves can participate. The composition of groups should vary. There are times for the security of a single-gender group, and there are times to check out the experiences and reactions of members of the other gender.

Top management can encourage the acceptance of women and their movement through the hierarchy by recognizing managers who train and promote women, and by making promotion difficult for those who neglect to do so.

Executives who hire women "get teased about it on the sly by their peers," says an article in the *Wall Street Journal.*[21] It's hardly called for—the man hired a manager, not a mistress. But somehow that connection gets made, and people have to make jokes to relieve the tension the fantasy creates. If you're subject to such teasing, take it for what it is—the other man's way of dealing with his anxiety. If you feel like teasing, restrain yourself. And ask yourself where the impulse comes from, and what else you could do instead.

The Difference That Makes A Difference
Sexuality is central to the level of comfort between men and women working together. One woman, a senior executive in a consumer industry, said, "Successful women are supposed to be neuter, and if a woman is clearly female, that presents a problem."[22] Whether or not it's true, it's plausible. But just imagine a male executive saying, "Successful men are supposed to be neuter, and if a man is clearly male, that presents a problem."

One thing that happens as women take on traditionally male roles is that boundaries are broken. The distinctions of "men's work" and "women's work" arose from a need people felt for segregation, along with the practical reasons. The reasons have become outdated and the boundaries artificial, so those boundaries needed to be broken. But the sexual drive still needs to be controlled. Clear boundaries within ourselves and between ourselves and our associates of the other sex are needed to replace segregated work roles.

The "sexual revolution" notwithstanding, sex and sexuality are difficult topics. But the feelings are real. Sidestepping them, denying them, hoping they'll go away if we ignore them, or saying they shouldn't exist and therefore we won't deal with them, doesn't help at all.

Confusion and ambivalence about one's feelings add to one's discomfort. They also are communicated to one's coworkers, adding to their discomfort. A good first step toward clearing the air is to distinguish your own feelings from the situation that engenders them. Did the remark, gesture, look, or course of action necessarily have the connotation you experienced, or could it be your own interpretation? Are you uncomfortable because your colleague is uncomfortable? Are you afraid your colleague will make an approach you'll have to rebuff? Are you afraid your colleague *won't* make an approach? Are you worried that something you do will be mistaken for an inappropriate approach? Perhaps you don't think an approach would be inappropriate at all, but everyone else does. You may even think a pass is expected. There are all kinds of possibilities, and most people feel several ways at once.

Some of the feelings are fantasy—it's the idea you like, not the reality. Recognizing that takes some of the pressure off. Fantasies don't hurt anyone, as long as we differentiate them from reality. Some of the feelings are real desires, but unwise to pursue. Again, recognizing the desire and realizing that you don't have to act on it eases the pressure to act, as well as the fear that you will. Sometimes fears mask desires. Discovering the desire behind the fear leaves you with a feeling you can understand and a situation you can control. Some of the worries are real and reasonable. The psychological contract suggested earlier could be framed to ease those anxieties, especially if they are based on experience.

Being sure of your own feelings and intentions makes it possible to communicate them clearly and definitely, even without direct discussion. And they are more likely to be taken seriously when they are not fuzzy or ambivalent. A quiet but definite "No" can be powerfully effective.

When the confusion of one person is communicated to a confused other, the result may be actions you both regret. Unadmitted feelings are nevertheless powerful. Admitting feelings increases our control over our actions. Some feelings frighten us or seem too terrible to admit. But suppressing them takes a lot of energy. Channeling that energy in more appropriate directions, with the help of clear boundaries, could be highly productive.

How might this look in practice? Perhaps you are a man with a woman subordinate whom you don't find especially attractive, but she seems to have eyes for you. You could maneuver to keep your distance, but you might do better to tell her directly that your interest in her is the same as your interest in Bob—you want to see her do well the work assigned to her, and you want to be able to give her the support she needs without worrying that she will read things into your efforts and attention.

Suppose you are a man with a new woman subordinate. You don't feel comfortable dropping in on her the way you do with the men reporting to you. Part of the problem, you realize, is that you find her attractive. But if you avoid her, your male subordinates will follow suit, and she'll remain an outsider.

First, make your intentions clear in your own mind. Next, make sure the woman knows about informal group gatherings—coffee breaks, drinks after work. If none exist, buy some donuts and get one going. Finally, discuss with the woman some acceptable settings and boundaries for one-to-one business. Is there an office with glass partitions? Could a third party be present? Is the company dining room sufficiently public and private at the same time? Could you agree to keep a certain amount of physical distance between you at all times? (Clearly, a sense of humor helps.) The woman will probably appreciate your concern and share your desire to keep the relationship professional. She may also be relieved by your straightforward approach.

Off The Guilt Trip
The mere presence of women in managerial roles stirs up feelings and raises questions about deep elements of our lives. What does it mean to be a man? What does it mean to be a woman? What will happen to families? Will my spouse still be there for me, or will I end up alone? The movement of women into management is not the superficial change it might seem. Comfortable acceptance of it will not come easily or quickly, but with hard work over decades. It may be easier to deny that anything is changing, to call the problems personality conflicts. We will all feel disappointed at times with our own and others' progress; angry at the need to change and at the ones we hold responsible for it; resentful of what we feel we must give up, or is being taken away, or is being withheld. We wouldn't be human if we didn't. The thing is to see our own imperfections, and still accept and respect ourselves. It makes the imperfections of others so much more acceptable. Certainly our perceptions are colored; often we are frightened when women and men won't stay in the molds we've made for them. The more we realize that we all have different versions of the same problem, the more we can support each other in making and benefiting from this change.

Education

As the pace of change accelerates, the need for education grows and the nature of education has to change. Business needs educated people, so it must invest in education—in the broadest sense of the word.

Thumbs Down

Scientific research didn't interest college freshmen in 1982 as a career possibility, and neither did teaching elementary or secondary school, according to a survey by UCLA and the American Council on Education. These students' top priority was "to be very well off financially," and their desires for personal authority and recognition were much greater than those of students during the mid-sixties. However, the decline in attitudes reflecting altruism and humanism was not as great as the increase in desire for money and power. This was attributed to women's increased interest in power and influence.[23]

These trends do not bode well for the future of our culture. The growing interests in personal authority and recognition are not necessarily bad—they could simply reflect higher self-esteem as young women begin to feel themselves to be the equals of men, and desire the compensation that their efforts are worth. But our society is unwilling to invest in education and basic research the way it invests in the production of goods. Elementary and secondary education have depended on the altruism and lower status of women, but can no longer do so. Since business depends on the educational system, it's worth considering what business can do to encourage qualified people to teach. One possibility is to encourage people to go into teaching as a second career, as their interests turn from getting ahead toward doing something for the next generation and society as a whole.

As H. G. Wells put it, "Human history becomes more and more a race between education and catastrophe." American business has to join that race, educating the skilled people it needs to outrun economic catastrophe.[24]

A Critical Defense

Behind each of two doors is either a hot meal or a poisonous snake. The first door says, "In this room there is a meal; in the other there is a snake." The second door says, "In one of these rooms there is a meal; in one there is a snake." You are told that one statement is true, the other false. Which door had you better open? In a review of Raymond Smullyan's collection of such puzzles, Hugh Kenner, Johns Hopkins U., makes an interesting point: "You'll notice . . . how careful thought left . . . only one option that wasn't self-contradictory. . . . Sharp kids find it obvious. But many grownups, accustomed to a complex world, fail to see self-contradiction as an absolute bar."[25] That's too bad, because they should. The complexity of the adult world notwithstanding, genuine self-contradiction *is* an absolute bar. To take one flagrant example from the rich treasury of advertising, it is not possible to look more natural by putting on more makeup. Better, maybe—that's a matter of opinion. But not more natural.

Why don't self-contradictions like that bother people more than they do? In my experience, most people don't really know what it means to be critical, to analyze statements for their logic and consistency. Some people aren't capable of it. Many just don't want to see the errors in a position they support. Others don't have the frame of reference and knowledge to detect flaws in the reasoning. That's why such pseudo-sciences as astrology and creationism can be passed off to the public as science. That's also why companies buy so many psychological gimmicks, and one of the reasons I try to provide a frame of reference for psychological analysis.

Critical analysis is a skill; if you don't have it, you can probably acquire it. It is supposed to be one of the products of education, but a good many people get all the way through college without having had any real critical effort demanded of them. That's a shame, because not only is it a pleasure in itself, it's the only defense against a great barrage of lies, delusions, and simple errors.

It Isn't What You Know, It's Knowing Where To Look

Would you be appalled if the only way your child could multiply 256 by 17 was on a pocket calculator? Well, what do you suppose your distant ancestors think of you if the only way you can have a chicken to eat is to buy it? What we consider the basics of knowledge are not immutable: reading, writing, and arithmetic have replaced hunting, fishing, and farming, and may be replaced in their turn. According to economist Herbert Simon, electronic information systems are already changing the nature of "knowledge." People were always taught in school that they "knew" something when they had the facts memorized. But increasingly, to "know" something will mean knowing where to get the facts. There is too much relevant information for anyone to memorize. That's a machine's job. The job for a human brain is to organize the facts, reflect upon them, and make use of them.[26]

This is apparent in the very fact that business students study "management"—how to handle business information—independent of any body of specific information. Learning the facts of mining coal or making shoes comes later, and facts can be dropped or added as the industry changes or the person switches jobs. As this trend continues, and the levels of abstraction needed for successful management increase, broader education will be necessary. In the future, an MBA may go back to school for a liberal arts education, just as managers go back for their MBAs today.

World Citizens

Faraway places are not far away any more, and political events can affect each of us. We can deny the dangers of world confrontation, or we can feel disconnected from them and powerless to change things. Or we can take an interest, take thought, and look for ways to use whatever power we have in being agents of change.

World Leaders Are People Too

Have you noticed in the headlines how much President Reagan and his administration talk about using rewards and punishments on Russia? Notice also that the Russians get their backs up in response. Apparently, the White House hasn't read *The Great Jackass Fallacy.* As I've noted repeatedly, manipulating rewards and punishments works only when you can control the total environment.

Does that mean nothing should be done? Not at all. It means some careful, strategic thinking should be done, based on psychological understanding not only of the key leaders, but also of the political forces that operate on them. It means careful consideration should be given to their personal ego ideals, as well as those of their nations. We probably could do more to destroy the Soviet threat by opening up all kinds of trade relations. That would require a good deal of interchange with the U.S. in the form of travel by Russian managers, scholars, scientists, and others. This would tend to open the Soviet system more, just as the need to compete with us scientifically required them to open communications a good deal in the 1950s. There's no way you can control people or information when there is so much mobility.

Birds Of Different Feathers

Discussions of conflict strategy are generally conducted as if strategy were purely a matter of facts and logic. In fact, strategy is largely a matter of the psychology of power. Take the debate about nuclear arms and Soviet first-strike capability, for example. As Leslie Gelb has pointed out, "It is mainly a debate about the psychology of power, more than about the likelihood of an actual attack. Because of the strategic balance, which side would act with confidence and which with fear—these are the key issues underlying the debate."[27]

Those who see power as something to be used in an attacking, controlling manner (feather them hawks) frequently have to reach premature closure on problems. That is, they can't take a wait-and-see attitude, consider all the possibilities, negotiate compromise, and so on. They need the situation resolved, now! So "attack and be done with it" is often their favored solution. At the other extreme are those who feel that aggression is not nice (feather them doves), and who therefore bend over backwards to avoid being aggressive.

Taking either of these extreme positions puts you in a fixed attitude, which quickly becomes a cliché (hawk, dove, the Russians are out to get us, the competition will stop at nothing, we can't take these people to court). And all the so-called logic of strategic debate flows from the assumptions embodied in these fixed attitudes. It's easy to get caught up in assumptions which reflect your own preferred way of handling aggression, but those assumptions may have little to do with the actual situation. The other party to the conflict may handle aggression in an entirely different way.

Rather than take a rigid, extreme position based on your own style of handling aggression, try to assess psychologically what the competition is doing and how they're going about it. Then you can respond to the actual situation, and do so on the basis of its psychological foundations. If you don't analyze the behavior of the other party, be it organization, department, individual, or nation, you're likely to find problems repeating themselves rather than being solved.

When you don't think psychologically about what's happening, you tend to depend on wielding power. That puts you in an escalating great jackass fallacy position—as we see in the arms race. Not that we shouldn't have arms and be prepared to protect ourselves. But the sticks just keep getting bigger, and the carrots lose their motivating power.

FOCUS ON . . . . Psychology Of World Confrontation

During a Russian-American disarmament conference, W. H. Ferry, a long-time writer on the arms race, stood up to say: "I raise the question here of what this is all about. What issue could possibly warrant the use of nuclear weapons?" No one answered; the question was dropped and never mentioned again.

Thomas Powers tells this story in his essay, "What Is It About?" in the January 1984 issue of the *Atlantic*. His own conclusion is that the Cold War is about nothing but itself. The two nations give economic and political reasons why they must confront each other, but "not one on a scale even close to the scale of the war we are preparing to fight with each other." It comes down to two strong powers, each unable to bear a rival that might be able to destroy it. "We fear each other," says Powers. "We wish each other ill. All the rest is detail."

But where's the logic of this rivalry? All around us every day are individuals who could destroy us—bigger, stronger, or just meaner—yet we don't try to wipe them out just to be on the safe side. Economic and political arguments can't fully explain what sets nations against each other.

A Basic Drive
Human behavior is driven by two basic forces: aggression and sex. Aggression is the capacity to attack the environment and to defend against attack. It is biologically based; survival in the animal kingdom depends on it. Most people no longer have to hunt and kill their food, but the genetic inheritance remains. This heritage shapes the behavior

of nations, too. In individuals, it is usually held in check by the superego; nations are not so controlled.

Is it valid to speak of a nation in psychological terms, as if it were a person? Nations are composed of many people who vary widely. Yet a nation can show the psychological behavior of an individual when its people share: 1) a collective belief about the world; 2) a characteristic style of behavior (such as the constraint of Swedes); 3) a common enemy; or 4) a common hero who becomes part of a national ego ideal (such as Juan Perón, Napoleon, or Queen Victoria). Like organizations, nations have personalities—there is an overall pattern to what their leaders will propose and what their citizens will do.

Get Off My Cloud
Aggression between groups often takes the form of rivalry. At the root of rivalry is the biological fact that anyone or anything that is or could become stronger is a deadly threat. The threat must be destroyed or defended against. That seems to be the case with the Soviet Union. It is not the only government we find odious; yet we find ourselves quite able to leave others, such as South Africa, alone and benefit from their resources. The Soviet Union's tremendous resources are not attractive enough to counterbalance the fact that it, alone among nations, can destroy us.

There are many historical precedents for this sort of rivalry and the wars that result. The war that ended the great age of Athens was not caused by the many hostile incidents that preceded it, according to the Greek historian Thucydides: "The real cause I consider to be . . . the growth of the power of Athens, and the alarm which this inspired in Sparta."[28] Sound familiar? Yet Athens and Sparta, too, had recently been allies in a major war.

Pointing Their Fingers And Beating Their Chests
Nations, like individuals, sometimes project their own hostility onto another, claiming—and believing—that it is the other who is hostile. Generally, the projection soon comes true. Sometimes a nation turns outward the hostility it would otherwise turn on itself. It's a well-known ploy for troubled governments to use war or threat of war to unify their nation behind them. This seems to have been one motivation for Argentina's Falklands invasion. The Russian people have historically been oppressed by their governments, both czarist and Communist, so they are ripe for turning their hostility outward to real and supposed enemies.

A nation also can exhibit narcissism, when it defines its self-image significantly in opposition to another. It overvalues its own characteristics and undervalues or denies those of its enemy. This can lead to prejudice, attack, and—in the extreme—slavery or genocide.

One of the main forms of aggression observed in animals is among males of the same species. It would follow that human beings do something similar; all too often, world leaders seem like gorillas in coats and ties, thumping their chests to see who'll back down first. The people in charge of nations and armies are almost all male. The few women in charge have succeeded in and are operating in a male system, surrounded by males. We don't know what "female politics" would be like or whether they would be any different. If there were true matriarchal societies in ancient times, no records remain to show what their power politics were like.

Is There Any Hope?

In the final chapter of *On Aggression*, ethologist Konrad Lorenz concludes that widespread knowledge of the genetic and biological nature of aggression can save the human race from itself. We cannot overcome aggression, since it *is* inherent, but we can avoid the worst manifestations (such as war) by redirecting it into ritualized and constructive channels, such as the Olympic Games. The boycotts of recent Olympics indicate that some connection does exist, and that neutral territory is needed if such contests are to serve that purpose.

What other ways could the U.S. and the U.S.S.R. channel some of their aggressive rivalry into activities other than the arms race?

1. Tackle jointly such relatively nonpolitical world problems as pollution, famine, acid rain, cancer, alcoholism, and mental retardation. It would cost billions—as do the weapons—but the money would be far better spent, bringing far more in return.
2. Put many more ordinary people into contact—not just a few scientists and exchange students. Business could contribute here by sponsoring more student exchanges and instituting employee exchanges, bringing people into the everyday life of each other's country.
3. Share more nonsensitive technology, such as farming techniques.
4. Stop calling each other names. Both nations have major crimes of persecution in their history. (Remember what we did to the Native Americans.)

I am not so naive as to say: These will work. There's no guarantee anything will "work," as long as the bombs are there. One can only say: these may help.

In Summary

1. *Business affects society, and increasingly is being held responsible for its negative effects. It makes sense for business to take the lead in countering the negative effects of its activity, and in creating and publicizing some positive effects. People are always prepared to see business as bad simply because it is big and has more power than individuals. If people see business using its power in positive ways, they may begin to see business as more trustworthy.*

2. *Equality among groups of people is a tricky concept, since each group is made up of individuals with unequal abilities. The best we can do is to try to understand our own feelings and try not to be swayed by the ones we know to be irrational. We can also try to change our prejudicial feelings, by taking every opportunity to get to know the unique individuals who make up minority groups.*

3. *Being educated—knowing how to think—becomes increasingly important as society, and therefore the business world as well, becomes increasingly complex.*

4. *The behavior of nations and national leaders follows psychological principles. When national leaders don't think psychologically, the control of aggression on the international scale remains a matter of who has the power to destroy whom, as we see in the arms race. Managers who think psychologically can use their own influence to encourage alternative approaches to international conflicts, improving our chances for survival and peace.*

NOTES

More Than Meets The Eye

1 *Administration in Mental Health*, Fall-Winter 1977.
2 Morris West, *The Shoes of the Fisherman* (New York: Dell, 1964).
3 *American Medical News*, Dec. 24-31, 1982.
4 *American Journal of Psychiatry*, December 1980.
5 *Harvard Business Review*, July-August 1980.

Tools For Your Trade

1 *Science*, July 17, 1981.
2 *Psychosomatic Medicine*, November 1980.
3 *Newsweek*, June 21, 1982.
4 *New York Times Book Review*, Dec. 19, 1982.
5 *Science*, March 1979.
6 *Boston Globe*, Dec. 4, 1980.
7 *Science*, Sept. 7, 1979.
8 *U.S. News & World Report*, Sept. 10, 1979.
9 *Smithsonian*, March 1984.
10 *American Journal of Psychiatry*, November 1981.
11 *The Levinson Letter*, "Focus On . . . . Personal Growth Workshops," Mar. 15, 1982.
12 *Fortune*, Aug. 6, 1984.
13 *Fortune*, Apr. 21, 1980.
14 Leonard Sayles, *The Behavior of Industrial Work Groups* (New York: Wiley & Sons, 1958).
15 *Academy of Management Journal*, December 1979.
16 Harry Levinson, Charlton R. Price, Kenneth J. Munden, Harold J. Mandl, and Charles M. Solley,
   Men, Management, and Mental Health (Cambridge: Harvard U. Press, 1962).
17 *International Management*, August 1981.
18 *Psychosomatic Medicine*, April 1980.
19 *American Journal of Psychiatry*, March 1983.
20 Charles Ford, *The Somatizing Disorders as a Way of Life* (New York: Elsevier, 1983).
21 Bruno Bettelheim, *Surviving* (New York: Knopf, 1979).
22 *Time*, Jan. 12, 1981.
23 *Time*, Mar. 9, 1981.
24 *American Medical News*, Feb. 20, 1981.
25 *American Sociological Review*, December 1979.
26 *Wall Street Journal*, July 7, 1980.
27 *Parabola*, vol. 8, no. 1.
28 *Harvard Medical Area Focus*, May 1, 1981.

Satisfying Work

1 *Boston Globe*, Mar. 25, 1980.
2 *Levinson Letter Addendum*, "Who's Promotable?" Mar. 1, 1983.
3 *Wall Street Journal*, Apr. 11, 1983.
4 *Parade*, June 17, 1979.
5 *Dun's Review*, April 1978.
6 *Skeptical Inquirer*, Spring-Summer 1977.
7 *Personnel Psychology*, Autumn 1979.
8 *Psychology Today*, May 1978.
9 *Boston Globe*, Dec. 4, 1978.
10 *Business Week*, Apr. 6, 1981.
11 Levinson, et al., *Men, Management, and Mental Health*.

Releasing Energy For Work

1 Nevitt Sanford, *Learning After College* (Orinda, Calif.: Montaigne, 1980).
2 Elliott Jaques, *A General Theory of Bureaucracy* (New York: Halsted, 1976).
3 *Boston Globe*, May 23, 1982.
4 *Fortune*, Apr. 23, 1979.
5 Harry Levinson, *Psychological Man* (Cambridge, Mass.: Levinson Institute, 1976).
6 Jay Fliegelman, *Prodigals and Pilgrims: The American Revolution Against Patriarchal Authority, 1750-1800*
   (New York: Cambridge U. Press, 1983).
7 *American Scholar*, Winter 1977.
8 Martin Gardiner, *Science: Good, Bad, and Bogus* (New York: Prometheus Books, 1982).
9 Opinion Research Corp. report presented at 9th Annual Personnel Policy Conference, February 1981.
10 Harry Levinson, *The Great Jackass Fallacy* (Cambridge: Harvard U. Press, 1973).
11 *Science*, Feb. 27, 1981.

12 Harry Levinson, *Emotional Health in the World of Work* (New York: Harper & Row, 1964).
13 *U.S. News & World Report*, Dec. 17, 1979.
14 *American Psychologist*, August 1982.
15 *New York Review*, Mar. 31, 1977.

Leading—More Than Managing

1 *Foreign Affairs*, Fall 1982.
2 *Foreign Affairs*, Fall 1981.
3 *Economist*, Mar. 28, 1982.
4 *Saturday Review*, December 1978.
5 *Wall Street Journal*, May 27, 1981.
6 *Atlantic Monthly*, January 1980.
7 *New York Review*, Dec. 9, 1976.
8 Michael Maccoby, *The Gamesman* (New York: Simon & Schuster, 1976).
9 *New York Review*, Feb. 22, 1979.
10 *Worldview*, January 1984.
11 *New York Times Magazine*, Aug. 3, 1980.
12 *New York Times*, Jan. 23, 1983.
13 *Wall Street Journal*, January 13, 1981.
14 *Issues & Observations*, February 1983.
15 *U.S. News & World Report*, Mar. 8, 1982.
16 *Academy of Management Journal*, September 1982.
17 *Saturday Review*, February 1981.
18 *New York Times*, May 15, 1983.
19 *Journal of the American Academy of Psychoanalysis*, January 1979.
20 *American Arts*, September 1980.
21 *Boston Business Journal*, Feb. 14, 1983.
22 Aleksandr Solzhenitsyn, *The Oak and the Calf* (New York: Harper & Row, 1980).
23 *New York Times Magazine*, Nov. 18, 1979.

Relationships That Work

1 Henry Mintzberg, "The Manager's Job: Folklore and Fact," in *Harvard Business Review* anthology, *On Human Relations* (New York: Harper & Row, 1979).
2 *Organizational Dynamics*, Winter 1979.
3 *Psychology Today*, January 1981.
4 David Halberstam, *The Best and the Brightest* (New York: Random House, 1972).
5 *U.S. News & World Report*, Mar. 9, 1981.
6 *Psychology Today*, October 1982.
7 *Sloan Management Review*, Winter 1978.
8 *Washington Monthly*, July-August 1980.
9 *New York Times*, Nov. 18, 1979.
10 June Jordan, *Civil Wars* (Boston: Beacon Press, 1981).

Managing Change

1 *Journal of Personality & Social Psychology*, June 1974.
2 *Business Week*, Sept. 7, 1981.
3 Harry Levinson, *Organizational Diagnosis* (Cambridge: Harvard U. Press, 1972).
4 *Science*, August 1980.
5 *Organizational Dynamics*, Winter 1979.
6 *Science*, Sept. 3, 1982.
7 *Harper's*, January 1981.
8 *Forbes*, Nov. 2, 1982.
9 *Administrative Science Quarterly*, June 1980.

Troubled Waters

1 Shirley Letwin, *The Gentleman in Trollope: Individuality and Moral Conduct* (Cambridge: Harvard U. Press, 1983).
2 *American Journal of Psychiatry*, September 1979.
3 *Archives of General Psychiatry*, May 1974.
4 *Psychosomatic Medicine*, June 1978.
5 Orville Brim, Jr. and Jerome Kagan, *Constancy and Change in Human Development* (Cambridge: Harvard U. Press, 1980).
6 *New York Times*, Aug. 19, 1980.
7 *International Journal of Group Psychotherapy*, January 1980.
8 *American Medical News*, June 9, 1975.

9 *American Journal of Psychiatry,* November 1980.
10 *Fortune,* Jan. 11, 1982.
11 *Wall Street Journal,* Jan. 13, 1983.
12 *Center Magazine,* January-February 1980.
13 *APA Monitor,* June 1980.
14 Karl Menninger, *Man Against Himself* (New York: Knopf, 1938).
15 *Newsweek,* May 28, 1979.
16 *Psychosomatic Medicine,* November 1980.
17 *Psychosomatic Medicine,* May 1979.
18 National Institute For Mental Health, Pub. No. (ADM) 76-383.
19 *Archives of General Psychiatry,* September 1980.
20 *American Journal of Psychiatry,* September 1982.
21 *American Psychologist,* January 1978.
22 *New Times,* June 26, 1978.
23 *Business Week,* Aug. 21, 1978.
24 *Psychology Today,* August 1978.
25 *Archives of General Psychiatry,* April 1977.
26 William H. Masters and Virginia E. Johnson, *Human Sexual Response* (Boston: Little, Brown, 1966).
27 *American Medical News,* Apr. 9, 1982.
28 *American Way,* October 1980.
29 Salvador Minuchin, "Psychosomatic Aspects of Diabetes in Children," in *Families Today 2,* NIMH Science Monographs vol. 1.
30 *Psychosomatic Medicine,* November 1979.
31 *Psychosomatic Medicine,* January 1980.
32 *Economist,* June 14, 1980.
33 *Science,* June 27, 1980.
34 U.S. Dept. HEW, Pub. No. (ADM 77-497), 1977.
35 *Science,* August 1978.

A Time For Every Purpose

1 *American Journal of Psychiatry,* July 1979.
2 *Saturday Review,* June 1982.
3 *National Business Employment Weekly,* Sept. 6, 1981.
4 *Washington Monthly,* January 1981.
5 Tom Wolfe, *The Right Stuff* (New York: Farrar, Straus, & Giroux, 1979).
6 *The Sciences,* July-August 1981.
7 *Atlantic Monthly,* November 1979.
8 *Fortune,* July 16, 1979.
9 *Psychology Today,* July 1979.
10 *Journal of the American Academy of Psychoanalysis,* October 1979.
11 *Newsweek,* Sept. 29, 1980.
12 *New York Review,* Feb. 2, 1980.
13 *New York Review of Books,* May 1, 1975.
14 *Science,* October 1978.
15 *Academy of Management Journal,* March 1975.
16 *Christian Science Monitor,* Feb. 13, 1981.
17 Erik Erikson, *Childhood and Society* (New York: Norton, 1963).
18 *Harvard Magazine,* March-April 1983.
19 *Bulletin of the Menninger Clinic,* July 1976.
20 *Boston Globe,* May 11, 1976.
21 *Psychology Today,* October 1978.
22 Morton Lieberman and Sheldon Tobin, *The Experience of Old Age* (New York: Basic Books, 1983).
23 Frederic Prokosch, *Voices: A Memoir* (New York: Farrar, Straus, & Giroux, 1983).

Family Matters

1 *American Journal of Psychiatry,* August 1978.
2 *New York Times Magazine,* Nov. 21, 1982.
3 *Boston Globe,* July 9, 1979.
4 *Social Science & Modern Society,* January-February 1981.
5 Pamela Daniels and Sara Ruddick, *Working It Out* (New York: Pantheon, 1977).
6 Barrie Greiff and Preston Munter, *Tradeoffs: Executive, Family and Organizational Life* (New York: New American Library, 1980).
7 *Fortune,* November 1951.
8 Mark Gerzon, *A Choice of Heroes: The Changing Faces of American Manhood* (Boston: Houghton Mifflin, 1982).
9 *Saturday Review,* Oct. 28, 1978.

10 *Science*, Oct. 7, 1977.
11 *International Review of Psycho-Analysis*, 1979.
12 *American Psychologist*, April 1980.
13 Fitzhugh Dodson, *How to Father* (Los Angeles: Nash, 1974).
14 *Psychology Today*, June 1979.
15 John Clausen, "The Mentally Ill at Home: A Family Matter," in *Families Today 2*, NIMH Science Monographs vol. 1.
16 *American Journal of Psychiatry*, December 1980.
17 *Journal of Clinical and Consulting Psychology*, April 1975.
18 *Harvard Gazette*, Jan. 19, 1979.
19 *Human Behavior*, February 1975.
20 John Gardner, *Morale* (New York: Norton, 1978).
21 *Human Nature*, February 1979.
22 *Human Nature*, March 1979.
23 Selma Fraiberg, *The Magic Years* (New York: Scribners', 1959).
24 Mark Kiefaber and Joseph Procaccini, *Parent Burnout* (New York: Doubleday, 1983).
25 *U.S. News & World Report*, Mar. 7, 1983.
26 *Journal of the American Academy of Psychoanalysis*, April 1979.
27 Ronald Blythe, *The View in Winter: Reflections on Old Age* (New York: Harcourt, Brace, 1979).

Manager As Citizen

1 *Wall Street Journal*, July 30, 1979.
2 *Atlantic Monthly*, December 1979.
3 *Journal of Business Research*, September 1977.
4 Harold Lasswell, *Psychopathology and Politics* (New York: Free Press, 1960).
5 *Personnel Administrator*, January 1981.
6 *Dun's Review*, January 1981.
7 *Road and Track*, June 1973.
8 *Personnel Journal*, March 1975.
9 *New York Review*, Feb. 3, 1977.
10 *Saturday Review*, Mar. 8, 1975.
11 *American Journal of Psychiatry*, December 1978.
12 *New York Times Magazine*, Oct. 17, 1982.
13 *Daedalus*, Fall 1979.
14 *New England Business*, Oct. 5, 1981.
15 *Personnel*, September-October 1981.
16 Harry Levinson, *Executive Stress* (New York: New American Library, 1975).
17 *Frequent Flyer*, October 1980.
18 *American Psychologist*, October 1980.
19 Joseph Pleck, *The Myth of Masculinity* (Cambridge, Mass.: MIT Press, 1981).
20 *American Psychologist*, September 1980.
21 *Wall Street Journal*, Apr. 14, 1981.
22 McLane, *Selecting, Developing, and Retaining Women Executives* (New York: Van Nostrand Reinhold, 1980).
23 *Science*, Feb. 18, 1983.
24 *Levinson Letter Addendum:* "Managing People in the 80s," Feb. 17, 1981.
25 *Harper's*, March 1983.
26 *Futurist*, August 1982.
27 *New York Times*, Oct. 4, 1981.
28 Thucydides, *The Peloponnesian War* (New York: Modern Library, 1981).

Reprints From *The Levinson Letter,* 1974-1984

ADDENDUM

Psychological Cost Accounting
The stress of change and loss: how to recognize and deal with it.

Performance Appraisal—Too Little, Too Late
Why many performance appraisals fail. An argument for the critical incident method, with a step-by-step model on how to implement it.

Organizations in Crisis
How human resources management and the psychological effects of change can block the forward movement of organizations.

The Executive as Internal Consultant
An analysis of the new executive role: coaching, counseling, preparing for change. How to step back from your organization and develop a more objective perspective.

Managing Termination: I
How to understand the psychology of termination and use that awareness when firing employees.

Managing Termination: II
How managers can ease the pain of termination for employees and organizations.

How to Speak Up to the Boss
What problems you must tell your boss about—and how to communicate them effectively.

Engineering Organizational Change
How to perform an in-house organizational diagnosis: an analysis of one company's success.

Up Through the Ranks: Mentoring for Leadership
How mentoring can enrich the work experiences of older managers, and develop leadership characteristics in young managers.

Leadership vs. Management: A Strategy for Action
How managers can develop personal strategies for leadership that meet their organizations' needs and enrich their own jobs.

Managing Organizational Stress
How stress symptoms spread through one organization. What managers can do to ease the impact of change and loss.

Mapping Your Managerial Education
Changing educational requirements for managers seeking advancement.

Men and Women in Management
Why men are uncomfortable with women as business associates. What men can do to ease their discomfort, and how they can support women in management.

Whose Successor Are You?
New managers inherit subordinates' attitudes toward the previous boss. Typical effects of three types of predecessor are described, and suggestions for coping with those effects are offered.

Problem-Solving Support for Handling Stress
Help with practical matters is as important to a person under stress as emotional support. How to provide practical support in a work setting.

Who's Promotable?
Who is promotable depends on what the person is being promoted to. How to define the prospective position. Four areas of individual capability to consider.

Behavioral Job Descriptions: How and Why
How to develop a behavioral job description, why the effort to do so pays off, and a sample behavioral job description.

The Three Rs of Change
How to take care of yourself in the new era of continuous organizational change.

Assessing High Potentials
What behavioral clues indicate that a manager should be able to handle a top-level position—or that promotion could be a disaster? Where do you start to look for clues, and how do you put them together?

Decentralization: How Much is Enough?
What can go wrong when decentralization isn't carried out selectively. How to repair the damage. How to avoid the mistakes.

FOCUS ON ....

Runs, Raids, and Reorganizations, February 15, 1980

Promotion: Stress and Stimulation, March 17, 1980

Mid-Career Misery: When Success Isn't Enough, May 15, 1980

Enriching Yourself to Enhance Your Career, June 16, 1980

The Rise of Neoconservatism, July 15, 1980

Educating Upward, August 15, 1980

Absenteeism, November 17, 1980

Identifying Organizational Purpose, December 15, 1980

Communicating Organizational Purpose, January 15, 1981

Career and Family: The Organization's Role, March 16, 1981

Doublespeak and Zerospeak: The Use of Language, June 15, 1981

In and Out the Mainstream, July 15, 1981

Criticism in Context, August 17, 1981

Support During Change, October 15, 1981

The Failure of Deinstitutionalization, December 15, 1981

Choosing an Employer, January 15, 1982

Personal Growth Workshops, March 15, 1982

Communicating a Merger, April 15, 1982

The Irrationality of Being Rational, June 15, 1982

Sudden Death in the Work Group, July 15, 1982

Participation, August 16, 1982

When Subordinates Can't Act, October 15, 1982

Loneliness, November 15, 1982

The Right to Know, January 17, 1983

Consensus and Organizational Survival, February 15, 1983

"Objective" Performance Appraisal, April 15, 1983

The Price of Success, May 16, 1983

Preventing Injuries in the Workplace, July 15, 1983

Being No. 2, August 15, 1983

Computerized Psychological Testing, November 15, 1983

The Flexible Corporation, January 16, 1984

Making Use of Advisers, February 15, 1984

Managing a Critical Boss, April 17, 1984

Compensation: Stop the Manipulation Game, May 15, 1984

Psychology of World Confrontation, July 16, 1984

The Manipulative Personality, August 15, 1984

The Too-Tough Boss, October 15, 1984

Father Hunger, November 15, 1984

Reprints may be ordered from:

The Levinson Institute, Inc.
Box 95
Cambridge, MA 02138